MW01107206

SHAREPOINT

SharePoint™ Portal Server: A Beginner's Guide

ANTHONY T. **MANN**

Osborne/**McGraw-Hill**

New York Chicago San Francisco
Lisbon London Madrid Mexico City Milan
New Delhi San Juan Seoul Singapore Sydney Toronto

Osborne/**McGraw-Hill**
2600 Tenth Street
Berkeley, California 94710
U.S.A.

To arrange bulk purchase discounts for sales promotions, premiums, or fund-raisers, please contact Osborne/**McGraw-Hill** at the above address. For information on translations or book distributors outside the U.S.A., please see the International Contact Information page immediately following the index of this book.

SharePoint™ Portal Server: A Beginner's Guide

1234567890 CUS CUS 01987654321

Book p/n 0-07-219401-4 and CD p/n 0-07-219402-2
parts of
ISBN 0-07-219400-6

Publisher
  Brandon A. Nordin
Vice President and Associate Publisher
  Scott Rogers
Acquisitions Editor
  Jane Brownlow
Project Editor
  Betsy Manini

Acquisitions Coordinator
  Emma Acker
Technical Editor
  Scott Schnoll
Production and Editorial Services
  Anzai! Inc.
Series Design
  Peter F. Hancik

This book was composed with Corel VENTURA™ Publisher.

SHAREPOINT

SharePoint™ Portal Server:
A Beginner's Guide

ABOUT THE AUTHOR

Anthony T. Mann, MCDBA, MCSD, MCT, is a veteran author of many popular computer-related books. In addition to this book, he has authored *Microsoft SQL Server 2000 for Dummies* and *Microsoft SQL Server 7 for Dummies* for Hungry Minds, Inc. He has also authored *Visual Basic 5 Developer's Guide*, *Real-World Programming with Visual Basic 4*, and *Real-World Programming with Visual Basic* for SAMS. He was also a contributing author on *Visual Basic 5 Development Unleashed* and *Visual Basic 4 Developer's Guide* for SAMS. For DigitalThink, he has authored a series of three courses designed to help individuals pass the Microsoft 70-029 (SQL Server 7 Implementation) exam.

When not writing, Mr. Mann is a National Solutions Center Principal with Internosis, based out of Arlington, VA, but resides in southern New Hampshire. Internosis is an award-winning, gold-level Microsoft consulting partner, where Anthony is responsible for the Business Intelligence Practice at a national level.

Mr. Mann is also the Steering Committee Chair for the Professional Association for SQL Server (PASS) Data Warehousing & Business Intelligence Special Interest Group (SIG).

If you have any questions or comments for him or to find out what Internosis can do for your organization, he can be e-mailed at **tmann@vbasic.com**.

To Alison,
my wife
of seven years.
She is my strength,
support, and love.

AT A GLANCE

CONTENTS

Part II

User Navigation and Management

Part III

General Administration

Part IV

Advanced Administration

ACKNOWLEDGMENTS

There are so many people who put in many long, hard, thankless hours that I wish to thank and acknowledge. The first is Judy Bass (Senior Acquisitions Editor), with whom I worked at Hungry Minds, but is now with Osborne/**McGraw-Hill**. She was instrumental in getting me involved with the right people at Osborne. Next, I want to acknowledge and thank Jane Brownlow (Senior Acquisitions Editor), who had the foresight to bring me into this project and keep me line. Emma Acker (Acquisitions Coordinator) had the incredibly difficult job of coordinating all materials in conjunction with this book, along with countless other books. Betsy Manini (Senior Project Editor) had the overall responsibility for managing the project and coordinating all people and departments to get this project finished on time.

A very hearty thanks goes out to Scott Schnoll and Gary Bushey, both Technical Editors. These guys are the ones who kept me on my toes and made sure that what I wrote was technically accurate. I appreciate their thoughts, ideas, and corrections.

Tom Anzai (Project Editor) was in charge of physically laying out the book and constructing the line-art drawings (the ones that aren't screen shots). Tom also coordinated with Betsy to ensure a timely delivery of materials. He did a phenomenal job. Lee Musick (Copy Editor) had the daunting task of ensuring that my thoughts actually make sense when they are transferred on paper. Lee made sure that the book was consistent in tone, copy, and organization. Thanks, Lee ☺ (inside joke). Also, thanks to Bert Schopf, Allan Shearer, Linda Shearer, and Robert Johns for helping Tom with the layout, proofs, and getting the manuscript ready for press. I also want to thank Ann Fothergill-Brown for her indexing efforts. Thanks, everyone! It is much appreciated!

INTRODUCTION

Microsoft SharePoint Portal Server is an exciting new product that was added to the growing list of .NET servers. This product is unlike any other product that Microsoft currently has in its arsenal. SharePoint Portal Server combines an enterprise portal with indexing and document management. I've found that many companies are struggling to figure out what SharePoint Portal Server is, how it can be used, and how it will benefit the company. This book was written, in part, to answer these questions and to give a clear understanding as to what SharePoint Portal Server is all about and how to administer the product.

Because every Windows operating system cannot be shown for every example in this book, it is assumed that you will be using Windows 2000. If you are using Windows NT, Me, 95, or 98, the menu commands listed in this book will be slightly different. Although the menus shown in this book are the same as those found in beta versions of Windows XP and Windows .NET Servers, neither of these products were released at the time of this writing. Therefore, this can change by the time the products are shipped.

SharePoint Portal Server can be administered in one of three ways, depending on the operation that you are trying to perform: Web browser, network place, SharePoint Portal Server Administrator. These are all described in great depth throughout the text of the book, but when using the SharePoint Portal Server Administrator, it is assumed that you know how to use the Microsoft Management Console (MMC). The MMC is also used to administer most other Microsoft products, such as SQL Server, Internet Information Services (IIS), Application Center, and others.

Who Should Read This Book

This book, while at a beginner level, is intended for anyone who is not familiar with SharePoint Portal Server. It explains in simple terminology, using examples, how to administer all aspects of a SharePoint Portal Server installation. This book is targeted for network administrators, executives, and even developers who want to get a better handle on what SharePoint Portal Server is all about. It should be known, however, that this book does not cover any programming topics. It does show where to go for additional programming information.

It is assumed that you have a basic understanding of general concepts within any of the Windows operating systems. This book does not go through any process required to setup network connectivity or domains. References are made to these concepts, but this book assumes that you have already set these things up.

How This Book Is Organized

This book is organized into thirteen chapters. These chapters are divided into four parts; SharePoint Portal Server Overview, User Navigation and Management, General Administration, and Advanced Administration.

SharePoint Portal Server Overview contains three chapters and is designed to give you an introduction to SharePoint Portal Server, explain the concepts, architecture, terminology, and installation of the product.

User Navigation and Management contains three chapters and focuses on how to use SharePoint Portal Server from a user's point of view. This part assumes that you have already setup your SharePoint Portal Server with a default configuration. It also cross-references chapters in other parts where administration is required.

General Administration contains three chapters that focus on day-to-day activities that an administrator might need to address. These activities include setting up workspaces, dashboards, discussions, folders, and much more.

Advanced Administration contains four chapters that help the administrator deal with more complex administration issues, such as security, optimization, backup, and troubleshooting. Even if you are an entry-level network administrator, you'll find this part to be very enlightening.

PART I

SharePoint Portal
Server Overview

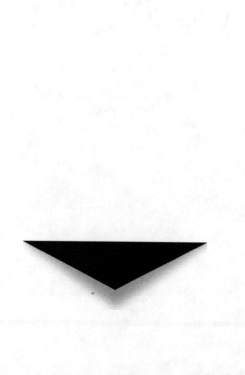

CHAPTER 1

Introduction to Microsoft SharePoint Portal Server

Welcome to the wonderful world of Microsoft's new product, SharePoint Portal Server 2001 (previously known by the code-name "Tahoe"). It is an exciting new product that allows for the effective collaboration and exchange of data, information, and ideas among peers and throughout a company or within a department.

The exchange of data is made possible by collecting information from disparate data sources and presenting it to the user in a customizable format. This format is either predetermined by an administrator, or customizable for each user. This concept is known as a *portal*. A portal is so named because all data elements must pass through the portal on its way to being presented to the user. In fact, there are three main areas that comprise SharePoint Portal Server. They are:

▼ Portal services

■ Document management

▲ Indexing and searching

Throughout this chapter, I introduce you to all of these concepts to get your creative juices flowing, your mouth watering, and adrenalin pumping. The rest of the chapters in the book show you all of these concepts in more detail. Are you ready? Let's get going.

PORTAL SERVICES

Not surprisingly, Microsoft SharePoint Portal Server provides, of course, portal services. The services provided are made available and accessed through the World Wide Web Publishing service, a component of Microsoft Internet Information Services (or IIS), version 5.0 or later. This is the version of IIS that comes with Windows 2000, all editions.

Portal services are used to gather bits and pieces of data from various sources and locations, and make them available in one handy place—your desktop. A good example of a portal is the home page at **www.msn.com**, as shown in Figure 1-1.

The data that is collected and shown via the MSN portal can be changed. To do so, you click on the appropriate link to change Content, Layout, and Colors. The Content link allows you to change the specific information that you see on the dashboard page. The Layout link allows you to change the positioning of the layout information on the dashboard page. Finally, the Colors link allows you to change the colors of the page to suit your desires.

Wouldn't it be great if you can construct a web site portal for your users just like MSN does? Well, you can. That's one of the great things about SharePoint Portal Server. Microsoft has made this *very* easy. In fact, you can provide as much or little functionality as you want; even allowing users to customize content, layout, and colors.

Collaboration is configured by setting up an *instance* of a portal by using a concept known as a workspace. A *workspace* allows for multiple portals to be set up on a single server. Each workspace requires its own set of server resources, such as memory and disk space. This sounds like a problem, but in fact, this can be a positive aspect. Separate

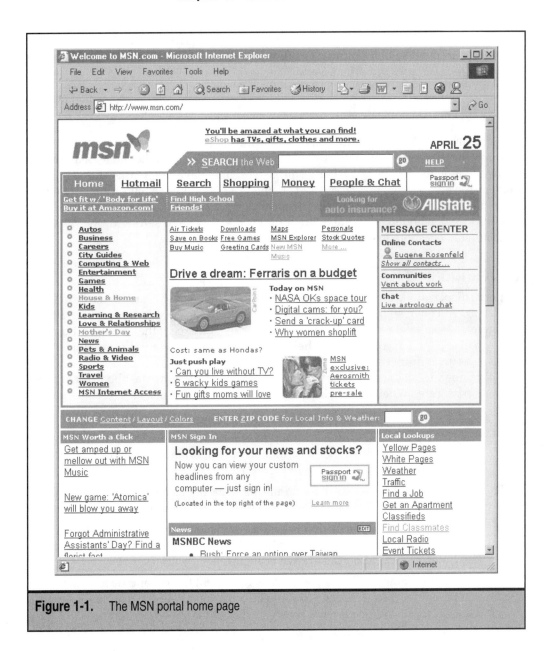

Figure 1-1.   The MSN portal home page

workspaces allow you to segregate departments, companies, or groups, if required. Each workspace has its own security settings as well. There is even a special type of workspace called an index workspace. An *index workspace* is a server dedicated to the resource-intensive work of creating and updating indexes. An index allows for fast retrieval of documents.

Index workspaces ensure that a *search server*—the server used to search for content—is not bogged down while the indexes are being created or updated. Workspaces are covered in more detail in Chapters 3 and 7.

To access the portal, you use a web browser and type in a URL in the form of:

```
http://server_name/workspace_name
```

In the above URL, substitute *server_name* with the name of your server where you have installed SharePoint Portal Server and *workspace_name* with the name of a defined workspace that you have set up. For example, you may have one workspace set up for people in the accounting department and another for executives. What's more is that you can set up security in such a way that you can restrict access to these workspaces. For more information about installing SharePoint Portal Server and setting up workspaces, see Chapter 3. For more information about security, see Chapter 10.

Digital Dashboards

The portal displays data back to a web browser using a digital dashboard. In the dashboard of your car, you have all the data you need right in front of you, like your speed, RPMs, mileage, etc. A digital dashboard is a very similar concept, except that it reflects business or personal information. You have all the data that you need (or want) to see right in front of you on your computer screen.

Although you can create your own dashboards, the following dashboards are automatically configured when the workspace is created:

▼ **Home** Provides web parts to view categories, quick links, news, subscription summary, and announcements. However, any of this can be configured and changed. For information how to do this, see Chapter 4. The Home dashboard is shown in Figure 1-2.

■ **Search** Allows you to search for documents in the portal. For more information on searching, see Chapter 8. The Search dashboard is shown in Figure 1-3.

■ **Categories** Allows you to view categories and documents that fall under those categories. For more information about categories, see Chapter 7. The Categories dashboard is shown in Figure 1-4.

■ **Document Library** Allows you to view document folders and documents that fall under those folders. For more information about the document library, see Chapter 5. The Document Library dashboard is shown in Figure 1-5.

■ **Subscriptions** Allows you to manage subscriptions. These are discussed in detail in Chapters 5 and 9. The Subscriptions dashboard is shown in Figure 1-6.

▲ **Management** Allows you to manage some distinct areas of the portal. These are discussed in Chapters 4, 7, and 9. The Management dashboard is shown in Figure 1-7.

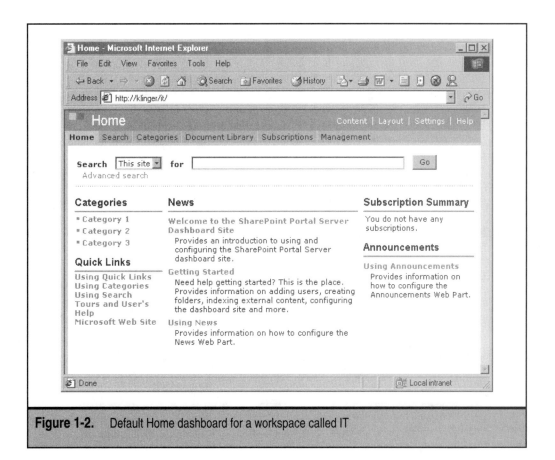

Figure 1-2.   Default Home dashboard for a workspace called IT

You can configure each dashboard for content and layout. The content refers to the data that will be presented in the dashboard. The layout refers to the physical positioning of web parts that are displayed within each dashboard. See the later section, "Digital Dashboards Are Made of Web Parts" for more information about web parts. To learn how to customize the layout and content of a dashboard, see Chapter 7.

Navigating Through the Portal

Because many of the chapters in this book discuss navigating to a specific area of the portal, I thought I would take this opportunity to discuss how to do that. *Navigation* refers to the action of getting from one screen (or area of a screen) to another. Typically, I refer to navigation as moving from one dashboard to another. For more information about dashboards, see Chapters 4 and 7.

To navigate from one dashboard to another, simply click the desired tab at the top of the screen. This will bring up the desired dashboard by contacting the web server where the portal server is installed and responding to an HTTP (or HTTPS) request for an Active

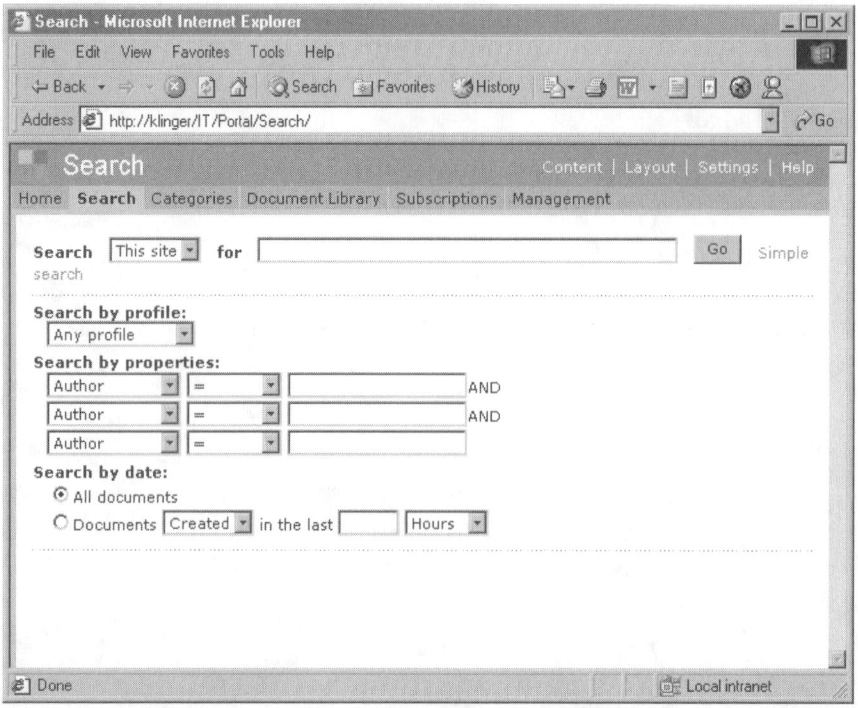

Figure 1-3.   Default Search dashboard for a workspace called IT

Server Page (ASP) that resides on that web server. These web pages are stored on the portal server in the following format:

```
http://portal_server/workspace/portal/dashboard
```

The following italicized words indicate a replacement that you must make in the format:

▼ *portal_server* is the Domain Name Server (DNS) name or TCP/IP address of the portal server. Depending on where the server is located, you may need to have a fully qualified domain name. For example, if you are trying to access my portal server called klinger in my vbasic.com domain, you will need to use klinger.vbasic.com as the fully-qualified domain name. On the other hand, if I'm trying to access the server in-house, I only have to use the name klinger.

■ *workspace* is the name of the workspace which contains the dashboard. You may only have one workspace installed on your server, but you still need to specify it!

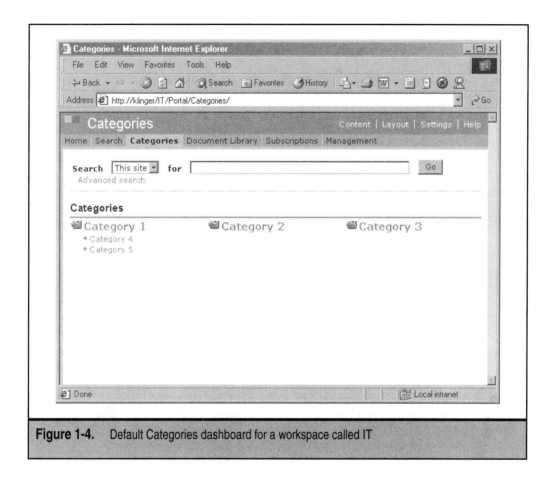

Figure 1-4. Default Categories dashboard for a workspace called IT

▲   *dashboard* is the name of the dashboard you wish to use, unless you are using the Home dashboard. In that case, you omit this part of the URL. See the last section in this chapter for a discussion about dashboards.

Digital Dashboards are Made of Web Parts

A digital dashboard is made up of smaller units, called web parts. You can write your own web parts using Microsoft Office XP, the Digital Dashboard Resource Kit (DDRK), Extensible Markup Language (XML), HTML, VBScript, or JavaScript. To learn how to customize your web parts, see Chapter 4.

Unless you customize your workspace, four web parts are automatically entered onto the Home dashboard: News, Announcements; Quick Links; and Subscriptions Summary. These web parts give basic information that a company may wish to present via the portal. In all likelihood, however, you will want to customize your Home dashboard.

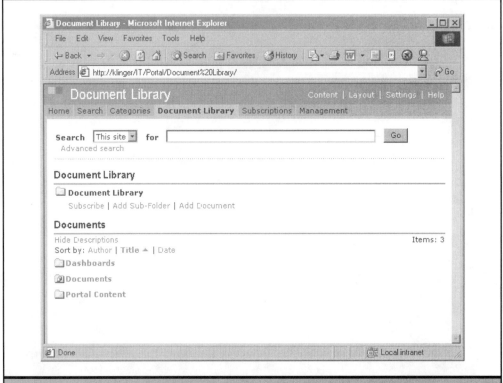

Figure 1-5.   Default Document Library dashboard for a workspace called IT

Online Catalogs

If you don't want to write your own web parts, you can choose them from a catalog of web parts. This catalog can be created and stored within your organization, or you can get them from Microsoft of course. Here is a partial listing of the types of web parts that are available from Microsoft:

▼   MSN Search

■   MSN Instant Messenger

■   MSN Money Central Stock Ticker

■   Expedia Maps

▲   Encarta Search

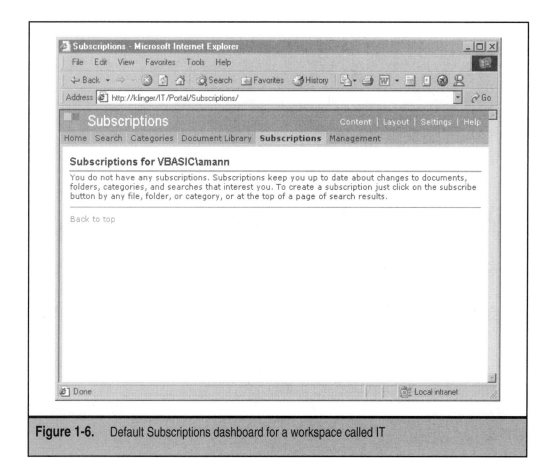

Figure 1-6.   Default Subscriptions dashboard for a workspace called IT

Client Program Extensions

In addition to using the web browser, the portal can be controlled, to a certain extent, by one of two client programs: Windows Explorer and Microsoft Office. For these client programs to interact with the SharePoint Portal Server, you must install special extensions to these programs. To learn how to install these extensions, see Chapter 3. To learn how to use these extensions, see Chapter 4.

DOCUMENT MANAGEMENT

Another main benefit of using SharePoint Portal Server is that it offers document management. Managing documents is broken into five categories:

▼   Profiling

■   Versioning

- Publishing
- Routing
▲ Security

Profiling allows you to prompt the user for specific properties—known as *metadata*—that aids in subsequent searches for the document. You can use standard properties, like Description, Author, and Title, or you can customize the properties that are stored with each document in any way that makes sense for your organization. For example, an IT

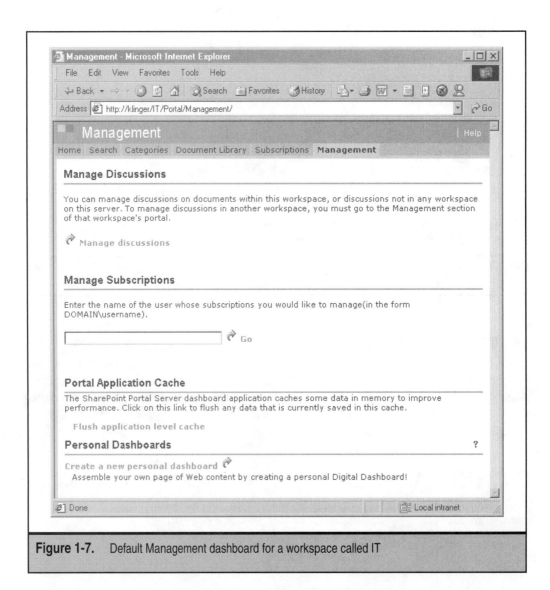

Figure 1-7.   Default Management dashboard for a workspace called IT

department might want to store the technologies specified in the document. Remember, the more granular the properties, the better searching capabilities you have. For more information about profiling, see Chapter 9.

Versioning refers to the ability of SharePoint Portal Server to store multiple versions of a document on the web server. Storing multiple versions of a document allows you to revert to a prior revision of a document. For added flexibility, you can make the latest version of your document either public or private. A public version of a document is available for searching by the general public. On the other hand, a private document can be searched, viewed, and edited only by the creator or owner, of the document. For more information about versioning, see Chapter 7.

Publishing refers to making a document available on your web server and searchable from SharePoint Portal Server, depending on the versioning scheme that you are using. If you publish a private document, only you can view it until it is made public. For more information about publishing, see Chapter 9.

Routing refers to SharePoint Portal Server's ability to route a document to one or more people for approval before publishing the document for public use. For more information about routing, see Chapter 7.

Security refers to the ability to restrict others from modifying, viewing, or searching for a document. Security in SharePoint Portal Server uses a role-based scheme. A role-based scheme is a concept whereby specific Windows 2000 security groups or users are granted specific, predefined privileges within SharePoint Portal Server. These predefined privileges are designed by Microsoft to allow for specific operations that can be performed within the product for a given folder or set of folders. These privileges are known as roles. There are only three possible roles, which are:

▼   **Author**   Can add new documents or modify existing documents within a folder.

■   **Coordinator**   Can manage content and manage categories for the portal. This role is similar to that of an administrator.

▲   **Reader**   Can only read an existing document within a folder.

In addition to the above stated roles, SharePoint Portal Server also allows you to deny a user access to specific documents, based on their individual domain account. Security is discussed in detail in Chapter 10.

INDEXING AND SEARCHING

What good is it if you have lots of stored documents if you can't find them? This question is answered by the indexing and searching features of SharePoint Portal Server. There are a few different indexing and searching features available in SharePoint Portal Server. Each is outlined on the following pages.

Keyword Searching

If you are familiar with Microsoft SQL Server 7 or SQL Server 2000, the concept of a keyword search is analogous to full-text searching. Keyword searching is performed by having the system create an index of all *non noise words* contained in the document. Non noise words are words that are not significant to the document. Such noise words that are eliminated are *the*, *a*, and *an*. The index created by the non noise words is highly optimized for fast text searching. However, the text search is only as effective as the data contained in the index. Therefore, the index must be kept current by populating it upon a specific schedule.

Categories

All documents that are stored in the SharePoint Portal Server are stored within one or more categories. For example, a category can be named Design Documents. This way, it is much faster to search because many categories can be eliminated from the search if they do not meet the criteria.

SharePoint Portal Server contains a really cool feature called the Category Assistant. This assistant will actually automatically categorize documents that don't already belong to a category. It does this by sampling the content of similar documents and makes a best guess for a category.

Best Bets

A *best bet* is a special category that can be assigned to documents that ensure that those documents appear first in a list returned from a search. In addition, a best bet is a way to indicate to users that one or more keywords have special relevance to the document(s) that match a search expression. For example, if you have a requirements document for a web site, you can search for any important words within the document, but you may want to indicate that the words "requirements" and "web" have special relevance by making them best bets. In addition to special keywords, you can include categories as a best bet.

Storage

You may be wondering about how your documents and settings are stored. Well, I cover that in detail in Chapter 2, when I discuss the architecture of SharePoint Portal Server, but it is important to begin to understand a relatively new concept of how the data in SharePoint Portal Server is stored.

In SharePoint Portal server, data is stored within a concept of web storage. The Microsoft Web Storage System is a file-based storage system that allows for unstructured data to be stored and retrieved. Web storage is a way to store data in a special database that is accessible by using your choice of many different protocols. These protocols include (but are not limited to):

▼   **HTTP**   Hypertext Transfer Protocol. As I'm sure you know, this is a universal protocol for getting data from a web server using a browser by conversing typically through TCP/IP port 80.

■   **WebDAV**   World Wide Web Distributed Authoring and Versioning. This protocol is an extension of the HTTP protocol that provides extensions for accessing content and properties of the web storage system.

■   **OLE DB**   (also version 2.5 or greater) Object Linking and Embedding for Databases. This low-level protocol allows for very efficient access to databases, which allows you to query the web storage system by using structured query language (SQL) calls.

■   **CDOEX**   Collaborative Data Objects for Exchange 2000. CDOEX is a convenient way to access Microsoft Exchange 2000 by offering a programmatic object model. These objects can be called from any programming language that supports the instantiation of COM objects, like all versions of Visual Basic or any other language in the .NET family.

■   **ADO**   (version 2.5 or greater) ActiveX Data Objects. If you have done any programming against a Microsoft SQL Server database in the last few years, you are undoubtedly familiar with ADO. If not, ADO is a language-neutral, high-level interface to the data exposed through OLE DB.

■   **MAPI**   Messaging Application Programming Interface. This API is a set of programmatic API functions (with an object model too) that allows for an industry standard way of communicating with mail storage systems. Not surprisingly, it works great with the web storage system also.

▲   **File System**   A way to access web storage by using a drive letter, such as D: or a UNC (Universal Naming Convention) path, such as **hawkeye**\ **WebStorage.**

The location of the web store is configurable, but by default the folder used to house the web storage database is c:\Program Files\SharePoint Portal Server\Data\Web Storage System. In this directory, there can be one or more of those special database files that I mentioned before. These files all have a file extension of MDB, which stands for messaging database. By default, the only file that is created when the web storage system is installed is called WSS.MDB.

NOTE: You may know of an MDB file as a Microsoft Access Database. However, as it relates to the Web Storage System, it is a Messaging Database. Therefore, the same file extension is used, but in a different format.

NOTE: The data that is retrieved by the portal from disparate sources is *not* stored in the web storage system. The disparate data is still stored and maintained within the original storage system, such as a Microsoft SQL Server database or a web site URL. Only documents that are to be stored within the SharePoint Portal Server are stored within the web storage system.

GETTING ADDITIONAL HELP

As surprising as it sounds, this book is not the only resource that you may need while using SharePoint Portal Server. If you do need additional help, I recommend that you use any of the compiled help modules (with a CHM file extension) that Microsoft ships with SharePoint Portal Server. Table 1-1 shows the available help files for SharePoint Portal Server.

Usage	File Name
Administrator's Help	\WINNT\Help\pkmadmin.chm
Planning and Installation	\WINNT\Help\pkmpig.chm
Managing Content	\WINNT\Help\pkmpmc.chm
User's Help	\WINNT\Help\webfoldr.chm

Table 1-1. SharePoint Portal Server help files

CHAPTER 2

Architecture

Before we really dive into the nitty-gritty of SharePoint Portal Server, I think it is important for you to understand the architecture and makeup of the product, as well as its supporting services. At the very heart of SharePoint is the Web Storage System, or WSS. This is a specialized database that stores all of your documents, files, settings, and links that are made available within SharePoint Portal Server. In this chapter, I explain to you all about the architecture and WSS. It also might help you to refer to the architecture blueprint in the center of this book.

WEB STORAGE SYSTEM

The Web Storage System, or WSS was introduced with Microsoft Exchange Server 2000. It is a storage system that is made up of a database system, file system, and web server all in one. These components allow for access to WSS in any of these ways:

▼ **HTTP**   Hypertext Transfer Protocol, as I'm sure you know, is a universal protocol for getting data from a web server using a browser by conversing typically through TCP/IP port 80.

■ **WebDAV**   World Wide Web Distributed Authoring and Versioning. This, too, is a protocol based on HTTP, but also provides extensions for accessing content and properties of the web storage system.

■ **OLEDB**   (version 2.5 or greater) Object Linking and Embedding for Databases. This low-level protocol allows for very efficient access to databases, which allows you to query the web storage system by using structured query language (SQL) calls.

■ **CDOEX**   Collaborative Data Objects for Exchange 2000 Server. CDOEX is a convenient way to access the Web Storage System by offering an object model which exposes programmable objects. These objects can be called from any programming language that supports the instantiation of COM objects, like all versions of Visual Basic or any other language in the .NET family.

■ **PKMCDO**   Publishing and Knowledge Management Collaborative Data Objects. PKMCDO is a programmable object model that is exposed by SharePoint Portal Server. This object model can be accessed just like the CDOEX object model, but shields you from the complexity of the Web Storage System. This is called *encapsulation*.

■ **ADO**   (version 2.5 or greater) ActiveX Data Objects. If you have done any programming that talks to a Microsoft SQL Server database in the last few years, you are undoubtedly familiar with ADO. If not, ADO is a set of programmable objects that allows you to access data from any OLEDB data source.

- ■ **MAPI**   Messaging Application Programming Interface. This API is a set of programmatic API functions (with an object model too) that allows for an industry standard way of communicating with mail storage systems. Not surprisingly, it works great with the web storage system also.

- ■ **File System**   A way to access web storage by using a drive letter, such as D: or a UNC (Universal Naming Convention) path, such as \\hawkeye\WebStorage.

- ▲ **XML**   eXtensible Markup Language. As I'm sure you've heard of by now, Microsoft is fully supporting XML in all of its .NET products. SharePoint Portal Server is no different.

WSS stores unstructured and semi-structured data in a hierarchical format. *Unstructured* data can be any random bit of data that has no structure or bearing on any other data. An example of unstructured data would be a binary stream of data representing an image. *Semi-structured* data, on the other hand, intrinsically has some basis of a hierarchical structure, but it does not have a storage mechanism. An example of semi-structured data is e-mail or a document.

ANATOMY OF SHAREPOINT PORTAL SERVER

At the core of WSS is an information store service. This service is called the Microsoft Exchange Information Store in the Services control panel applet. Then, to access this information store, many different protocols and methods can be used.

To understand Figure 2-1, let's start with the Information Store Service. Below this box in the figure, the Information Store Service talks to a storage database, known as the Web Storage System. Also, when certain events take place, calls can be made to the workflow engine or other external services. The workflow engine, as it is implemented in SharePoint Portal Server, is limited because it processes approval routing. However, the workflow engine, as it is implemented in Exchange Server 2000, is quite a bit more extensive. The external services box shown in Figure 2-1 indicates that you can write your own services or programs that respond to events generated by the Information Store Service.

In Figure 2-1, above the Information Store Service box is a series of four boxes that shows the various ways one can access the Information Store. The first is an *Installable File System Driver*, or IFS. IFS allows you to access the Information Store Service by using a drive letter. This drive letter is mapped to a workspace, which becomes available through the Windows Explorer, or any other program that can access files through a drive letter.

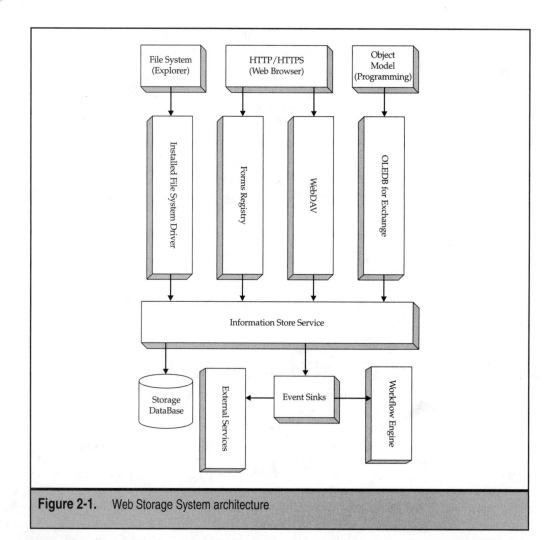

Figure 2-1. Web Storage System architecture

NOTE: The help files refer to drive M: being automatically mapped to a workspace. This was true in the beta versions of SharePoint Portal Server, but the shipping version does not automatically map a drive letter. Also, it is recommended that you do not use IFS to do any of the following:

- Create folders
- Create documents
- Assign security settings
- Edit properties

IFS is mainly used for read-only access to documents or web storage system development.

The second box is the forms registry. Although SharePoint Portal Server does not implement the forms registry, I thought I would leave it in because it is an important part of the Web Storage System in Exchange 2000 Server. The forms registry is a way to implement custom forms that are stored within the Web Storage System. The third box is the WebDAV protocol. WebDAV stands for World Wide Web Distributed Authoring and Versioning. This is a cutting-edge protocol that allows access to the information store. Both the forms registry and WebDAV are accessed using HTTP or HTTPS (Secure HTTP) with a web browser.

The fourth box is a low-level service called OLEDB for Exchange, or sometimes referred to as *EXOLEDB*. EXOLEDB allows for programmatic access to the Web Storage System by using an object model, such as CDOEX, PKMCDO, and ADO. A description of each of these object models is described earlier in this chapter, under the heading, "Web Storage System."

Folders

Folders allow you to create a structure and hierarchy in which your documents will reside. This is analogous to creating folders on your hard drive to store files. If you didn't create folders on your hard drive, you would have thousands of files located on the root of your C: drive.

Folders can be either standard or enhanced folders. Each is described in the next two sections. You should know that when you create a folder, it will be created as the same type as its parent. This is known as *inheritance*. For example, if you have a folder called Proposals, which is an enhanced folder, creating a folder called Internal under the Proposals folder will also be created as an enhanced folder. However, you should know that you can make any folder either enhanced or standard, regardless of its type when it was created.

Enhanced Folders

An enhanced folder is just like a standard folder, but as you might expect, it allows for additional functionality. These additional capabilities are:

- ▼ **Document Profiles**   Helps to organize folders and documents by allowing you to create a set of properties that are to define documents, then selecting that profile for use with specific documents.

- ■ **Check out documents**   The ability to reserve the right to make modifications to one or more documents, while all other users have to wait.

- ■ **Check in documents**   Indicating to SharePoint Portal Server that you are finished with your changes to one or more documents and you want to allow others to make changes. Other users will automatically get your changes when they check out the document(s).

- ■ **Track version history**   Allows reporting on the check in, check out, and publishing of documents.

- ▲ **Approval routing**   Specifies that one or more people must approve a document before it is published.

Standard Folders

A standard folder does not support any of the features that are available with an enhanced folder. So why would anyone create a standard folder over an enhanced folder? Well, the answer is that it depends on your organization and what you want to do. If documents contained within a folder do not need any approvals before they are published, simply use a standard folder.

Folder Locations

When you create a folder within SharePoint Portal Server, the folder is not exactly created within the Windows File System. What I mean is that if you create a folder, called Internal Docs, you cannot locate that folder by searching for it in Windows. This is because it resides within the Web Storage System. See discussion of the Web Storage System earlier in this chapter, under the heading, "Web Storage System." Although the Web Storage System can be accessed in a multitude of ways, it can be helpful to understand where the SharePoint Portal Server files are located.

Table 2-1 shows the Windows SharePoint folder locations and description of the types of files that are contained within these folders. To save space, I have used place holders, based on the choices you make when you install SharePoint Portal Server (see Chapter 3), as follows:

- ▼ <ProgFolder> = C:\Program Files\SharePoint Portal Server
- ■ <DataFolder> = C:\Program Files\SharePoint Portal Server\Data
- ▲ <workspace> is the name of the workspace that you've created

Windows SharePoint Folder Location	Description
<ProgFolder>	Main parent folder that contains SharePoint Portal Server files.
<ProgFolder>\Bin	Contains the binary program files that allow SharePoint Portal Server to run.
<ProgFolder>\ClientDrop	Sub-Folder that contains setup programs for client installations.

Table 2-1.   SharePoint Portal Server Folder Locations

Windows SharePoint Folder Location	Description
<ProgFolder>\ClientDrop\Languages	Sub-Folder that contains one folder for each available client language.
<ProgFolder>\ClientDrop\Languages\enu	Sub-Folder for client installation programs in English.
<ProgFolder>\ClientDrop\Languages\enu\MSI	Sub-Folder that contains the client setup program for English.
<DataFolder>	Main parent folder used to store SharePoint data. If you accept the default installation locations, this directory will actually be under the <ProgFolder>.
<DataFolder>\FTData	Sub-Folder that contains other folders for holding Full-Text data. Most likely, this full-text data is only for SharePoint server, but could be for other services as well.
<DataFolder>\FTData\SharePointPortalServer	Sub-Folder that contains other folders for holding Full-Text data for SharePoint Portal Server.
<DataFolder>\FTData\SharePointPortalServer\AutocatPlugin	Folder for holding plug-ins for auto-categorization rules for the server.
<DataFolder>\FTData\SharePointPortalServer\Config	Sub-Folder that contains configuration files for SharePoint Portal Server. Such files include noise word files, which are discussed in Chapter 8.
<DataFolder>\FTData\SharePointPortalServer\GatherLogs	Sub-Folder that contains other folders for holding log files.
<DataFolder>\FTData\SharePointPortalServer\GatherLogs\<workspace>	Contains log files for the workspace
<DataFolder>\FTData\SharePointPortalServer\GatherLogs\<workspace>_train$$$	Contains log files for the trained Category Assistant in the workspace
<DataFolder>\FTData\SharePointPortalServer\Projects	Sub-Folder that contains other folders for workspace-related files

Table 2-1.   SharePoint Portal Server Folder Locations *(continued)*

Windows SharePoint Folder Location	Description
<DataFolder>\FTData\ SharePointPortalServer\ Projects\<workspace>	Sub-Folder that contains data for a given workspace.
<DataFolder>\FTData\ SharePointPortalServer\ Projects\<workspace>\ AutocatPlugin	Folder for holding plug-ins for auto-categorization rules for the workspace.
<DataFolder>\FTData\ SharePointPortalServer\ Projects\<workspace>\Build	Sub-Folder that is a container for indexes in a workspace
<DataFolder>\FTData\ SharePointPortalServer\ Projects\<workspace>\Build\ Indexer	Sub-Folder that contains other folders and files for indexed-related activities.
<DataFolder>\FTData\ SharePointPortalServer\ Projects\<workspace>\Build\ Indexer\CiFiles	Stores files generated while building indexes.
<DataFolder>\FTData\ SharePointPortalServer\ Projects\<workspace>\Build\ Indexer\NlFiles	Stores files generated while building indexes.
<DataFolder>\FTData\ SharePointPortalServer\ Projects\<workspace>\Build\ IxBuild	Sub-Folder that is a container for temporary files used while building indexes
<DataFolder>\FTData\ SharePointPortalServer\ Projects\<workspace>\Build\ IxBuild\PropInfo	Stores property information for indexes that are being built.
<DataFolder>\FTData\ SharePointPortalServer\ Projects\<workspace>_train$$$	Contains training data for the Category Assistant in the workspace

Table 2-1. SharePoint Portal Server Folder Locations *(continued)*

Windows SharePoint Folder Location	Description
\<DataFolder>\FTData\ SharePointPortalServer\ Projects\\<workspace>_train$$$\ AutocatPlugin	Contains plug-ins for auto-categorization rules for the Category Assistant in the workspace
\<DataFolder>\ Web Storage System	Folder that contains the web storage system database, WSS.MDB
\<ProgFolderDir>\Ows	Folder containing files for the Office Web Server for integration with Microsoft Office

Table 2-1.   SharePoint Portal Server Folder Locations *(continued)*

WORKSPACES

A workspace is the main container for all of your documents, folders, files, settings, categories, and data. Before you can do anything in SharePoint Portal Server, you must create a workspace. In fact, the setup process will force you to do so. However, you can create additional workspaces.

NOTE: You can create a maximum of 15 workspaces on a server. However, unless your server is loaded with resources, you probably want to move some of the processing off to another server.

So, when should you create more than one workspace? Well, that depends. Many organizations will need only one workspace for access to a portal. It is more likely that you will need another workspace to crawl content to create indexes (known as an index workspace) than you will need to create another workspace for portal access. To see how to create an index workspace, see Chapters 3 and 8.

There may be times that you want to create additional workspaces other than index workspaces. You see, each workspace is assigned its own set of resources. One workspace really has nothing to do with other workspaces. Although security is covered in Chapter 10, you should know that one of the most common reasons to set up additional workspaces is for security purposes. Suppose you have a departmental workspace, called IT, for use in the Information Technology department. You give all members of the IT department access to this workspace. However, you don't want them to have access to special confidential information that executives need. Therefore, you decide to implement an additional workspace called Executive. This way, you can give only executives access to that workspace.

Another similar scenario is that of an Application Service Provider (ASP). Typically, an ASP would host a SharePoint Portal Server workspace. However, just because another client wishes to use SharePoint Portal Server, the ASP will not necessarily dedicate another box for that client. Therefore, creating another workspace gives the separation of clients because each workspace has its own set of resources.

> **NOTE:** If the SharePoint Portal Server computer that hosts multiple clients is also used for indexing, then one client's indexing tasks can actually affect data retrieval in another client. Therefore, in an ASP model, you must consider your architecture very seriously.

MICROSOFT DOWNLOADS

This is a good point to let you know that you can extend the architecture of WSS and SharePoint Portal Server itself. Microsoft provides some great resources to help with this in the form of Software Development Kits (SDKs). The use of these SDK's are outside the scope of this book, but I wanted to let you know that they exist.

Web Storage System SDK

The web storage system SDK provides mostly detailed, in-depth programming information; there is some great architectural documentation in the SDK. It can be downloaded at:

```
http://msdn.microsoft.com/downloads/default.asp?url=/downloads/
sample.asp?url=/msdn-files/027/001/654/msdncompositedoc.xml
```

SharePoint Portal Server SDK

Although this SDK is more for programmers than administrators, it does provide help files that tell you much about the overall concepts and architecture of SharePoint Portal Server. It can be downloaded at:

```
http://www.microsoft.com/sharepoint/downloads/tools/SDK.asp
```

Web Storage System Developer Tools

This is one toolset that is not just for developers. Although it does come with developer-related tools, one of the most useful tools that you'll ever use with SharePoint Portal Server and WSS is the Web Storage System Explorer. The WSS Explorer is shown in Figure 2-2.

The Web Storage System Explorer allows you to browse all objects in WSS and their properties. It can be downloaded at:

```
http://msdn.microsoft.com/downloads/default.asp?URL=/code/
sample.asp?url=/MSDN-FILES/027/001/557/msdncompositedoc.xml
```

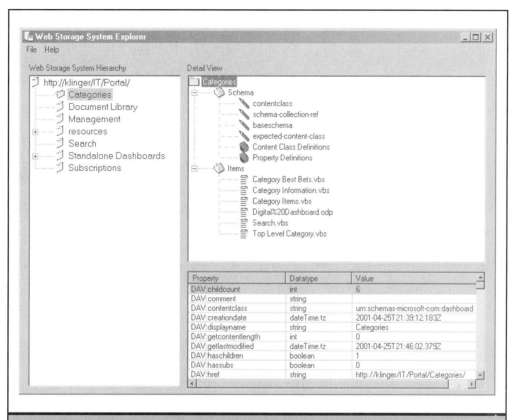

Figure 2-2. Web Storage System Explorer

SHAREPOINT TEAM SERVICES

You may have heard that there is another "sister" product to SharePoint Portal Server, called SharePoint Team Services. This product shares the same name, "SharePoint," but really has little in common with SharePoint Portal Server, except that they both allow you to collaborate on documents.

SharePoint Team Services is designed for small workgroups to publish documents and make those documents searchable by team members. It is a good collaborative solution, but is scaled-down considerably from SharePoint Portal Server.

Table 2-2 shows a comparison between the two products. As you can see, there are many advantages to using SharePoint Portal Server, which includes the use of the Web Storage System. This allows for lots of different types of data to be stored because it doesn't have to be structured like it does in other databases, such as SQL Server. On the other hand, there are some nice features of SharePoint Team Services, like the fact that you can customize security roles and that it has surveys.

Functionality	SharePoint Portal Server	SharePoint Team Services
Portal	Yes	Yes
Search Scope	Enterprise	Within team web only
Discussions	Yes	Yes
Notifications	Yes	Yes
Surveys	No	Yes
Uses Web Parts	Yes	No
Document Management	Yes	No
Document Publishing	Yes	Yes
Customizable Security Roles	No	Yes
Administrator Role	Yes	Yes
Coordinator Role	Yes	No
Author Role	Yes	Yes
Advanced Author Role	No	Yes
Contributor	No	Yes
Browser/Reader	Yes	Yes
Storage Mechanism	Web Storage System	SQL Server
Server License Required	Yes	Yes, but a FrontPage 2002 Server License, not SharePoint
Client Licenses Required	Yes	No
Targeted Users	75+	5 - 75
Clients can use a Browser	Yes	Yes
Clients can use Windows Explorer	Yes	No
Clients can use FrontPage 2002	No	Yes
Clients can use Office 2000	Yes	No
Clients can use Office XP	Yes	Yes

Table 2-2.   Comparison Between SharePoint Portal Server And SharePoint Team Services

Need a Survey?

OK, here's a cheap plug. Do you need additional survey capabilities? Do you wish your SharePoint Portal Server could support surveys? Do you need surveys that can be used over the web or via XML-based web services? If you answered "yes" to any of these questions, then I've got something for you. Check out the web site at **http://www.transport80.com**, or e-mail me at **tmann@vbasic.com** for more information.

CHAPTER SUMMARY

In this chapter, you learned about how SharePoint Portal Server stores the files needed to function properly. This chapter also discussed the storage mechanism behind storing documents within SharePoint Portal Server. You discovered the basics of how folders are used to manage the plethora of documents that you will make available from within the portal. The details of managing folders is shown in Chapter 7.

This chapter also showed some topics that are not covered in this book in too much depth. Such topics include using the Web Storage System SDK and the SharePoint Portal Server SDK. Additionally, the book focuses on SharePoint Portal Server, not SharePoint Team Services. SharePoint Portal Server is a separate, licensed product, whereas SharePoint Team Services comes with Office XP. Therefore, besides comparing and contrasting these products, SharePoint Team Services is not mentioned in this book.

CHAPTER 3

Installation

Installing SharePoint Portal Server is quite simple. However, there a few considerations that you must understand. In this chapter, I'll show you all about installing SharePoint Portal Server and let you know about the prerequisites. If you would like to know more about how to scale your SharePoint installation into more than one server, see Chapter 11.

As with most Microsoft products, there are two types of installations:

▼ Server

▲ Client

A *server* installation allows you to install the parts of SharePoint Portal Server that will respond to client requests. These parts include:

▼ **Microsoft Search**   Service to provide full-text searching throughout documents

■ **Portal Server components**   Miscellaneous components are installed on the web server, which make up the server itself.

▲ **Client Components**   Client components are automatically installed with a Server installation.

A *client* installation allows you to perform certain actions within Windows Explorer or Microsoft Office. These are not actual applications, but extensions to Windows Explorer or Microsoft Office. For more information about using these extensions, see Chapter 4.

PREREQUISITES

Before you install SharePoint Portal Server, you must make sure that your hardware and software conform to a minimal level. This minimal level is known as a *prerequisite*. There is a different prerequisite depending on whether you are installing server components or client components. These hardware and software requirements are outlined on the next few pages.

Server Components

For server components, you must be using Microsoft Windows 2000 Server or Advanced Server editions. SharePoint Portal Server is not supported on Windows 2000 Professional or Datacenter editions. In addition, you must be running Windows 2000 Service Pack 1 or greater. If you need to download Service Pack 1, direct your browser to:

```
http://www.microsoft.com/windows2000/downloads/servicepacks/sp1/default.asp
```

Windows 2000 Service Pack 2

Although not required for SharePoint Portal Server, it is a good idea to install the latest service pack available. At the time of this writing, Service Pack 2 was the latest available. Generally, Microsoft incorporates prior service packs and hot fixes into the latest service pack, so the latest one is all you'll need. Service Pack 2 can be downloaded at:

`http://www.microsoft.com/windows2000/downloads/servicepacks/sp2/default.asp`

In addition to the operating system with Service Pack 1, you'll need to have three options installed, all of which are included with Windows 2000:

▼ Internet Information Services (IIS) 5.0

■ World Wide Web Publishing Service

▲ Simple Mail Transport Protocol (SMTP) Service to send e-mail

Hardware

The hardware requirements for installing server components are:

▼ **Computer Processor**   Intel Pentium III or higher

■ **Memory**   256MB recommended, but 512MB or greater is a good idea

▲ **Hard Disk**   550MB minimum space, broken up like this:

A minimum of 160MB is needed on the drive that contains the operating system, plus a minimum of 60MB is needed for SharePoint Portal Server program files, plus a minimum of 330MB is needed on the drive that contains data files.

Software

If you are going to install the server components, you will have the following software issues to consider:

▼ *Exchange Server 5.5 or earlier* cannot co-exist on the same server as SharePoint Portal Server.

■ *Exchange 2000 Server* can co-exist with SharePoint Portal Server, but Exchange 2000 Server must be installed first and must have Exchange 2000 Server Service Pack 1 or greater installed prior to installing SharePoint Portal Server.

■ *Site Server* (any version) cannot co-exist on the same server as SharePoint Portal Server.

■ *Windows 2000 Cluster Service* cannot be installed on a SharePoint Portal Server computer. Also, you should not attempt to have a SharePoint Portal Server computer join a Windows 2000 Cluster.

■ *SharePoint Team Services* cannot co-exist on the same server as SharePoint Portal Server.

▲ *SQL Server 7 or 2000* can co-exist with SharePoint Portal Server. Also, you should know these versions of SQL Server come with the Microsoft Search service for full-text indexing.

For additional information about the coexistence of programs with SharePoint Portal Server, refer to the Microsoft "Q" article, Q295012 by using the URL:

```
http://support.microsoft.com/support/kb/articles/Q295/0/12.ASP
```

Client Components

The client components that can be installed from the SharePoint Portal Server CD are not actually applications, but extensions to Windows Explorer and Microsoft Office. For these extensions to be installed, you must conform to the minimum requirements for hardware and software as outlined next.

Hardware

The hardware requirements for installing client components are:

▼ **Computer Processor**   Intel Pentium 200 MHZ or higher.

■ **Memory**   64MB recommended, but 128MB or greater is a good idea. In fact, if you plan to do a lot of searching, 1GB is not unreasonable.

▲ **Hard Disk**   30MB minimum space on Windows 2000, 50MB on all other supported platforms.

Software

For client components, you must be using Microsoft Windows 2000 Professional, Server, or Advanced Server editions as well as any version of Windows XP. The client components will not run on Windows 2000 Datacenter edition.

Netscape Limitation

There is a limitation in Netscape whereby advanced searches are not supported. For additional information, refer to the Microsoft "Q" article, Q274711 by using this URL:

```
http://support.microsoft.com/support/kb/articles/Q274/7/11.ASP
```

You can also use Windows 98 or Windows NT 4 (with Service Pack 6a installed), but you will not have full functionality. If you are using either of these two operating systems for a client installation, you will not be able to manage coordinator features, such as:

▼ Content sources (see Chapter 7)

■ Scheduled updates (see Chapter 8)

■ Subscriptions (see Chapters 5 and 9)

■ Categories (see Chapter 9)

▲ Profiles (see Chapter 9)

You'll be glad to know that the majority of the functionality of the SharePoint Portal Server is accessed by using a web browser. Internet Explorer 4.0.1 or greater or Netscape 4.7.5 or greater is required. These browsers can run under most operating system that supports them, such as Windows 95, Windows 98, Windows NT, Windows Me, all editions of Windows 2000, and Windows XP.

SERVER INSTALLATION

Installing SharePoint Portal Server is very easy. Installation is performed by answering questions in a series of steps. Most of the time, you simply accept all the defaults presented in these steps and the installation program does the rest. This section guides you through installing Microsoft SharePoint Portal Server 2001 on your server. After you install SharePoint Portal Server, you may want to to install the client-side components. I discuss installing client components later in this chapter under the heading "Client Installation."

NOTE: The installation process can take up to 15 minutes, depending on the speed of your computer.

Server Components

Three separate components make up a server installation. They are:

▼ **Web Storage System**   Special storage system that stores unstructured or semi-structured data, such as that which is available in SharePoint Portal Server. The web storage system is discussed in Chapter 2.

■ **Microsoft Search**   Search service used to find your documents and data.

▲ **SharePoint Portal Server**   Programs, files, and components that make up the SharePoint Portal Server.

Microsoft Search Service

The version of Microsoft Search service that comes with SharePoint Portal Server is later than that which comes with SQL Server 2000. This is generally not a problem, but uninstalling SharePoint Portal Server does not uninstall this version of the service. Additionally, uninstalling SharePoint Portal Server on a computer that contains SQL Server 2000 might render SQL Server's Microsoft Search service inoperative.

To install the server components, follow these simple steps:

1. Start the Setup program.

   Place the SharePoint Portal Server CD-ROM into the CD-ROM drive. If your CD-ROM is configured to run automatically when a disc is inserted, the SharePoint Portal Server setup program runs automatically. If your CD-ROM is not configured to run automatically when a disc is inserted, choose Start | Run. then type D:\launch.exe in the Open text box. If D: is not the letter corresponding to your CD-ROM drive, then substitute your drive letter for D:.

   In either case, the Setup program begins with the choices shown in Figure 3-1.

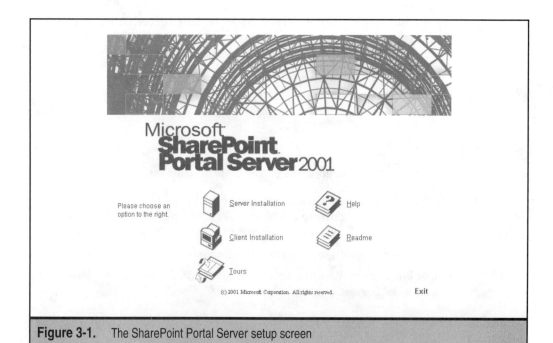

Figure 3-1.   The SharePoint Portal Server setup screen

2. Enter the Server Welcome screen.

   Click Server Installation to start the installation program for a server installation. After a few moments needed to load the setup program, you'll see the welcome screen, as shown in Figure 3-2. This is the first screen in a series of steps that the program will guide you through.

3. Accept the License Agreement.

   Click Next to enter the License Agreement screen. Read the agreement and click I Agree. Doing so will enable the Next button to continue with the installation. The License Agreement screen is shown in Figure 3-3.

4. Choose installation folders.

   Click Next to enter the Installation Folders screen. This screen is shown in Figure 3-4. To change any of the paths, simply click Change Folder and choose the desired path. You can change the path of these folders:

   ■ **Program Files** This is the path where the SharePoint Portal Server installation files will be installed. You probably want to select a drive where you have placed other program files on the server. If you have multiple disk drives or partitions, you may want to place operating system files on the C: drive and program files on the D: drive.

   ■ **Data Files** This path is where your data will reside. Most likely this will be the same drive that the program files reside on, or perhaps you have a separate drive where you store your data.

   If you are unsure of how much disk space you have on each of your drives, click Disk Information. Doing so brings up a listing of requested and remaining space available on each drive. Clicking this button brings up this dialog box:

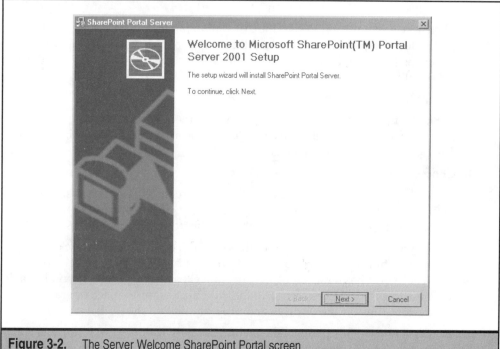

Figure 3-2. The Server Welcome SharePoint Portal screen

NOTE: You will see all drives listed in this dialog box, including CD-ROM drives, even though you cannot write data back to a CD-ROM drive.

5. Specify Indexing Settings.

Click Next to enter the Indexing Settings screen. Although indexing is not covered until Chapter 8, you can specify indexing information on this screen. If you already know about indexing and wish to enter this information now, you can. Otherwise, we won't enter indexing information now. We'll defer that until Chapter 8. Therefore, uncheck Enter This Information Now. You'll notice all fields become disabled, as shown in Figure 3-5.

6. View Installation Progress.

Click Next to begin copying files. As files are copied and the system is being set up, you can view the progress of the installation of all three server components. Figure 3-6 shows the screen that allows you to view the progress of the installation.

7. Review and fix errors.

After installation, if there were any errors, the Component Messages screen appears. The information displayed is not too detailed, but you will be prompted

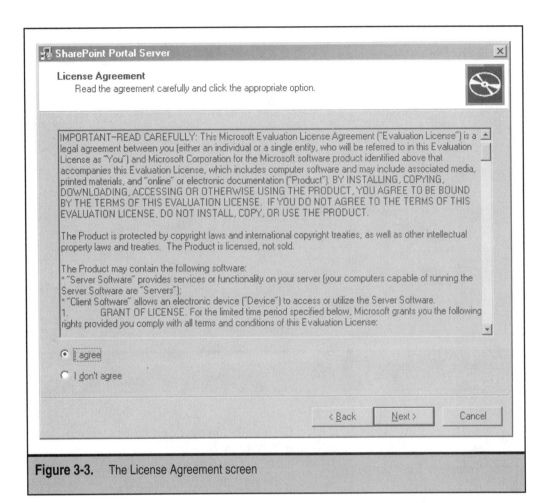

Figure 3-3. The License Agreement screen

where to go for more detailed information about the error. Figure 3-7 shows this screen.

To help you understand the types of error messages that you might see, this is the error message that was listed in the C:\Program Files\Microsoft Integration\ SharePoint Portal Server\Logs\errorlog.txt file, as shown in Figure 3-7:

```
[05/06/01,21:43:12] SharePoint Portal Server: [2]
CPkmSetupComponent::CreateSearchApplication, Error setting
default access account. The account specified during setup or in
the unattended install file is not valid.  hr=0x8007052e
```

This error occurred because the network cable became unplugged during the installation. However, normally, the installation goes off without a hitch. If you

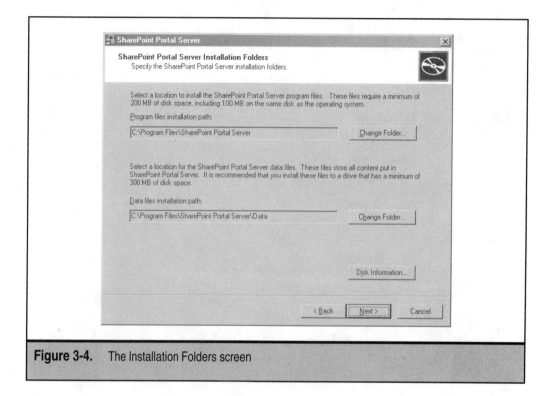

Figure 3-4. The Installation Folders screen

experience any errors at all, start the installation over or refer to Chapter 13 to see if there are any troubleshooting tips that will help.

8. Complete the installation.

   If no errors occur (see step 7), finish the installation by clicking Finish, as shown in Figure 3-8.

Workspace Installation/Setup

Setting up a new workspace is also quite easy. You can setup a new workspace by using the New Workspace Wizard. This wizard is invoked in one of two ways:

▼ Automatically at the completion of the SharePoint Server installation

▲ Manually by following the procedure noted in Step 1 below

To create a new workspace, follow these simple steps:

1. Start the New Workspace Wizard.

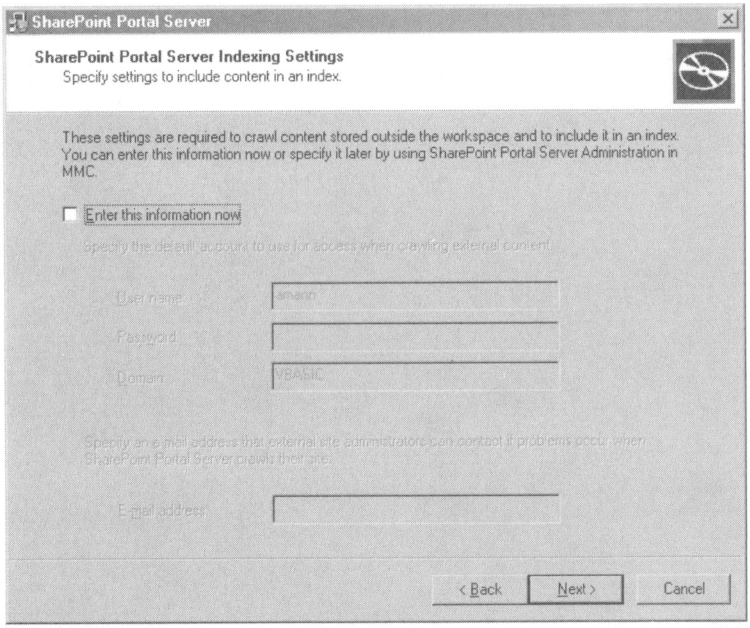

Figure 3-5.   The Indexing Settings screen

If the New Workspace Wizard is not already shown, but you have already installed the server components, you can still bring up the New Workspace Wizard manually. To do so, you can use these steps:

a. On the server, open the SharePoint Portal Server Administration MMC console by selecting Start | Programs | Administrative Tools | SharePoint Portal Server Administration.

b. Drill-down to the name of your server.

c. Right-click the details pane and select New | Workspace.

If you are setting up the server components, after successful installation, the New Workspace Wizard will appear automatically, as shown in Figure 3-9.

2. Define your workspace.

Click Next to enter the Workspace Definition screen, shown in Figure 3-10. Give your workspace a name. You can also give your workspace a description. Although a name is required, a description is not. You will refer to your workspace in a web browser by this name, so make sure that you use a name that is germane to the way you will use the workspace. For example, if the

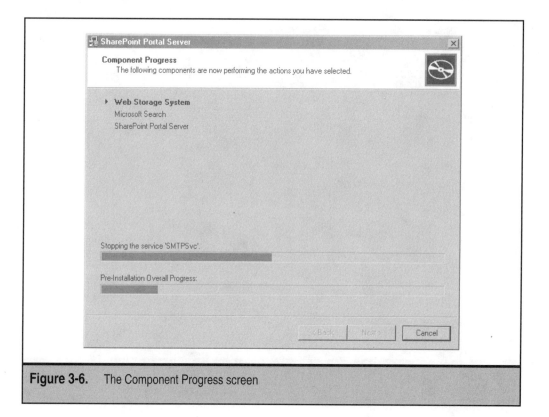

Figure 3-6. The Component Progress screen

workspace is to be used only by IT personnel, you may want to name the workspace IT. It is entirely possible that you may need only one workspace for your organization.

NOTE: Each workspace uses its own set of resources, so be aware that creating many workspaces will require more resources.

Once you enter a workspace name, the Advanced button becomes enabled. This button allows you to configure the workspace as an indexed workspace. Index workspaces are covered in more detail in Chapter 8.

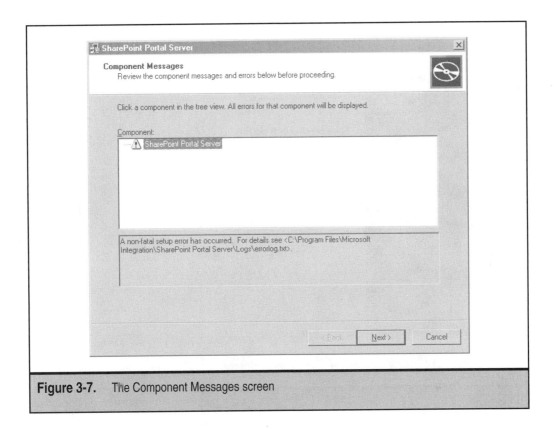

Figure 3-7. The Component Messages screen

If you do decide to make this an indexed workspace, follow these steps:

    a. Click Advanced. This brings up this dialog box:

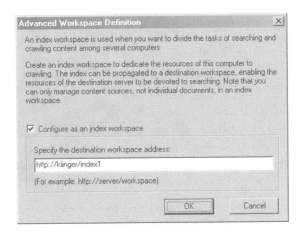

Figure 3-8.   Completing the installation

    b. Click Configure As An Index Workspace. Doing so enables the only text
       box field in the dialog box.

    c. In the text box provided, enter the destination workspace address. Because
       an index workspace is only used to crawl content (which is described in
       Chapter 8), enter the HTTP URL that will be used to access this workspace.
       Such a name could be **http://klinger/index1** .

    d. Click OK to save your changes and close the Advanced Workspace Definition
       dialog box.

3. Enter Contact Information.

   Clicking Next shows you the Workspace Contact screen shown in Figure 3-11.
   Simply specify the name and e-mail address of the administrative person to
   contact for the workspace. Both of these fields are required to continue.

4. Review your settings.

   Clicking Next shows you the Completing the New Workspace Wizard screen
   shown in Figure 3-12. Review all the information on this screen, as this will be

Figure 3-9.   The New Workspace Wizard welcome screen

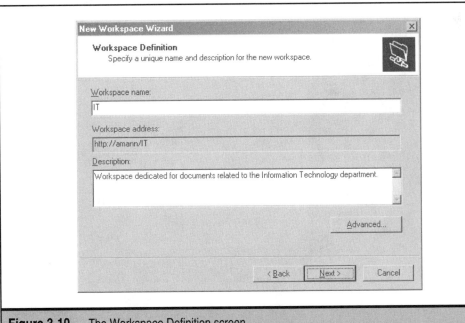

Figure 3-10.   The Workspace Definition screen

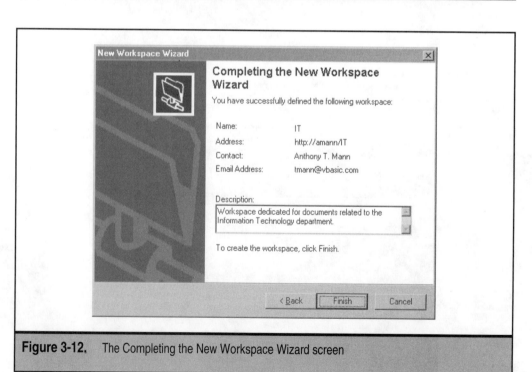

Figure 3-11.   The Workspace Contact screen

Figure 3-12.   The Completing the New Workspace Wizard screen

your last chance to change anything before the workspace is created. If you wish to change anything, click Back.

5. Create your workspace.

   Clicking Finish creates your new workspace using the criteria and settings that you've specified in the wizard steps. Doing so shows this message while you are waiting:

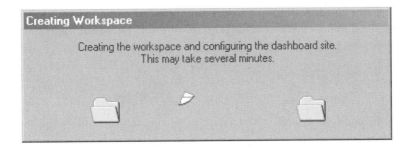

6. Create a shortcut to your workspace.

   After the workspace is created, you will be given a choice to create a shortcut to the workspace in My Network Places, as shown here:

   I would suggest clicking OK, as this shortcut is referenced many times throughout this book.

CLIENT INSTALLATION

There is not a specific client program that is used to access SharePoint Portal Server. Instead, you can access the portal by using any of the following:

▼ **Web browser**   Standard web browser, such as Internet Explorer 4.0.1, or Netscape 4.7.5, or greater. The browser does not need any special installation. To use the portal, simply access it using a URL. Portal usage is discussed in Chapter 4.

- **Office 2000 and Office XP extensions** Extensions that allow access to the portal server directly from Office 2000 or Office XP. The use of the Office extensions is covered in Chapter 4. The Office extensions are installed as part of the client installation.

▲ **Windows Explorer** Extensions that allow access to the portal server directly from Windows Explorer. The Windows Explorer extension usage is also covered in Chapter 4. The Windows Explorer extensions are installed as part of the client installation.

Installing the client extensions could not be simpler. To install the client extensions, follow these steps:

1. Start the Setup program.

   Place the SharePoint Portal Server CD-ROM into the CD-ROM drive. If your CD-ROM is configured to run automatically when a disc is inserted, the SharePoint Portal Server setup program runs automatically. If your CD-ROM is not configured to run automatically when a disc is inserted, choose Start | Run then type D:\launch.exe in the Open text box. If D: is not the letter corresponding to your CD-ROM drive, then substitute your drive letter for D:.

   In either case, the Setup program begins with the choices shown in Figure 3-13.

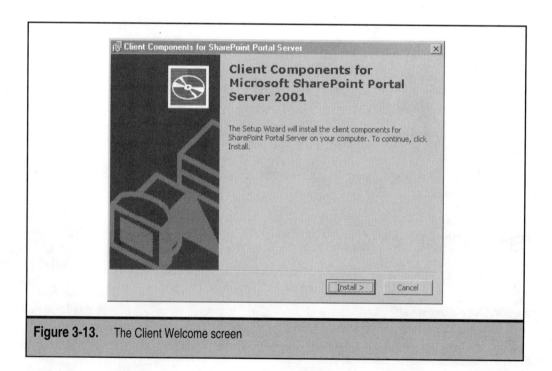

Figure 3-13.   The Client Welcome screen

2. Enter the Client Welcome screen.

   Click Client Installation to start the installation program for the client extensions. A welcome screen appears, as shown in Figure 3-13.

3. Begin the installation process.

   Click Install to install the client extensions.

4. View the installation progress.

   During the installation process, you can view the progress. Figure 3-14 shows the screen that allows you to view the progress.

5. Finish the installation.

   Clicking Finish, as shown in Figure 3-15, closes the installation program and completes installing the client extensions.

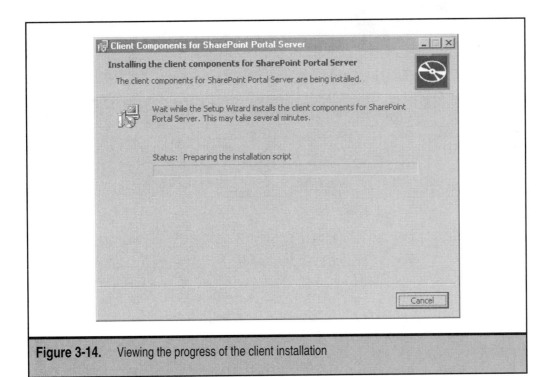

Figure 3-14. Viewing the progress of the client installation

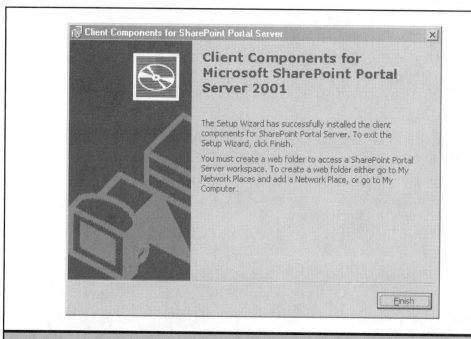

Figure 3-15. Finishing the client installation

PART II

User Navigation and Management

CHAPTER 4

Portal Navigation

I f you have been reading this book from the beginning, you now have an understanding about the overall concepts and architecture of SharePoint Portal Server. In addition, you learned how to install SharePoint Portal Server, and the client components. Now, before any administration or document management, in this chapter, I'm going to show you how to use the portal as if you were a regular user and not an administrator. This is an important concept because, as an administrator, you'll have to do some testing before you release the product to your audience.

NETWORK PLACES

Most chapters in this book show you how to access SharePoint Portal Server by using a network place. What is a network place? Quite simple! If you minimize all of your open windows to show your Windows 95, 98, Me, NT, XP, or 2000 desktop, you'll notice an icon called My Network Places or Network Neighborhood. Double-clicking this icon shows you all of the network places that have been configured on your system. A *network place* is a shortcut to a resource located somewhere on the network. Network places can be any of the following resource types:

▼ **Shared folder**   folder that has been explicitly shared on your LAN or WAN. The format is:

`\\server_name\share_name`

An example would be a network share called Download on a server named Klinger, or \\Klinger\Download.

■ **Web folder**   folder that is available on a web site. These folders are available through HTTP or HTTPS, just as you would use in a web browser. Note that this is the type of resource you'll be accessing when you create a network place for use with SharePoint Portal Server. The format of this share is similar to that of a shared folder, but uses the HTTP protocol. The format is:

`http://webserver_name/share_name`

For SharePoint Portal Server, *share_name* is the name of the workspace. An example would be a workspace called IT on a server named winchester, or http://winchester/IT.

▲ **FTP site**   FTP is a protocol that allows the transfer of actual files (instead of web pages) over the internet. An FTP site is an explicit share on an FTP server that has been configured for use with the FTP protocol. The format of this share is similar to that of a shared folder or web folder, but uses the FTP protocol. The format is:

```
FTP://ftp_server_name/share_name
```

An example would be the softlib share on the Microsoft FTP site called ftp.microsoft.com, or FTP://ftp.microsoft.com/softlib.

I cannot show how to create a network place in all operating systems. Therefore, to create a network place in Windows 2000, Windows XP, or any of the Windows .NET Servers, you use the Add Network Place wizard. For all other operating systems, refer to the system documentation. To use the Add Network Place wizard, follow these steps:

1. Close or minimize all windows.

   Closing or minimizing all windows shows the Windows desktop.

2. On the Windows Desktop, double-click My Network Places.

   Opening this icon brings up a window that shows all the network places that have been configured already, like this:

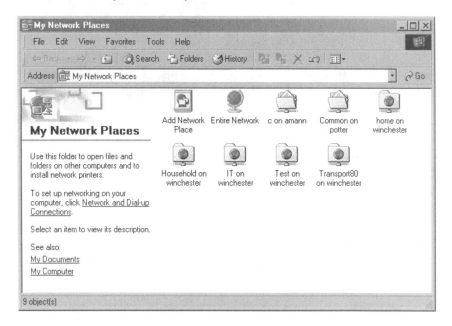

3. Double-click Add Network Place.

   Double-clicking this icon invokes the Add Network Place wizard, showing the welcome screen, like this:

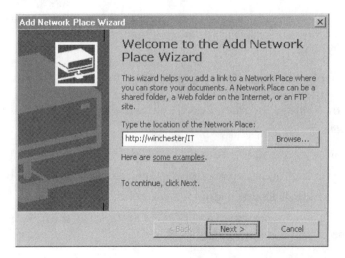

4. Type the location of the Network Place.

   Again, for SharePoint Portal Server workspaces, you will be creating a network place that points to a web folder. For example, if you want to create a network place that points to the IT workspace on the winchester server you would type:

   ```
   http://winchester/IT
   ```

NOTE: The Add Network Place Wizard will validate that the location exists before you can continue.

5. Click Next.

6. Enter a name for the connection.

   By default, the name of the connection will be in the format of *workspace_name* on *server_name*. Therefore, the name of the connection in the above example is IT on winchester. This is illustrated here:

7. Click Finish.

    You have now set up a new network place. If you open the My Network Places folder, you'll see your new network place. To open it, simply double-click it.

DASHBOARDS

The "portal" part of SharePoint Portal Server serves as a focal point for data from disparate systems. These disparate systems can include:

▼   Web pages

■   XML documents

■   Custom programs

■   Data from databases

▲   Many other resources

To help organize the portal, SharePoint Portal Server allows you to break-up your disparate systems into logical pages that make sense to you. These pages are known as dashboards.

As an example of how you may want to implement the SharePoint Portal Server product in your business, I refer you to what I've termed the "enterprise" scenario. To illustrate this point, consider that you might want to organize your corporate data using the following dashboards:

▼ **Home**   Home page to serve as a welcome page and display news and info

■ **Search**   Web page to allow for searching enterprise documents

■ **IT**   Web page dedicated to the information technologies department

■ **Executives**   Web page dedicated to executives

■ **Personal**   Web page that allows for personalization

▲ **Administration**   Web page that allows administrators to change settings

SharePoint Portal Server is not necessarily just a business application. You can also use this on a personal network if you have one setup. I refer to this as the "home" scenario. It is designed as a 'mish-mash' of information presented through the portal:

▼ **Home**   Upcoming events, To Do lists, instant messaging, and stock ticker

■ **Shopping**   Displays and allows entry of shopping lists

■ **Search**   Allows for document searching

▲ **Inventory**   Allows for the entering of personal inventory items and serial numbers

In the two examples presented above, you'll notice that the different dashboards have virtually nothing in common. They are bits of unrelated or somewhat-related data that needs to be displayed in the portal. All of the dashboards together are contained within a workspace. A single SharePoint Portal Server can have up to 15 workspaces.

To access and navigate from one dashboard to another, simply click the dashboard name. Take a look at Figure 4-1. It shows the Home dashboard for a workspace called IT on a server called winchester. To change from the Home dashboard to the Search dashboard, just click Search. Likewise, if you wanted to change from the Search dashboard to the Subscriptions dashboard, simply click Subscriptions.

PERSONAL DASHBOARDS

Most dashboards are not configurable by general users. To configure a dashboard's contents and layout, you must have Coordinator privileges. However, even Authors can configure personal dashboards. For more information about security, see Chapter 10.

TIP: You need Coordinator privileges to configure a personal dashboard's content and layout. However, when a personal dashboard is first created, the owner of that dashboard is given Coordinator access to that dashboard.

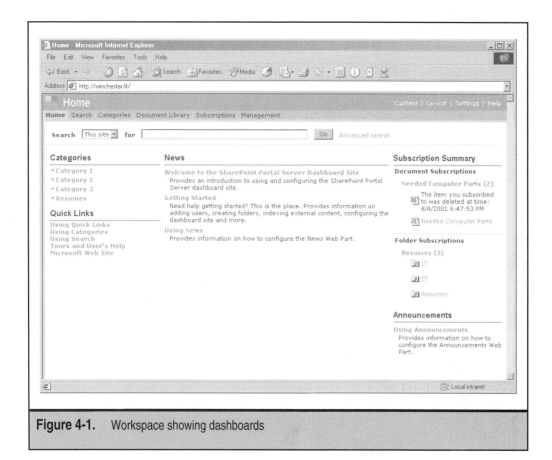

Figure 4-1.   Workspace showing dashboards

Adding and removing dashboards, as well as web parts, from the server's perspective is covered in Chapter 7. However, the workspace coordinator can set up a personal dashboard that allows the user to change the settings of this specific dashboard. Configuring a personal dashboard is quite simple. To do so, follow these easy steps:

1. Open the web browser on the client's computer.

   On the client's computer, open the web browser. If you are using Internet Explorer, go to Start | Programs | Internet Explorer.

2. Type in the base URL of the portal's workspace.

   The portal's workspace follows this syntax:

   ```
   http://server_name/workspace_name
   ```

   Therefore, to open the workspace called Home on the server winchester, type:

   ```
   http://winchester/home
   ```

3. Click the Management dashboard tab. This brings up the screen shown in Figure 4-2.

Notice that Figure 4-2 displays the word "Portal" in the URL. This is placed in the URL automatically by SharePoint Portal Server:

TIP: To see the Management dashboard, you must be either assigned to the Coordinator role for the workspace, be a member of the Domain Admins Windows NT or Windows 2000 Active Directory groups, or a member of the local Administrators group. If you choose to add yourself as a member of the Domain Admins group, you must reboot your workstation for the changes to take effect.

4. Click Create A New Personal Dashboard.

Doing so brings up the settings screen shown in Figure 4-3.

5. Type in the name of your dashboard, give it a caption, and a description.

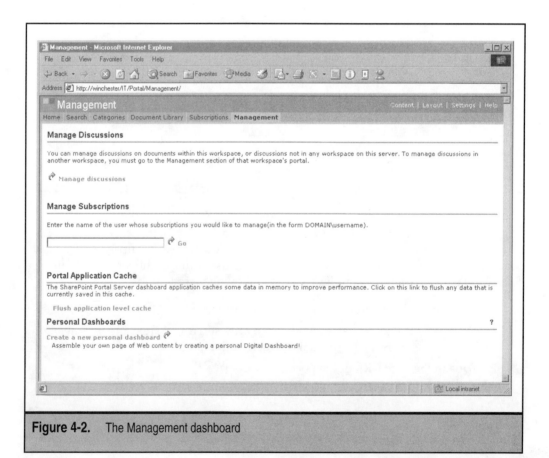

Figure 4-2. The Management dashboard

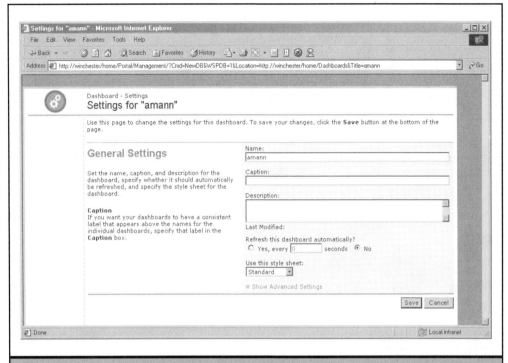

Figure 4-3.   The Settings screen for a new personal dashboard

By default, your user name will appear as the name of the dashboard site. This name will be used in the URL to access the dashboard. The caption will appear above the dashboard name in smaller type. The description will appear as a tooltip when the mouse hovers over the dashboard name. Both the caption and description are optional.

6. Click Save to create your dashboard site.

TIP: You must have either Author or Coordinator privileges on the Dashboards folder to save a dashboard. If you change these settings for the workspace, you do not need to reboot or even close the browser. You need only to refresh the page in the browser.

7. Add content to your dashboard.

Your dashboard is physically created at the completion of the last step. However, it has no content. To create content, click Content at the top of the page. This brings up the screen shown in Figure 4-4.

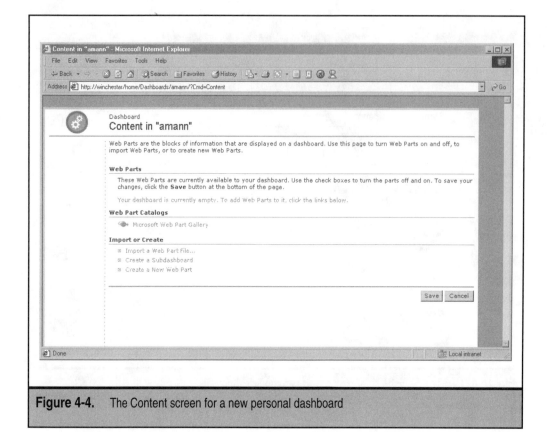

Figure 4-4. The Content screen for a new personal dashboard

8. Select web parts to be placed on the page.

    You have the following options to define where the web parts should come from:

    ■ **Web Part Gallery** The only gallery available after you install SharePoint Portal Server is the Microsoft Web Part Gallery. You can create your own galleries by using the SharePoint Portal Server SDK.

    ■ **Import a Web Part File** This option allows you to import a saved web part file (with a DWP file extension) or an XML web part file (with an XML extension). This allows you to easily exchange web parts with other users.

    ■ **Create a Subdashboard** Allows you to create another dashboard that is visible in the line at the top of the portal (where Home, Search, Categories, etc., are displayed). Dashboard and subdashboard creation is covered in Chapter 7.

CAUTION: The link to create a subdashboard seems to be ill-placed. You think of a dashboard as a part of a portal, so it would make sense to configure the dashboards at that level. However, the placement of the new dashboard item depends on what page is currently displayed when you click the subdashboard link. If you are at the home dashboard, then the link is created on the top line. If you are positioned on any other dashboard, the subdashboard will be created hierarchically beneath that dashboard. Therefore, you can actually have multiple dashboards placed under a current dashboard. This is particularly useful when you have too much content to display on a single dashboard. For example, suppose you wish to display additional web parts for scanned documents, as opposed to other types of documents. You might have a Scanned dashboard, as well as an Other dashboard created as subdashboards under the Documents dashboard.

- **Create a New Web Part**   Lets you create a web part "on-the-fly." With this option, you can specify individual parameters for either HTML, VBScript, JavaScript, or XML content. Choosing this option does not provide the best editor in the world. In fact, it is quite difficult to create complex web parts using this method. However, if you want to create a simple script or provide a link to another web site, this is a "quick and dirty" way to do it.

9. Click Save to add your web parts to your dashboard site.

10. To access the personal dashboard, use this syntax:

```
http://server_name/workspace_name/dashboards/dashboard_name
```

Therefore, to access the personal dashboard named amann (that's me) on the server named Winchester in a workspace called home, here's what you type in the browser's URL:

```
http://winchester/home/dashboards/amann
```

WEB PARTS

Notice the dashboard examples that I presented earlier in this chapter, in the section "Dashboards". Each dashboard is fairly dissimilar to the other dashboards, but each dashboard contains bits of data that *are* related to the dashboard. For example, in the home scenario, the Upcoming Events and To Do lists are both considered to be general information that is germane to the home page. Another thing they have in common is that they both can be stored in Microsoft Exchange. These parts that make up a dashboard are called web parts.

So where do you get these web parts? There are three main places where you can get web parts:

▼ **Microsoft**   Microsoft provides a web part catalog for free and trial downloads. It is located at:

```
http://www.microsoft.com/sharepoint/downloads/webparts/
default.asp
```

■ **Third parties**   Individual vendors can provide web parts on their web sites.

▲ **Build them yourself**   You can write your own web parts to suit your needs. I don't go into too much detail on how to do this, as it requires knowledge of either HTML, VBScript, JavaScript, or XML. I do not teach any of these concepts in this book, but if you are familiar with these languages, see the section later in this chapter on creating web parts.

The next few sections describe web parts in more detail.

Web Part Catalogs

Microsoft provides many different web parts for your usage through the use of a catalog. A web part catalog is simply a collection of web parts that are organized into a logical grouping. However, they are located in two separate places; from the digital dashboard web site, and from within the content page on any dashboard.

Microsoft Digital Dashboard Web Site for Microsoft and Third-party Tools

To access Microsoft's digital dashboard web site, point your browser to this URL:

```
http://www.microsoft.com/sharepoint/downloads/webparts/default.asp.
```

There you will find over 100 web parts that are available with more web parts being added as they are available. Some of the web parts are available from Microsoft and some are from other companies. Some of them are free; some are not. Some of the web parts that are available for download are shown in Table 4-1. Even though the web parts available will change over time, you can get an idea of what is available.

Each web part comes with its own instructions. However, most likely, you will use Import a Web Part File when you change or add content to your personal dashboard. See Chapter 7 for more information about dashboards and web parts.

Working with Web Parts from Within the Portal

From within the portal, you can download web parts. This is done when you customize the content of a dashboard. This concept is touched on thus far in this chapter. Altering content is described in more detail in Chapter 7. When you change the content of a dashboard, you have the option of downloading web parts from a catalog. The only catalog that is displayed is the Microsoft Web Part Gallery. When you click this link, you can download most of the Microsoft products that are available in Table 4-1.

The main difference in installing the web parts through the portal is that you can simply check all of the desired web parts and download them all at once. Figure 4-5 shows what the Microsoft web part catalog web site looks like. You'll receive an error if you attempt to point your browser to the Microsoft web part gallery. It must be accessed from within the portal. Doing so provides the web part gallery with calling server information.

TIP: You'll receive an error if your proxy settings are not correctly set up when trying to grab web parts from the gallery. See Chapter 10 for more information on how to set up your proxy server.

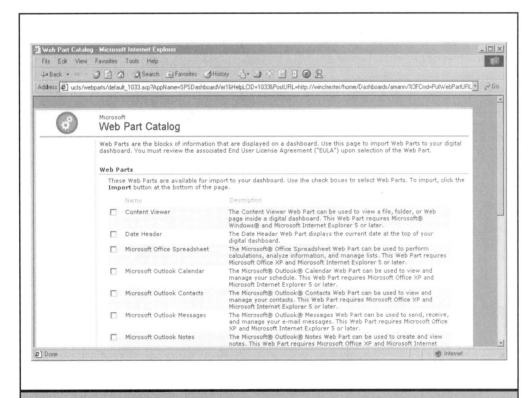

Figure 4-5. The Microsoft Web Part Gallery

Category	Company	Web Part	Status	Registration Required
Information Delivery	Bridge	BridgeInform	Free	No
Business Intelligence	Business Objects	SharePoint Portal Integration Kit	Free, but only if existing customer	Yes
Business Intelligence/CRM/ERP/Knowledge Management/Project Management/Tools	Correlate Technologies	Correlate K-Map	Trial	Yes
Business Intelligence	Crystal Decisions	Report Alerts	Demo	Yes
Business Intelligence	Crystal Decisions	Report Listing	Demo	Yes
Business Intelligence	Crystal Decisions	Report Viewer	Demo	Yes
Business Intelligence	Crystal Decisions	Report Thumbnails	Demo	Yes
Business Intelligence	Decision Support Panel	DSP Trend Arrow	Demo	Yes
Information Delivery	DotNetWire	.NetWire News Headlines	Free	No
Information Delivery	Factiva	Search and Track Modules	Trial	No
Information Delivery	Hoovers	Misc. Financial News and Info	Charge, but Downloadable	Yes
Tools	InfoImage	InfoImage Portal Object to Microsoft Web Part Conversion	Free	Yes

Table 4-1. Web Parts Available From The Microsoft Digital Dashboard Site

Category	Company	Web Part	Status	Registration Required
Business Intelligence	Knosys	ProClarity Web Parts	Demo	No
Business Intelligence/ERP	Microsoft	GreatPlains	Purchase	Yes
CRM	Microsoft	Siebel Miscellaneous Web Parts	Free	No
ERP	Microsoft	SAP Toolbox	Free	No
Information Delivery	Microsoft	Web Links	Free	No
Information Delivery	Microsoft	MSNBC Weather	Free	No
Information Delivery	Microsoft	MSNBC Stock Quotes	Free	No
Information Delivery	Microsoft	MSNBC Stock News	Free	No
Information Delivery	Microsoft	MSNBC Business News	Free	No
Information Delivery	Microsoft	MSN Money Central Stock Quotes	Free	No
Information Delivery	Microsoft	MSN Money Central Search	Free	No
Information Delivery	Microsoft	MSN Search	Free	No
Information Delivery	Microsoft	MSN Money Central Stock Ticker	Free	No
Information Delivery	Microsoft	MSN Encarta Reference	Free	No
Information Delivery	Microsoft	Simple HTML Viewer	Free	No
Information Delivery	Microsoft	Date Header	Free	No
Information Delivery	Microsoft	Content Viewer	Free	No
Knowledge Management/ Tools	Microsoft	Instant Messenger	Free	No
Microsoft Apps	Microsoft	Misc. Outlook Tools	Free	No
Microsoft Apps	Microsoft	Office XP Spreadsheet	Free	No

Table 4-1.   Web Parts Available From The Microsoft Digital Dashboard Site *(continued)*

Category	Company	Web Part	Status	Registration Required
ERP	Navision	Portal Web Parts	Demo	No
Business Intelligence/ Information Delivery	NQL	Phone Messenger	30-day Trial	Yes
Business Intelligence/ Information Delivery	NQL	Any POP3 Anywhere	30-day Trial	Yes
Business Intelligence/ Information Delivery	NQL	Dynamic Video	30-day Trial	Yes
Business Intelligence/ Information Delivery	NQL	Web Chat	30-day Trial	Yes
Business Intelligence/ Information Delivery	NQL	NQL Text to Speech Quote Reader	30-day Trial	Yes
Business Intelligence/ Information Delivery	NQL	SQL 2000 Script	30-day Trial	Yes
Project Management	PCubed	Project Central Web Parts	Demo	No - User ID and Password Given on Site
Business Intelligence/CRM	SAS	WebHound Report	Free, but can't be customized without purchasing software	No
Business Intelligence/Project Management	Tactical Marketing Ventures	TMS Marketing Calculator	Free	Yes

Table 4-1.   Web Parts Available From The Microsoft Digital Dashboard Site *(continued)*

Creating Web Parts

Creating a web part can be as simple or as complex as you want it to be. Your web parts are made up of scripts, so you must take the following into consideration:

▼ In what language will your web parts be written? You have a choice of HTML, VBScript, JavaScript, or XML.

■ How will you develop your web parts? Yourself? A team of developers?

■ How will you test your web parts? Yourself? Do you have a QA department?

▲ How will you implement and deploy your web parts? Will you have a web parts catalog?

TIP: To create or edit web parts, you must have Author or Coordinator privileges.

To begin creating your web parts, click Content in the upper right-hand corner of the portal page. This brings up Content page, similar to the one shown in Figure 4-4. Click Create A New Web Part at the bottom of the screen to begin. Clicking this link brings up the Settings screen shown in Figure 4-6.

Table 4-2 shows a listing of the fields on this screen and what they are used for. For simplicity sake, I have abbreviated the names of some of the fields shown on the screen to save space.

When you are finished editing the fields relating to your web part, click Save to save your web part.

Importing and Exporting Web Parts

A web part can be exported by clicking Export while editing or creating a web part. A web part is exported to a file with an extension of DWP. Exporting a web part makes it a very easy way to share web parts.

Likewise, if you have exported (or obtained an exported) DWP file, you can import it. You can even edit it, change its name, and save it as a different web part. This gives you sort of a "Save As" functionality for web parts. To import a web part, from the Content page, click Import A Web Part File. This allows you to select a previously saved DWP file, which adds it to the list of web parts.

To edit a web part, simply click Content on any dashboard. Once the content screen is displayed, you simply click the web part listed. This will bring up the settings screen that was described in the previous section.

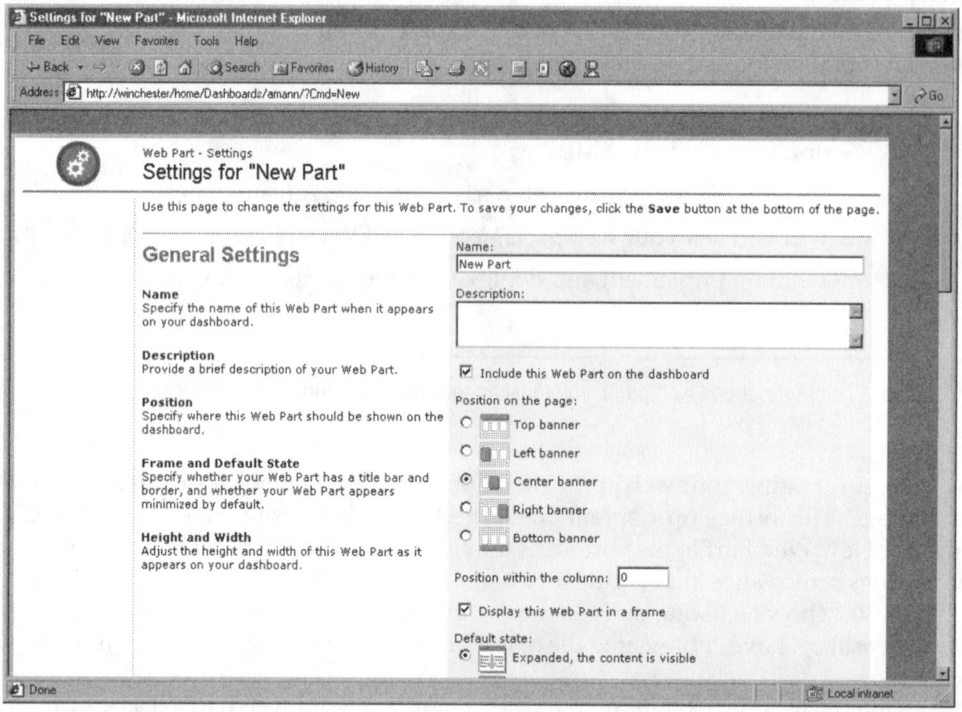

Figure 4-6. Settings screen for creating a new web part

Field	Type	Description
Name	Text Box	Used to identify the web part.
Description	Text Box	Used to further clarify what the web part is for. The Name and Description together identify the web part.
Position on the page	Option Button	You can choose which location on the page the web part will appear, but you can change it later by changing the layout. You can choose from Top, Left, Center, Right, or Bottom.

Table 4-2. Fields Available For Defining A New Web Part

Field	Type	Description
Position within the column	Text Box	Used to indicate which position within the Top, Left, Center, Right, or Bottom columns in which the web part will be displayed. There can be more than one web part in a position.
Display this Web Part in a frame	Check Box	If checked, will place the web part in a frame, allowing for a border to be shown.
Default State	Option Button	You can choose from Expanded or Minimized. If you choose Expanded, the entire content of the web part is visible, but if you choose Minimized, only the title of the web part is shown. However, the user can change the state manually at any time.
Fixed Height?	Option Button	You can choose from Yes and No. If you choose Yes, you must specify the height of the web part and the unit of measure. If you choose No, scroll bars will automatically appear if the web part is too tall for the browser.
Fixed Width?	Option Button	You can choose from Yes and No. If you choose Yes, you must specify the width of the web part and the unit of measure. If you choose No, scroll bars will automatically appear if the web part is too wide for the browser.
Type of Content	Drop-down List	You must specify the type of the content. You can choose from HTML, VBScript, JavaScript, and XML. Many of the new web parts created today are XML-based.
Get content from the following link	Check Box	If you check this box, the content of the web part will come from an HTML link. Checking this box enables a text box to type in the link.

Table 4-2. Fields Available For Defining A New Web Part *(continued)*

Field	Type	Description
Isolate web part's content	Check Box	If checked, other web parts cannot access the script specified in this web part. You may want your web parts to interact with each other. In this case, you want this field unchecked. However, this field is only enabled when you get content from another link.
Embedded content	Text Box	For VBScript or JavaScript, the actual script goes into this field. For HTML or XML, the code for the web part goes here, or the error message text goes in this field. In the later example, when the HTML or XML link is not available, the content (error message) comes from this field.
Use XSL to transform the content	Check Box	If you check this box, your script will be formatted and translated using an XSL stylesheet by specifying the link to the XSL stylesheet in the box provided. On the other hand, you can provide your own XSL code in the box provided if the link isn't available, or you wish for the stylesheet to be embedded in the web part. Note that any of your scripts, including VBScript, can be formatted using XSL. The content does not have to be XML.
Master web part matching	Check Box	If checked, the content and properties that are specified in the web part will automatically be updated when the links change.

Table 4-2.   Fields Available For Defining A New Web Part *(continued)*

Field	Type	Description
Allow users to remove web part	Check Box	If checked, a user can remove the web part from the dashboard. If not checked, the web part will be forcibly displayed on the dashboard. This is useful for corporate communications that the company wants each employee to read. *You must have Coordinator privileges to remove a web part. You cannot be an Author.*
Allow users to minimize web part	Check Box	If checked, a user can minimize the web part on the dashboard. Just like allowing the removal of a web part, a company may not want users to minimize a web part. *You must have Coordinator privileges to minimize or maximize a web part. You cannot be an Author.*
Make this web part visible on the dashboard	Check Box	If checked, the web part will be visible on the dashboard. If unchecked, the web part will be invisible. This might be advantageous if you have a web part whose main purpose in life is to communicate with other web parts, but has no visible interface.
Use the following namespace	Check Box	If checked, you must fill in the namespace in the text box provided. It is a good idea to specify a namespace when XML is the content type.
Provide content personalization	Check Box	If checked, allows you to type in a link that will allow for web part personalization. Such a web part would be a stock ticker.

Table 4-2.   Fields Available For Defining A New Web Part *(continued)*

Field	Type	Description
Provide detailed content	Check Box	If checked, allows you to type in a link to provide additional content for the web part. This is only needed if your web part is not complete in content. You may want to specify this if more than one web part shares content. This way you don't have to duplicate code.
Provide help	Check Box	If checked, allows you to specify a link to HTML help for the web part.
Store data for the web part	Check Box	If checked, you can enter data that is available to the web part. This is much like passing parameters to a program.
Should the content be cached?	Option Button	If selected, allows the content to be cached in memory. Doing so can speed-up performance. If you select this option, you can also specify whether the web part should be cached for all users or each user individually. You also specify the number of seconds to cache the web part.

Table 4-2. Fields Available For Defining A New Web Part *(continued)*

CLIENT PROGRAMS

In addition to accessing the portal from a web browser, you can also access the portal from client programs. These are implemented in the form of client extensions to existing programs. They are not new programs. Each is described in the following sections.

Before you can use either of these client extensions, you must install them. See Chapter 3 to find out how to install the client extensions. It might also help to view the Installation Diagram Blueprint in the middle of this book.

Windows Explorer

Windows Explorer utilizes the SharePoint Server extensions by allowing file-based access to the web folders. Windows Explorer does not allow you to access the portal via

HTTP directly. If you wish to access the portal using HTTP directly, you'll have to use a web browser, like Internet Explorer.

To use Windows Explorer, you must create a network place under My Network Places. To set up a network place, see the earlier section in this chapter, "Network Places." Figure 4-7 shows what the Windows Explorer looks like when you view the web folders.

After you have set up a network place, to use it you must expand your new network place. Doing so shows you these web folders, as set up by SharePoint Portal Server:

▼ **_TEMP_**   Used by SharePoint to manage temporary files. This is a hidden folder.

■ **Categories**   Stores the hierarchy of categories.

■ **Dashboards**   Stores all personal dashboards, not the main dashboards that you see at the top of the portal.

■ **Documents**   Contains hierarchy of folders and documents stored in the portal.

■ **LOCKS**   Used by SharePoint to manage concurrency locking. This is a hidden folder.

■ **Management**   Stores settings for portal and workspace-level settings.

■ **Portal**   Contains scripts for all aspects of the portal. This is a hidden folder.

■ **Portal Content**   Contains folders for displaying web parts on the Home dashboard only.

■ **SHADOW**   Contains duplicate documents used by SharePoint Portal Server. This is a hidden folder.

▲ **system**   Stores all system-related data for the portal, like users and subscriptions. This is a hidden folder.

NOTE: Of the web folders shown in the above list and in Figure 4-7, some are hidden folders that are used by SharePoint Portal Server internally and are not meant to be changed by a user or administrator. They are shown only for completeness.

Office

Similar to Windows Explorer, Microsoft Office (both 2000 and XP) are integrated into SharePoint Portal Server. However, with Office 2000, you must install the client extensions. For more information on how to install the client extensions, see Chapter 3. From Microsoft Office, you can perform any of these actions:

▼ Check-in

■ Check-out

■ Open a document

▲ Publish

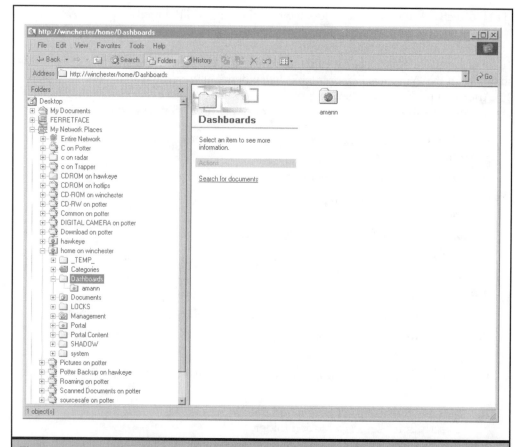

Figure 4-7.   Viewing web folders in Windows Explorer

If you are using Office XP, you will be prompted for all of these actions with dialog boxes when you save your documents. There is one caveat, however. For these additional features to be enabled, the folder that you are saving the document into must be an enhanced folder. Enhanced folders are covered in Chapter 7.

To use Microsoft Office with SharePoint, simply open the desired Office application, such as Word, Excel, or PowerPoint.

NOTE: FrontPage is not integrated with SharePoint Portal Server.

Construct your document as you normally would. The integration into SharePoint begins when you save the document. The details of saving documents (which is part of document management) into SharePoint Portal Server are discussed in Chapter 5.

CHAPTER SUMMARY

In this chapter you learned how to navigate through the portal using a web browser. In addition, you also learned how to use the Windows Explorer and Microsoft Office extensions to aid in your portal navigation and administration.

If that wasn't enough, you also learned how to add web parts to your web pages from web part catalogs. I also showed you how to create your own script-based web parts, but I didn't teach you anything about scripting. I left that up to you because it's outside of the scope of this book.

CHAPTER 5

Document Management

D ocument Management refers to the concept of (what else?) managing your documents. This includes the addition of new documents, modifying those documents, deleting, renaming, approving, and publishing. Arguably, approving and publishing could be considered outside the scope of document management because these items do not manage the content of the document; only actions to that document. However, I've included these items in this chapter because I want to show, from a user's perspective, how to manage the document as a whole, not just the content of that document.

Again, this chapter shows you about document management features of SharePoint Portal Server from the perspective of a user sitting in front of a client computer. There are some other document management-related actions that can be performed, but those are mostly in the form of configurations on the server. These configurations are shown in Chapter 9. This chapter focuses on document management from a client computer. You'll see what I mean as you read on. This chapter makes reference to actions that can be performed through the portal. This refers to using a web browser as a portal interface.

ADDING DOCUMENTS

Before you can search on a document, of course it needs to be added into the portal. You can add a document into SharePoint Portal Server in one of two ways. You can add a document through the portal or by using a network place. Each of these ways is described in the following sections.

TIP: You must be assigned to the Author or Coordinator security roles to add documents.

Using the Portal

To use the portal to add documents, you must use the Document Library dashboard. Follow these easy instructions:

1. Open the web browser on the client's computer.

   On the client's computer, open the web browser. If you are using Internet Explorer, select Start | Programs | Internet Explorer.

2. Type in the base URL of the portal's workspace.

   The portal's workspace follows this syntax:

   ```
   http://server_name/workspace_name
   ```

   Therefore, to open the workspace called IT on the server winchester, type:

   ```
   http://winchester/IT
   ```

3. Click the Document Library dashboard tab. This brings up the screen shown in Figure 5-1.

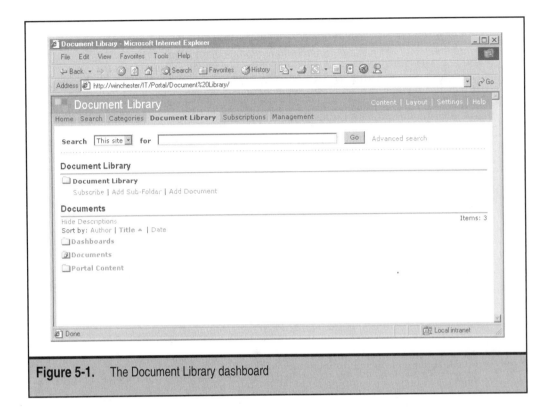

Figure 5-1.   The Document Library dashboard

4. Navigate to the desired folder.

    You can also create a new folder in which you will store documents. Creating
    folders is covered in Chapter 7. Once you create a folder, navigate to that folder
    before you add a document.

    You'll notice in Figure 5-1 that, by default, there are three folders listed in the
    Documents section of the screen. This means that hierarchically, there are
    three folders contained one level down from the Document Library dashboard.
    They are:

    ■ Dashboards

    ■ Documents

    ■ Portal Content

    Most likely, you want your documents to be stored in a folder hierarchy
    under the Documents folder, but not always. For example, if you are creating a
    news item, you would place it in the News folder, which is located under the
    Portal Content folder. You must either navigate to one of these three folders or
    create your own. You cannot add a document into the Document Library
    dashboard directly. If you do, you'll receive the error shown in Figure 5-2.

5. Click Add Document.

   Clicking this link brings up the screen shown in Figure 5-3. Notice that in the top left-hand corner of the screen is the folder that you navigated to when you clicked the Add Document link.

6. Click Browse.

   Clicking this button allows you to search your hard drive or a network share for the file that you wish to add into the web storage system. Doing so brings up the standard Windows dialog for opening a file, like this:

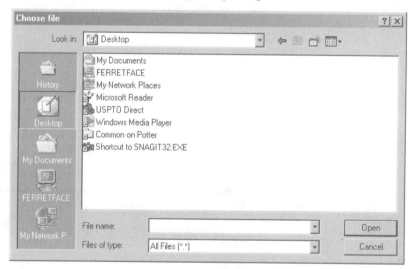

Once you locate the desired file, click Open, as you would using any other Windows program. The file I used in Figure 5-3 is named Computer Parts.xls in the McGraw-Hill folder under My Documents.

7. Choose the desired option.

   You can choose one of two additional options:

   ■ **Check in the document** Checks in the document, making it available for others to check out and work on. This would be the option to choose if you do not want it to be available for searching and reviewing by general users in the portal.

   ■ **Publish the document** Checks in the document and also publishes it. This would be the option to choose if you are finished editing the document and want to make it available to general users from within the portal. However, if any approval routing is configured on the folder where you are checking in the document, it must be approved before it is made available for searching in the portal.

8. Click Continue.

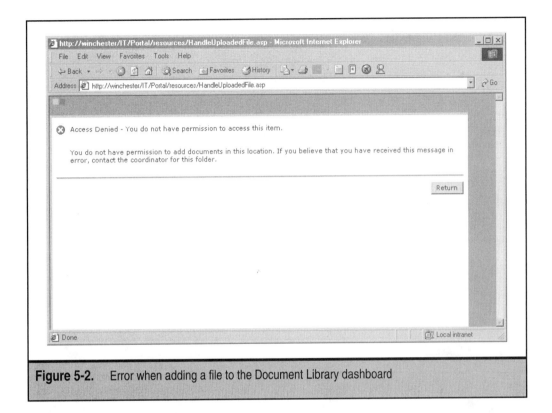

Figure 5-2.   Error when adding a file to the Document Library dashboard

Clicking this button brings up the screen shown in Figure 5-4.

9.   Select and enter the desired document profile and properties.

The Document Profile screen is divided into two sections:

- **Version comments**   Allows you to enter information relating to what you changed between the time you checked out the document and the time you checked it in. When you are adding a new document, you might want to place a descriptive note in the Enter Your Version Comments field, like Initial Document Check-In on 6/24/2001.

- **Document Profile**   Selects the desired profile (which is just a collection of properties) that you wish to use to save the document. The system administrator can decide which is the default profile (which is automatically shown when the screen comes up). Also, there may be only one profile available, as shown in Figure 5-4. If no additional profiles are created, the default profile Base Profile is used, which contains the properties also shown in Figure 5-4. Profiles are covered in Chapter 9.

You must fill in required fields (noted with a red asterisk) before you can save the document.

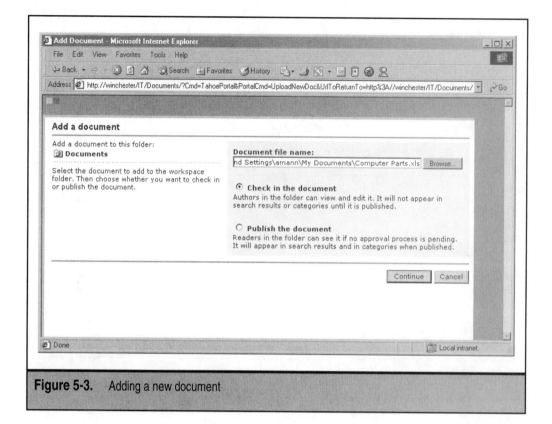

Figure 5-3. Adding a new document

10. Click Save.

FYI: If you opted to publish the document, it will not be available until after it is approved (assuming that you have configured the folder for approval routing). For more information on approval, see the section "Approval Routing" later in this chapter.

Using a Network Place

To use a network place to add a document, you can follow these easy steps:

TIP: When using a network place, you can perform bulk operations by dragging and dropping to copy files or selecting multiple files (with the SHIFT or CTRL keys while clicking the mouse) before right-clicking.

1. Open the network place that represents the workspace on your portal.

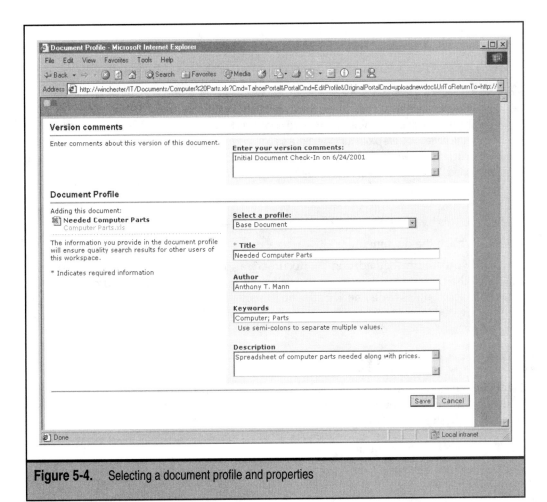

Figure 5-4.   Selecting a document profile and properties

In my example, I open the network place for a workspace called IT (for information technology) on the SharePoint Portal Server called winchester. This network place is called IT on winchester. For more information about creating a network place, see Chapter 4.

2. Navigate to the Documents folder.

3. Navigate to the desired folder under the Documents folder (we'll call this window 1).

   You can also create a folder structure at this time to hold your documents.

4. Open another Explorer window or network place (we'll call it window 2).

5. In window 2, navigate to the folder containing the document(s) that you wish to add into your portal.

6. Drag and drop the desired document(s) from window 2 to window 1.

NOTE: Adding a document to a window in this fashion does have a slight difference from adding a document through the portal. This difference is the way SharePoint checks in your documents. When using the portal, you are prompted to make a selection to check in or publish your document. However, when using a network place, none of this happens. Your documents are neither checked in nor published. You must do all of that manually.

7. Check in the document.

Do this by right-clicking the document and selecting Check In.

8. Publish the document.

If you are finished editing the document and you wish to publish it, do so by right-clicking the document and selecting Publish. This menu will not be enabled unless you check in the document first. Publishing documents is covered later in this chapter in the section, "Publishing Documents."

EDITING DOCUMENTS

Once you have added documents into the portal, you can, of course, edit them. You should know that there is no specific menu that you use to edit a document. Editing documents consists of these actions:

▼ Check out the document
■ Perform any necessary edits
■ Check in the document
▲ Publish the document if you want it to be available for searching

As with most document management features, you can edit a document through the portal or by using a network place. Each of these ways is described in the following sections.

TIP: You must be assigned to the Author or Coordinator security roles to edit documents.

Using the Portal

To use the portal to edit documents, you must use the Document Library dashboard. Follow these easy instructions:

1. Open the web browser on the client's computer.

   On the client's computer, open the web browser. If you are using Internet Explorer, select Start | Programs | Internet Explorer.

2. Type in the base URL of the portal's workspace.

   The portal's workspace follows this syntax:

   ```
   http://server_name/workspace_name
   ```

   Therefore, to open the workspace called IT on the server winchester, type:

   ```
   http://winchester/IT
   ```

3. Click the Document Library dashboard tab. This brings up the screen shown in Figure 5-1.

4. Navigate to the desired folder containing the document.

5. Click Check Out.

6. Click Open.

   Clicking this button opens the document using the appropriate program.

7. Make the desired changes to the document.

8. Save your document changes.

9. Close the program that was automatically invoked when you opened the document.

   If you are using Office XP (not Office 2000), then closing the program brings up this dialog:

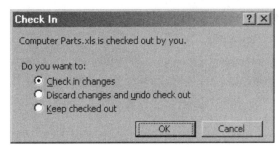

Because you have checked out the document, you are prompted to choose one of a few options:

- **Check in changes** Checks in your changes, making the document available for publishing. Additionally, if you have not saved your file first, the option is called Save changes and check in.

- **Discard changes and undo check out** Acts as if you never checked out the document and made changes.

- **Keep checked out** This option only appears if you have saved your changes before you close the program. This option closes the program, but does not check in your changes. In fact, the document is still checked out by you. This enables you to make changes later. If you have not saved your changes, the option is called Save changes only, but performs the same functionality.

10. If you are using Office 2000 (not Office XP), check in your changes.

    To check in your changes, simply right-click the file and choose Check In.

11. Select a profile and property values in the presented dialog box.

    Selecting a profile and editing property values is done exactly as it was when you added a document using the portal through a browser.

Using a Network Place

To use a network place to edit a document, you can follow these easy steps:

1. Open the network place that represents the workspace on your portal.

   In my example, I open the network place for a workspace called IT (for information technology) on the SharePoint Portal Server called winchester. This network place is called IT on winchester. For more information about creating a network place, see Chapter 4.

2. Navigate to the Documents folder.

3. Navigate to the desired folder and locate the document you wish to edit.

4. Check out the document.

   Do this by right-clicking the document and selecting Check Out.

5. Open the document.

   Opening the document entails only right-clicking the document and selecting Open.

6. Make the desired changes to the document.

7. Save your document changes.

8. Close the program that was automatically invoked when you opened the document.

If you are using Office XP (not Office 2000), closing the program will prompt you to check in your changes. For more information on these options, see "Using the Portal" under the "Editing Documents" heading. Follow this procedure to check in changes and edit properties.

9. If you are using Office 2000 (not Office XP), check in your changes.

   To check in your changes, simply right-click the file and choose Check In.

10. Publish the document.

    If you are finished editing the document and you wish to publish it, do so by right-clicking the document and selecting Publish. This menu will not be enabled unless you check in the document first. Publishing documents is covered later in this chapter in the section, "Publishing Documents."

DELETING DOCUMENTS

Inevitably, there comes a time when you must delete a document from SharePoint Portal Server, just as you must sometimes delete documents from your operating system folders. You should know that when you delete a document from SharePoint Portal Server, it is deleted from the workspace, not its original location.

In other words, suppose you have a file called Software Development Plan.doc on the C: drive. You add it to the SharePoint Portal Server using one of the methods described earlier in this chapter. Then, you decide to delete it from the portal. The file still exists on your C: drive, just as it did before you added it into SharePoint Portal Server. This is because when you add a file, you are making a copy of it from its original location to the Web Storage System. All further work on the file is done in the Web Storage System, not the original location.

Once again, to delete a file you can either use your browser in SharePoint Portal Server or use a network place. Each is described in the following sections.

TIP: You must be assigned to the Author or Coordinator security roles to delete documents.

Using the Portal

To use the portal to delete a document, follow these easy steps:

1. Open the web browser on the client's computer.

   On the client's computer, open the web browser. If you are using Internet Explorer, choose Start | Programs | Internet Explorer.

2. Type in the base URL of the portal's workspace.

   The portal's workspace follows this syntax:

   ```
   http://server_name/workspace_name
   ```

Therefore, to open the workspace called IT on the server winchester, type:

```
http://winchester/IT
```

3. Click the Document Library dashboard tab. This brings up the screen shown in Figure 5-1.

4. Navigate to the desired folder that contains the document.

   Alternatively, you can certainly search for the desired document instead of navigating through a complicated set of folder hierarchies. To learn how to do this, see the section, "Searching for Documents" later in this chapter.

5. Click Show Actions.

   Clicking this link brings up the screen shown in Figure 5-5. Notice all of the possible actions that can be performed on a document.

6. Click Delete.

   You will be prompted to confirm the delete action.

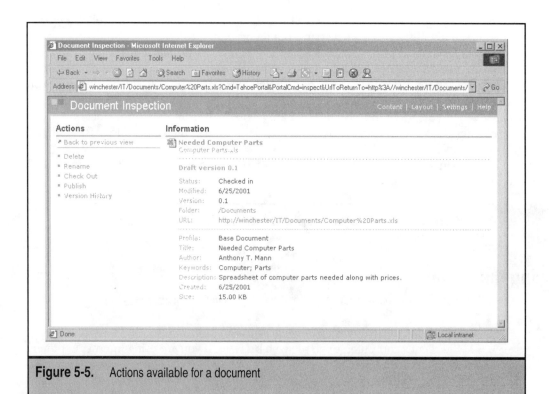

Figure 5-5.   Actions available for a document

Using a Network Place

Using a network place to delete a document from the workspace is exceedingly simply. Just follow these easy steps:

1. Open the network place that represents the workspace on your portal.

    In my example, I open the network place for a workspace called IT (for information technology) on the SharePoint Portal Server called winchester. This network place is called IT on winchester. For more information about creating a network place, see Chapter 4.

2. Navigate to the Documents folder.

3. Navigate to the desired folder that contains the document you wish to delete.

4. Simply select one or more documents to delete.

5. Press DEL or DELETE on your keyboard.

    Alternatively, you can right-click on the selected files and click Delete.

6. You are prompted to confirm deletion before the action actually takes place.

RENAMING DOCUMENTS

Just as simple as deleting a document is, renaming is probably even easier. The same rules and concepts that apply to deleting a document also apply to renaming a document. This means that you can rename a document through the portal with a browser or with a network place. Each of these are described in the next two sections.

TIP: You must be assigned to the Author or Coordinator security roles to rename documents.

Using the Portal

To use the portal to rename a document, follow these easy steps:

1. Open the web browser on the client's computer.

    On the client's computer, open the web browser. If you are using Internet Explorer, go to Start | Programs | Internet Explorer.

2. Type in the base URL of the portal's workspace.

    The portal's workspace follows this syntax:

    ```
    http://server_name/workspace_name
    ```

Therefore, to open the workspace called IT on the server winchester, type:

```
http://winchester/IT
```

3. Click the Document Library dashboard tab. This brings up the screen shown in Figure 5-1.

4. Navigate to the desired folder that contains the document.

   Just as with deleting a document, you can search for the desired document instead of navigating through a complicated set of folder hierarchies. To learn how to do this, see the section, "Searching for Documents" later in this chapter.

5. Click Show Actions.

   Clicking this link brings up the screen shown in Figure 5-5. Notice all of the possible actions that can be performed on a document.

6. Click Rename.

   Clicking this link brings up the screen shown in Figure 5-6.

7. Enter the desired new name.

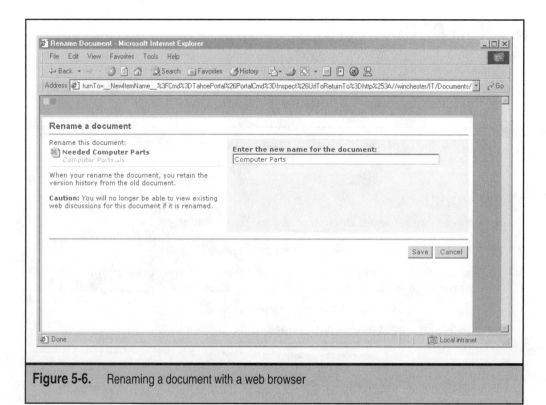

Figure 5-6.   Renaming a document with a web browser

8. Click Save to rename the document.

> **NOTE:**   The two pieces of information about the document in Figure 5-6 are the title and the file name. The title is Needed Computer Parts. This was the title entered when the file was checked in (as a property contained within a document profile). This title is a property and can be edited the way all properties can.

The file name is the actual name of the file as it existed in the original source file in the operating system. The file name in Figure 5-6 is Computer Parts.xls. This file name is what you are changing by using the rename command. However, you are not affecting the original file name; only the represented file in the Web Storage System.

Using a Network Place

Using a network place to rename a document from the workspace is also very simple. Here's how you do it:

1. Open the network place that represents the workspace on your portal.

    In my example, I open the network place for a workspace called IT (for information technology) on the SharePoint Portal Server called winchester. This network place is called IT on winchester. For more information about creating a network place, see Chapter 4.

2. Navigate to the Documents folder.

3. Navigate to the desired folder that contains the document you wish to rename.

4. Simply select one or more documents to rename.

5. Right-click on the selected files and click Rename.

    Alternatively, you can press the F2 key to enter the rename command. This is true of any Windows folder.

6. Type in the desired new name.

SEARCHING FOR DOCUMENTS

One of the major features of SharePoint Portal Server is its ability to index documents very efficiently for searching. Although I cover indexing in detail in Chapter 8, that is from the server's perspective. In this section, I show you how to perform searches from the user's perspective.

There are two types of searches that can be done in SharePoint Portal Server. You are probably relieved to know that these searches are performed only from a web browser, not from a network place. Therefore, this section becomes quite a bit simpler than the preceding sections in this chapter.

The two types of searches that are available are:

▼ **Simple**   Allows searching of keywords and the selection of search scope.

▲ **Advanced**   Allows a simple search, plus additional criteria, such as specifying property values, etc.

You'll see how to use each of these options shortly, but first, you need to be aware of something. Searching is available, by default, from four different dashboards. All of these places allow for simple or advanced searching, but the starting point of the search can actually be from one of these four different dashboards.

TIP: You must have at least Reader privileges to search for documents.

The dashboards that allow searching are:

▼ Home

■ Search

■ Categories

▲ Document Library

Although you can decide to perform a simple or advanced search at any time, from any of these four dashboards, only the Search dashboard is configured to present to you an advanced search by default. The other three dashboards present a simple search by default.

You might ask why there is duplication among dashboards. The answer is that it makes sense to search for documents from each of these, as the concept is to perform required and related activities from within a single dashboard, if possible. Although the functionality is duplicated, the code is not. Each of the four dashboards that contain searching capability do so through the Search web part. In fact, you can create your own dashboard or subdashboard and actually include this same functionality if it makes sense to do so.

Simple Searches

Again, simple searches allow only the specification of search scope and keywords. Setting up search scopes is covered in Chapter 8. A *search scope* is a way to limit the catalogs in which searching takes place. By default, search scopes are set to search the entire site, but if the system administrator sets up additional search scopes, searching can be limited and therefore much quicker.

To see how search scopes can be beneficial is to consider this example. Suppose you are a company that maintains two separate types of documents. One is for purchase orders and one is for e-mail attachments. If you are searching for a specific purchase order, you don't want to waste time searching for e-mail attachments when you know your search phrase won't produce any hits there. Therefore, limiting the search scope to only purchase orders will be faster.

To perform a simple search, follow these steps:

1. Open the web browser on the client's computer.

   On the client's computer, open the web browser. If you are using Internet Explorer, go to Start | Programs | Internet Explorer.

2. Type in the base URL of the portal's workspace.

   The portal's workspace follows this syntax:

   ```
   http://server_name/workspace_name
   ```

   Therefore, to open the workspace called IT on the server winchester, type:

   ```
   http://winchester/IT
   ```

3. Click the Home, Categories, or Document Library dashboard tab. This brings up the screen shown in Figure 5-7.

4. Select the desired search scope from the Search drop-down list.

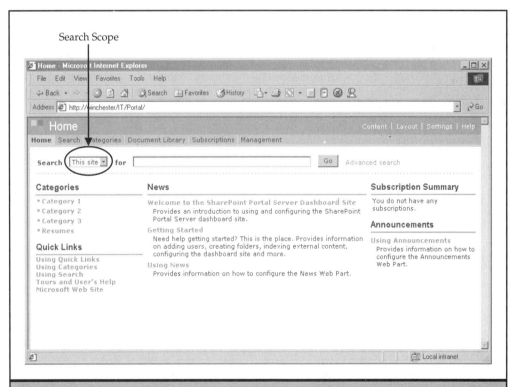

Figure 5-7.   Home dashboard, showing a simple search

5. Enter the desired search terms in the For text box provided.

    For example, type in the word Computer.

6. Click Go to begin the search.

    Search results will look similar to those shown in Figure 5-8.

NOTE: At any time, you can click Advanced Search to perform an advanced search from a simple search.

Advanced Searches

To perform an advanced search, follow these steps:

1. Open the web browser on the client's computer.

    On the client's computer, open the web browser. If you are using Internet Explorer, go to Start | Programs | Internet Explorer.

2. Type in the base URL of the portal's workspace.

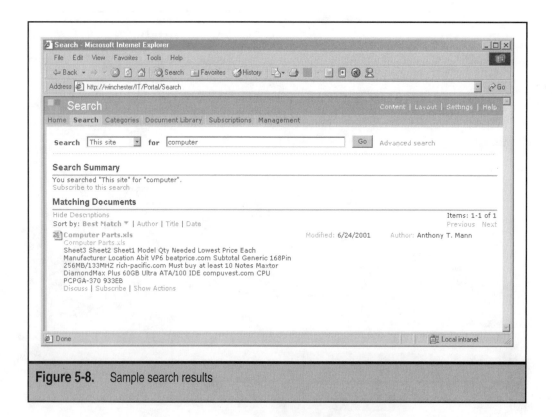

Figure 5-8. Sample search results

The portal's workspace follows this syntax:

```
http://server_name/workspace_name
```

Therefore, to open the workspace called IT on the server winchester, type:

```
http://winchester/IT
```

3. Click the Search dashboard tab. This brings up the screen shown in Figure 5-9.

4. Select the desired search scope from the Search drop-down list.

5. Enter the desired search terms in the For text box provided.

6. Click the desired document profile from the Search By Profile drop-down list to use to limit the search.

   By default, Any Profile is selected. However you can choose one profile to use for the search. You cannot choose more than one profile.

7. Limit the search by specifying values of properties in the Search By Properties section.

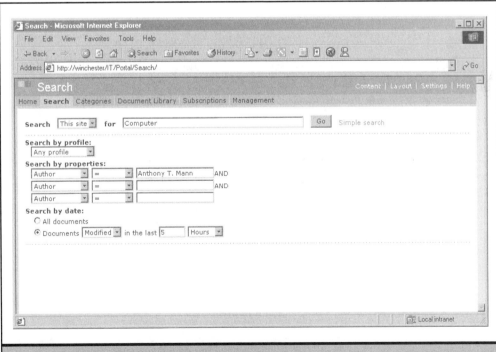

Figure 5-9.   Search dashboard showing an advanced search

You can specify up to three separate property/operator/value combinations in the Search By Properties section. If you do specify more than one combination, all of them will be considered in the search. This is known as performing an AND operation. The reason for this is that the first AND second combination must provide results, which is also known as evaluating to True. If you specify three separate values, all three must evaluate to True.

In other words, suppose you have two sets of values, like this:

```
Author_LastName = Mann
Author_FirstName = Fred
```

Suppose you have a document that was written by me, Anthony Mann. The Author_LastName property will have a value of Mann, which evaluates to True. However, the second property, Author_FirstName, will have a value of Fred, which does not evaluate to True. Therefore, the document will not be returned. Again, all conditions that you specify must evaluate to True.

This option is quite powerful because you can specify a property, a value, and a comparison to that value. For example, you specify a search where the Title property equals Computer. However, in this case, the title must exactly match the word Computer. Probably a more relevant search is to indicate that the Title property must contain the word Computer. The comparison operator in the middle drop-down list allows you to select from these operators:

- = Property value must equal the value specified.
- > Property value must be greater than the value specified. This is only useful for numerical and date fields.
- < Property value must be less than the value specified. This is only useful for numerical and date fields.
- >= Property value must be greater than or equal to the value specified. This is only useful for date fields.
- <= Property value must be less than or equal to the value specified. This is only useful for date fields.
- Contains   Property value must contain the values specified. This is only useful for text fields.

8. Limit the search by date using the options in the Search By Date section.

Document Profiles and Properties

If you have a specific document profile selected for searching when you specify your search property values and the property does not exist in the profile, no results will be displayed.

By default the search will be performed regardless of date, as noted by the selection of All Documents. If you want to limit the search based on date, click Documents and select from the next drop-down list to test for the Created Date or Modified Date. Then enter the date value that you wish to test. Finally, choose from the drop-down list of available time periods (Hours, Days, Months, or Years).

For example, if you wanted to limit your search to those documents that were modified within the last month, select Modified in the first drop-down list, type 1 in the text box, and select Months from the second drop-down list.

9. Click Go to begin the search.

Search results will look similar to those shown in Figure 5-8.

NOTE: At any time, you can click the Simple Search link to perform a simple search from an advanced search.

PUBLISHING DOCUMENTS

Publishing a document is the process of making it available to everyone from within the SharePoint Portal Server. This availability includes the ability to search for the document. However, you should know that there is one situation where you publish a document and it is not available in the portal. This situation is when approval routing is configured for a folder that contains the document. I cover setting up approval routing on a folder in Chapter 7. I cover performing the approvals (or rejections) later in this chapter, under the heading "Approval Routing."

You can publish a document by using either a web browser or by using a network place. You should know this routine by now ☺. Each is discussed in the following sections.

TIP: You must be assigned to the Author or Coordinator security roles to publish documents.

Using the Portal

To use the portal to delete a document, follow these easy steps:

1. Open the web browser on the client's computer.

    On the client's computer, open the web browser. If you are using Internet Explorer, go to Start | Programs | Internet Explorer.

2. Type in the base URL of the portal's workspace.

    The portal's workspace follows this syntax:

    ```
    http://server_name/workspace_name
    ```

Therefore, to open the workspace called IT on the server winchester, type:

```
http://winchester/IT
```

3. Click the Document Library dashboard tab. This brings up the screen shown in Figure 5-1.

4. Navigate to the desired folder that contains the document.

    Alternatively, you can certainly search for the desired document instead of navigating through a complicated set of folder hierarchies. To learn how to do this, see the section, "Searching for Documents" earlier in this chapter.

5. Click Show Actions.

    Clicking this link brings up the screen shown in Figure 5-5. Notice all of the possible actions that can be performed on a document.

6. Click Publish.

    You will be prompted to confirm that you want to publish the document. This actually makes the document "publishable." If approval routing is configured for the folder that contains the document, it won't actually be published by SharePoint Portal Server until it is approved. A visual diagram of approval routing can be seen in the blueprint section of this book. The documents that you publish must be in the Checked-in or Checked-out state or you will not be able to publish the documents.

Using a Network Place

Using a network place to publish a document from the workspace is also very easy. Just follow these easy steps:

1. Open the network place that represents the workspace on your portal.

    In my example, I open the network place for a workspace called IT (for information technology) on the SharePoint Portal Server called winchester. This network place is called IT on winchester. For more information about creating a network place, see Chapter 4.

2. Navigate to the Documents folder.

3. Navigate to the desired folder that contains the document you wish to publish.

4. Simply select one or more documents to publish.

    The documents that you publish must be in the Checked-in state or you will not be able to publish the documents.

5. Publish the document.

    Right-click the document(s) and select Publish. This menu will not be enabled unless you check in the document first. You will not receive a confirmation prompt.

APPROVAL ROUTING

The approval routing built into SharePoint Portal Server is very thorough. It allows one or more people to approve or reject a document before it is published into SharePoint Portal Server. Although I discuss setting up approval routing in Chapter 7, I'll go over some of the concepts here.

Approval routing is configured at the folder level, not the document level. The "trigger" mechanism for approval routing is when a user publishes a document into a folder that is setup for approval routing. Here is the general workflow process of a document:

1. Add into SharePoint
2. Check out the document
3. Edit the document
4. Check in the document
5. Publish the document
6. Approve or reject the document, if required

This is discussed more in Chapter 7, but a folder can be configured to have multiple approvers on a document. To aid in your understanding of approval routing, see the blueprint in the center of the book. In addition, you can specify the order in which approvers must approve a document, or even that only one person needs to approve a document.

There are quite a few approval and rejection actions that are available for a document, depending on the state of the document. Each is outlined in Table 5-1.

Action	Security	Description
Publish	Author or Folder Coordinator	Publishes a document and makes it available for approval
Cancel Publishing	Folder Coordinator	Cancels the publishing of a document
Approve	Approver	Approves a document
Bypass Approval	Folder Coordinator	Bypasses approval and directly publishes a document
Reject	Approver	Rejects approval for a document

Table 5-1. Approval And Rejection Actions For A Document

Requiring Approval

If you have not configured a folder to require approvals, the only actions that are available on a document are Publish and Check Out. Also, when you publish a document, it is immediately available to everyone that has Reader privileges or greater if the folder containing the document doesn't require approvals.

Versioning comes into play with approvals as well. As a document version primer, a version is in the form of:

```
Major.Minor
```

These version numbers help to identify changes to documents. This is also true in software. For example, version 3.0 of a piece of software is considerably enhanced in functionality over version 2.0. However, version 2.1 adds only minor fixes and enhancements over version 2.0.

The *Major* version is incremented when a document is published (and approved, if required). The *Minor* version is incremented when a document is checked out. The Minor version is decremented when the user performs an Undo Check Out action. This, in effect, reverses the Check Out action, so the minor version must be decremented to the state the document was in before the Check Out action.

Approval or rejection actions for one or more documents can be performed by using a web browser in the portal or a network place. See the next two sections to see how each of these is performed.

Using the Portal

To use the portal to approve or reject a document, follow these easy steps:

1. Open the web browser on the client's computer.

    On the client's computer, open the web browser. If you are using Internet Explorer, go to Start | Programs | Internet Explorer.

2. Type in the base URL of the portal's workspace.

    The portal's workspace follows this syntax:

    ```
    http://server_name/workspace_name
    ```

    Therefore, to open the workspace called IT on the server winchester, type:

    ```
    http://winchester/IT
    ```

3. Click the Document Library dashboard tab. This brings up the screen shown in Figure 5-1.

4. Navigate to the desired folder that contains the document.

   Alternatively, you can certainly search for the desired document instead of navigating through a complicated set of folder hierarchies. To learn how to do this, see the section, "Searching for Documents" earlier in this chapter.

5. Click Show Actions.

   Clicking this link brings up the screen shown in Figure 5-10. Note that this is similar to Figure 5-5, but it shows approval-related actions.

6. Click the desired link to Approve or Reject.

Using a Network Place

Using a network place to approve or reject a document from the workspace is also very easy. Just follow these easy steps:

1. Open the network place that represents the workspace on your portal.

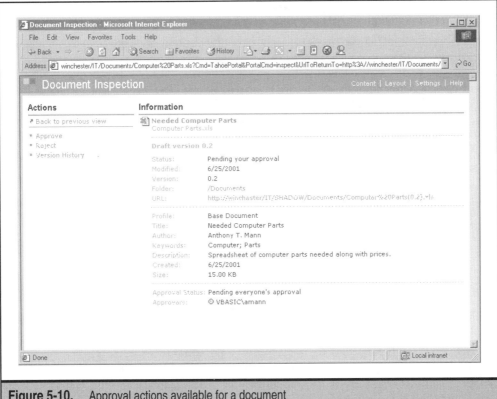

Figure 5-10. Approval actions available for a document

In my example, I open the network place for a workspace called IT (for information technology) on the SharePoint Portal Server called winchester. This network place is called IT on winchester. For more information about creating a network place, see Chapter 4.

2. Navigate to the Documents folder.

3. Navigate to the desired folder that contains the document you wish to approve or reject.

4. Select one or more documents to approve or reject.

5. Select the desired menu.

   Depending on the permissions you have, you will see one or more of the menus shown in Table 5-1 when you right-click on the selected document(s).

6. For some of the actions, you are prompted to confirm.

PERSONAL SUBSCRIPTIONS

A *subscription* in SharePoint Portal Server is similar to a subscription to a magazine or any other service. Once you subscribe, you are automatically notified of changes to that subscription content. In the magazine example, the content changes are scheduled on a periodic basis; hence the term, periodical.

A *personal* subscription is one that you personally subscribe to. Nobody else can subscribe to a publication on your behalf. You have to initiate it.

Subscriptions are created by using a web browser. You can subscribe to any or all of these items:

▼ Documents

■ Folders

■ Categories

▲ Search Results

Managing Subscriptions

Two thoughts on managing subscriptions that I want to share with you. The first is that even though you must initiate your own personal subscriptions, anyone with Coordinator privileges can delete subscriptions on your behalf. The second is that there are only two actions for subscriptions: Adding and Deleting. There is no modification of subscriptions.

NOTE: It is important to know that a single subscription can contain multiple documents. This isn't true if you subscribe to a document because the document contained within the subscription *is* the document itself. However, in the case of folders, categories, and search results, each of these subscriptions can contain multiple documents. See the next section that discusses limitations on these subscriptions.

Subscription Limitations

You cannot subscribe to an unlimited number of documents or subscriptions because a subscription consumes system resources. Although setting up subscription limitations is discussed in Chapter 7, Table 5-2 shows what the default limitations are on subscriptions.

Subscribing to a Document

To subscribe to a document, follow these steps:

1. Open the web browser on the client's computer.

   On the client's computer, open the web browser. If you are using Internet Explorer, go to Start | Programs | Internet Explorer.

2. Type in the base URL of the portal's workspace.

   The portal's workspace follows this syntax:

   ```
   http://server_name/workspace_name
   ```

Item	Limitation	Description
Maximum subscriptions for a workspace	5000	Specifies the maximum number of subscriptions for the entire workspace. Even if a user has not met their personal limit, this limit comes into effect.
Maximum subscriptions per user	20	Specifies the maximum number of subscriptions that a user can actually subscribe to. This is irrespective of the number of documents that are contained within the subscription
Maximum results per subscription	20	Specifies the maximum number of documents that can belong to a single subscription. With all default values set, a user can only subscribe to a maximum of 400 documents.

Table 5-2.   Default Subscription Limitations

Therefore, to open the workspace called IT on the server winchester, type:

`http://winchester/IT`

3. Click the Document Library dashboard tab.

4. Navigate to the desired folder that contains the document.

   Alternatively, you can certainly search for the desired document instead of navigating through a complicated set of folder hierarchies. To learn how to do this, see the section, "Searching for Documents" earlier in this chapter.

5. Click Subscribe.

   Clicking this link brings up the screen shown in Figure 5-11.

6. Specify the name of the subscription.

   By default, the name of the subscription will be the title of the document. However, you can change this to any non-blank value, as it is a required field.

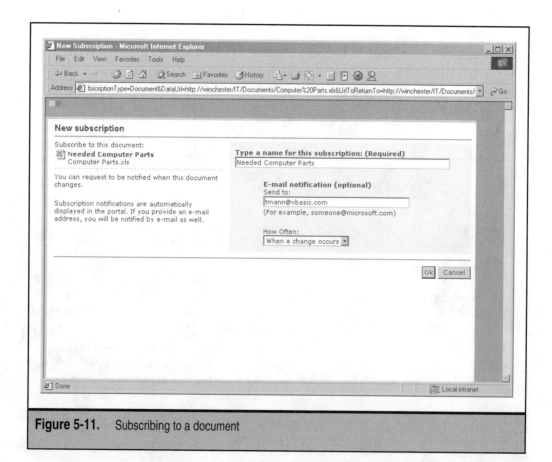

Figure 5-11.   Subscribing to a document

7. Specify e-mail notification.

   If you enter an e-mail address, which is optional, this address will be sent a message about the subscription, based on the frequency option specified next.

8. Specify the frequency.

   In the How Often field, select from the drop-down list of choices. You can choose to be notified once a day, once a week, or when a change occurs. You might choose the once a day or once a week option if you expect changes to be very frequent. This would avoid a situation whereby a document changes 10 times within a day and you get notified 10 times (by selecting the When A Change Occurs option).

9. Click OK.

Subscribing to a Folder

To subscribe to a folder, follow these steps:

1. Open the web browser on the client's computer.

   On the client's computer, open the web browser. If you are using Internet Explorer, go to Start | Programs | Internet Explorer.

2. Type in the base URL of the portal's workspace.

   The portal's workspace follows this syntax:

   ```
   http://server_name/workspace_name
   ```

   Therefore, to open the workspace called IT on the server winchester, type:

   ```
   http://winchester/IT
   ```

3. Click the Document Library dashboard tab.

4. Navigate to the desired folder.

5. Click Subscribe next to the name of the folder.

   This link for a folder is shown in Figure 5-12.

6. Specify the name of the subscription.

   By default, the name of the subscription will be the name of the folder. However, you can change this to any non-blank value, as it is a required field.

7. Specify e-mail notification.

   If you enter an e-mail address, which is optional, this address will be sent a message about the subscription, based on the frequency option specified next.

8. Specify the frequency.

   In the How Often field, select from the drop-down list of choices. You can choose to be notified once a day, once a week, or when a change occurs. You might

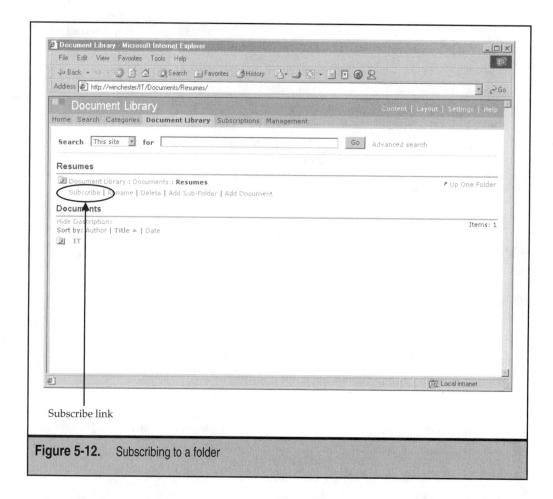

Subscribe link

Figure 5-12.   Subscribing to a folder

choose the Once A Day or Once A Week option if you expect changes to be
very frequent. This would avoid a situation whereby a document changes
10 times within a day and you get notified 10 times (by selecting the When A
Change Occurs option). If you choose the When A Change Occurs option, you
will be notified when there is any change to the folder, sub folder, or a
document contained within the folder or sub folders.

9. Click OK.

Subscribing to a Category

To subscribe to a category, follow these steps:

1. Open the web browser on the client's computer.

On the client's computer, open the web browser. If you are using Internet Explorer, go to Start | Programs | Internet Explorer.

2. Type in the base URL of the portal's workspace.

   The portal's workspace follows this syntax:

   ```
   http://server_name/workspace_name
   ```

   Therefore, to open the workspace called IT on the server winchester, type:

   ```
   http://winchester/IT
   ```

3. Click the Categories dashboard tab.

4. Navigate to the desired category.

5. Click the Subscribe To This Category link next to the name of the category.

   This link for a category is shown in Figure 5-13.

6. Specify the name of the subscription.

   By default, the name of the subscription will be the name of the category. However, you can change this to any non-blank value, as it is a required field.

7. Specify e-mail notification.

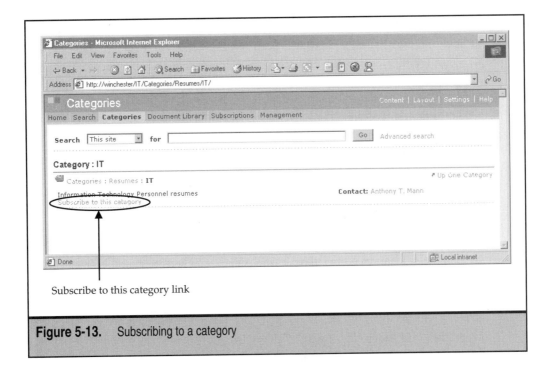

Subscribe to this category link

Figure 5-13. Subscribing to a category

If you enter an e-mail address, which is optional, this address will be sent a message about the subscription, based on the frequency option specified next.

8. Specify the frequency.

   In the How Often field, select from the drop-down list of choices. You can choose to be notified once a day, once a week, or when a change occurs. You might choose the Once A Day or Once A Week option if you expect changes to be very frequent. This would avoid a situation whereby a document changes 10 times within a day and you get notified 10 times (by selecting the When A Change Occurs option). If you choose the When A Change Occurs option, you will be notified when there is any change to the category, subcategory, or a document contained within the category or subcategories.

9. Click OK.

Subscribing to Search Results

To subscribe to search results, follow these steps:

1. Open the web browser on the client's computer.

   On the client's computer, open the web browser. If you are using Internet Explorer, go to Start | Programs | Internet Explorer.

2. Type in the base URL of the portal's workspace.

   The portal's workspace follows this syntax:

   ```
   http://server_name/workspace_name
   ```

   Therefore, to open the workspace called IT on the server winchester, type:

   ```
   http://winchester/IT
   ```

3. Click the Search dashboard tab.

4. Perform a search.

   Searching is discussed earlier in this chapter under the heading, "Searching For Documents." For example, you could search on the word Resumes.

5. Click the Subscribe To This Search link next to the name of the category.

   This link for search results is shown screen shown in Figure 5-14.

6. Specify the name of the subscription.

   By default, the name of the subscription will be a description of the search that you made, including the keywords and search scope. However, you can change this to any nonblank value, as it is a required field.

7. Specify e-mail notification.

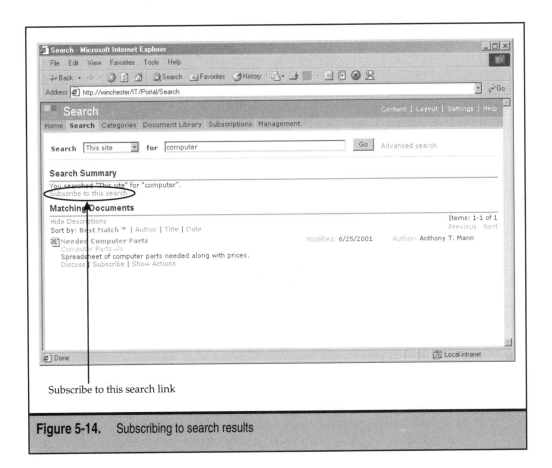

Subscribe to this search link

Figure 5-14.   Subscribing to search results

If you enter an e-mail address, which is optional, this address will be sent a message about the subscription, based on the frequency option specified next.

8. Specify the frequency.

   In the How Often field, select from the drop-down list of choices. You can choose to be notified once a day, once a week, or when a change occurs. You might choose the Once A Day or Once A Week option if you expect changes to be very frequent. This would avoid a situation whereby a document changes 10 times within a day and you get notified 10 times (by selecting the When A Change Occurs option). If you choose the When A Change Occurs option, you will be notified when documents are added or changed that now satisfy the search criteria.

9. Click OK.

Managing Subscriptions

To manage your subscriptions, you must use the Subscriptions dashboard. As mentioned earlier, you can only delete subscriptions, not modify them. Therefore, this dashboard only lets you delete either a single subscription or all subscriptions.

To manage subscriptions, follow these easy steps:

1. Open the web browser on the client's computer.

    On the client's computer, open the web browser. If you are using Internet Explorer, go to Start | Programs | Internet Explorer.

2. Type in the base URL of the portal's workspace.

    The portal's workspace follows this syntax:

    ```
    http://server_name/workspace_name
    ```

    Therefore, to open the workspace called IT on the server winchester, type:

    ```
    http://winchester/IT
    ```

3. Click the Subscriptions dashboard tab.

    Clicking this tab brings up the screen shown in Figure 5-15.

4. Click the desired delete link.

    At the top of the screen, you'll see a link labeled Delete All Subscriptions. Click this link to delete every subscription that you are subscribed to. Alternatively, below that, each individual subscription is listed. Click the desired Delete Subscription link associated with the specific subscription that you are trying to delete. If you are a Coordinator and you wish to delete subscriptions for another user, you must "switch-to" that user from the Management tab. This is shown in Chapter 9.

5. You are prompted to confirm before deletion will take place.

About Subscriptions...

Notice in Figure 5-15 that the subscription to the Resumes folder has no notifications. This means that no changes have been detected to the subscription. However, the second subscription for the Needed Computer Parts document does have a notification. This is one of two ways that SharePoint Portal Server notifies you about your subscriptions. You can view these changes by simply clicking the name of the document. The other way that you can be notified about changes is with the Subscription Summary web part on the Home dashboard. However, this web part does not show all of your subscriptions, only the top three.

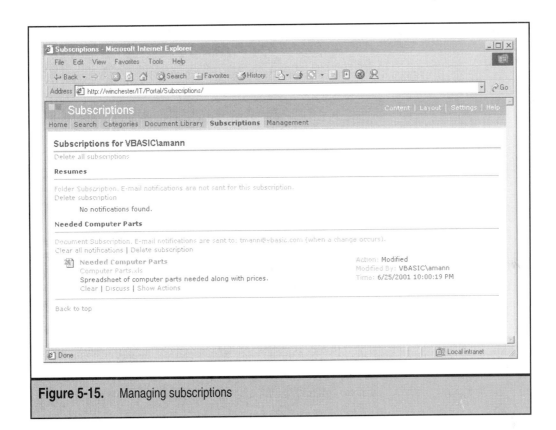

Figure 5-15. Managing subscriptions

CHAPTER SUMMARY

This chapter was jam-packed with lots of information. You learned how to manage your documents from the user's perspective. You learned how a user can add documents into the portal, as well as rename, edit, and delete those documents.

In this chapter, you also learned how to search for documents. This included simple and advanced searching, as well as search scopes. Finally, you learned how to publish, approve, or reject documents. Furthermore, this chapter discussed the security credentials that are needed to perform all actions on documents from a user's perspective. Chapter 7 covers the administrative end of document management.

CHAPTER 6

Web Discussions and Collaboration

Web discussions are a collaboration facility that are built into SharePoint Portal Server. The main concept is that users can collaborate on and discuss a document before it is published. This can be a much easier way to communicate with your peers about a document than sending it through e-mail. Sending a document through e-mail poses these problems and risks:

▼ E-mail messages containing documents can be moved into folders or deleted, making them hard or impossible to find.

■ There is no version tracking with e-mail, so if you have multiple e-mails, you will not necessarily know which document to use.

▲ With multiple e-mails from several simultaneous peers, you have to deal with merging changes.

Throughout this chapter, you'll see how and why to use discussions. However, please note that what I show you is from a client perspective. I cover configuring the server for discussions in Chapter 8.

OVERVIEW

To participate in web discussions, you must have the web discussion extensions installed. These extensions come built-in with Office XP, but must be installed as part of the client installation with Office 2000. Installing the client components is discussed in Chapter 3. The rest of the discussion software is built-into SharePoint Portal Server. Also, discussions must be enabled for a workspace, which they are by default. If discussions have been disabled, enable them according to the directions in Chapter 8.

TIP: You must be assigned to at least the reader security role or higher to participate in discussions.

You may think that you can only discuss documents, but SharePoint Portal Server allows more than that. You can actually discuss:

▼ **Dashboards** Search, Categories, Document Library, and others can be discussed. Others like Home cannot be discussed.

■ **Web Parts** Some web parts like Subscription Summary, Announcements, and Quick Links can be discussed. Others like News cannot be discussed.

▲ **Web Part content if it is document-based** Most web part content like Categories (which actually contains links to categories), and other documents can be discussed. Such documents include the Using Announcements document that shows you how to use announcements. This is a document contained within the Announcements web part. Some documents cannot be discussed, such as Using Quick Links under the Quick Links web part.

So, how do you know what can be discussed? It's simple! SharePoint Portal Server makes a discussion icon available when a document can be discussed. To illustrate the point, first look at Figure 6-1, which shows the standard Home dashboard for a newly created workspace, called IT.

Next, look at Figure 6-2, which shows the discussion icons available. In addition to the discussion icons shown in Figure 6-2, also notice the discussion bar at the bottom of the figure, along with the Discuss toolbar button. I'll be mentioning this within the chapter.

OPENING WEB DISCUSSIONS

Using web discussions is quite simple, as SharePoint Portal Server gives you menus and buttons to perform the discussions. You can perform web discussions from either a web browser or from within Microsoft Office XP or Office 2000. The usage of web discussions is presented throughout this chapter.

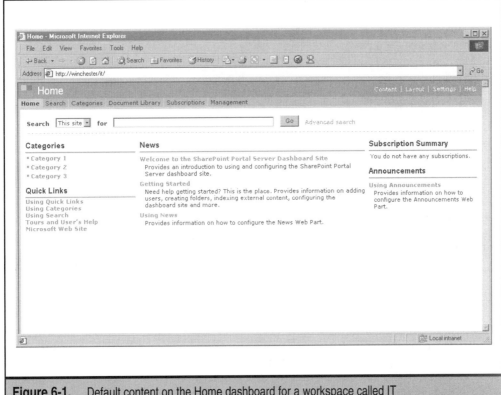

Figure 6-1. Default content on the Home dashboard for a workspace called IT

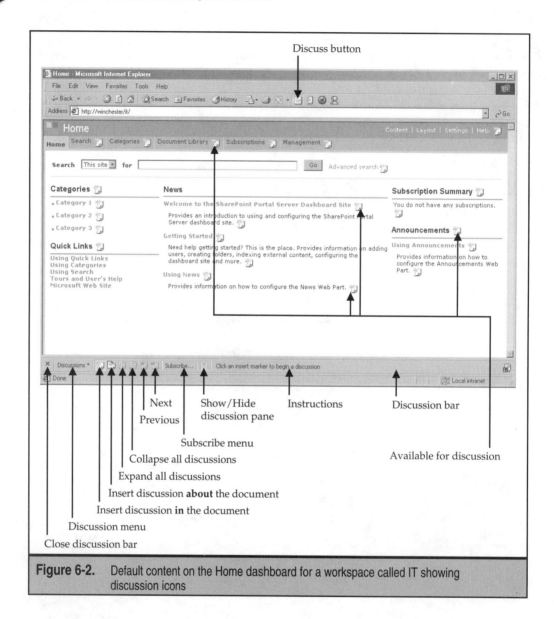

Figure 6-2. Default content on the Home dashboard for a workspace called IT showing discussion icons

To start either a new discussion, participate in an existing discussion, or delete a discussion, you must have access to the discussion bar. The procedure for opening a discussion bar depends on which program you are using. To open a web discussion using Internet Explorer, click the Discuss toolbar button, as shown in Figure 6-2.

To open a web discussion using Office 2000 or Office XP, click Tools | Online Collaboration | Web Discussions.

Regardless of how you open the discussion bar (Office XP, Office 2000, or Internet Explorer), once it opens, the procedure for discussions is the same because the discussion bar is the same in all three programs. From the discussion bar, you control all aspects of the discussion. Remember, you can discuss not only documents, but also other components within the portal. However, for ease of understanding, I will group the things you can discuss into the following categories:

▼   **Documents**   An actual document stored within the web storage system.

▲   **Non-Documents**   A part of the portal, such as a dashboard, web part, or link.

Because non-documents are all discussed the same way, I place them all into the same category. Check out the next couple of sections for information about document and non-document discussions.

Document Discussions

Discussing a document can be done in one of two ways. The first is by using the discussion bar. The second is by using the discussion menu. As with many things in all versions of Windows, there are multiple ways of doing things. Discussions are no exception, so I'll show you both and you can take your pick.

Using the Discussion Bar

To perform a document discussion by using the discussion bar, follow these easy steps:

1.   Open the web browser on the client's computer.

    On the client's computer, open the web browser. If you are using Internet Explorer, go to Start | Programs | Internet Explorer.

2.   Open the discussion bar.

    Click either Discuss or View | Explorer Bar | Discuss in Internet Explorer. Depending on the browser version that you are using, the menu may be View | Explorer Bar | Discussion.

3.   Navigate to the desired document.

    You can search for the document using the Search dashboard, or perhaps click another dashboard that contains your document.

4.   Insert a discussion.

    If you wish to insert a discussion into a document, click Insert Discussion In The Document (see Figure 6-2) or click Discussions | Insert In The Document menu on the discussion bar. Doing so places an icon directly next to your document (if it is HTML-based). This is shown in Figure 6-2 also with a callout labeled "Available for Discussion." Click the icon next to the desired document to create an in-line discussion at that point. Jump to the next step.

Difference Between Discussing IN and ABOUT a Document

Notice that Figure 6-2 shows a button on the discussion bar that lets you insert a discussion IN the document and one that inserts a discussion ABOUT the document. The difference between these is that inserting a discussion IN the document actually displays and stores the discussion within the document. This can only happen in HTML documents. A discussion ABOUT the document is stored as more of an attachment to the document, not actually within the document.

A discussion IN a document actually appears with the text of the discussion in-line with the document text. On the other hand, a discussion ABOUT a document brings up a separate window where the discussion takes place.

If you wish to insert a discussion about a document, click Insert Discussion About The Document (see Figure 6-2) or click Discussions | Insert About The Document menu on the discussion bar.

5. Enter discussion text.

Regardless of whether you are entering a discussion IN or ABOUT the document, you will now be at the same point. You must enter text relating to the subject and a description of the discussion. For example, if you want your peers to verify the technical content of the document, you can enter Tech Review for the subject and Please Verify All Technical Content In This Document as the discussion text. If the text that you are entering is a reply to existing discussion text, the reply will be indented, showing that each part of the discussion is part of that discussion thread. A *discussion thread* is a single path from which a single discussion and all replies are tied together in a hierarchical structure.

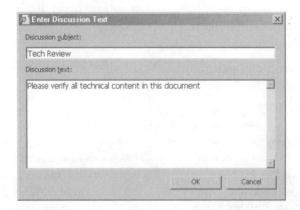

If you insert a discussion about the document, a new window pops up, showing you the discussion text, as shown in Figure 6-3.

If you insert a discussion in the document, a new window is not displayed, but your discussion is available inside the document, as shown in Figure 6-4.

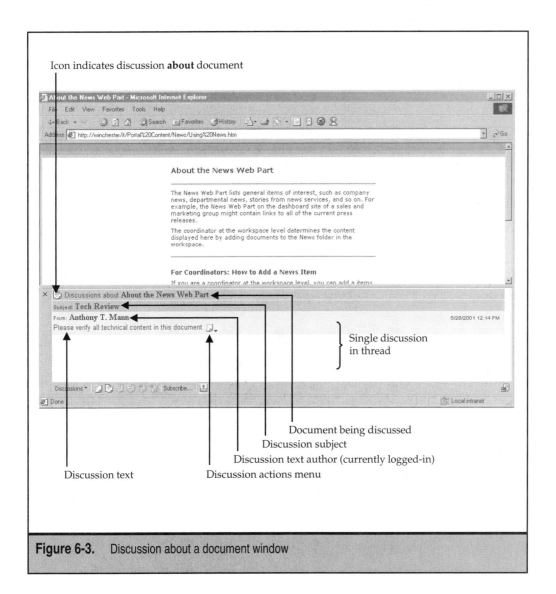

Figure 6-3.   Discussion about a document window

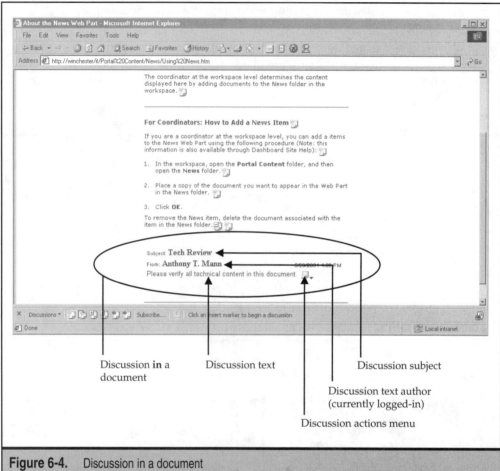

Figure 6-4. Discussion in a document

A Note About the Discussion Text Author

You may wonder about how the system knows what name to place as the discussion author. Well, this is not rocket science. Since you must have Office 2000 or Office XP running for discussions to function, it actually gets this name from the registry. Remember when you first installed Office on your computer and you were asked for your user name and initials? The name used as the discussion author is this user name. If you wish to change the user name, from within Microsoft Office, you can choose Tools | Options, then select User and change the desired value.

NOTE: Sometimes it is much clearer to use discussions ABOUT a document, rather than IN a document. This is because it makes the original document less cluttered.

6. Select additional commands, if necessary.

    Clicking the Discussion Actions menu (shown adjacent to or under discussion text), as shown in Figure 6-3, gives you a list of additional commands available for the discussion, as follows:

    ■ **Reply**   Allows you to add discussion text at the end of the discussion thread.

    ■ **Edit**   Allows you to edit the currently selected instance of discussion text.

    ■ **Delete**   Allows you to delete the currently selected instance of discussion text.

    ■ **Close**   Closes the current discussion text.

    ■ **Close Item and Replies**   Closes the current specific discussion thread, including all of the replies in the thread.

    ■ **Activate**   Activates the current discussion thread.

See the section later in this chapter called "Discussion Security" for more information about security requirements for the above actions.

Discussion Menu

The discussion menu is only available from the Document Library dashboard. It performs the same functionality as the discussion bar, just in a different way. In fact, I would say that it is more awkward to enter discussions in this manner, which you'll see as you read on.

To perform a document discussion by using the discussion menu, follow these steps:

1. Open the web browser on the client's computer.

    On the client's computer, open the web browser. If you are using Internet Explorer, choose Start | Programs | Internet Explorer.

2. Navigate to the desired document.

    You can search for the document using the Search dashboard, or perhaps clicking the Document Management dashboard and navigating to the desired document. Notice that in the list of possible actions is the Discuss link.

3. Click Discuss.

    Clicking this link brings up the discussion bar, but first prompts you to open or save the document if you don't already have it saved on your local hard drive. This is the awkward part that I mentioned earlier.

4. Choose Open, if it is displayed.

    Choosing Open opens the document in the window. Saving the document does nothing for you, as the document is already saved.

5. Follow the instructions for using the discussion bar.

    Follow the same discussions mentioned under the heading "Discussion Bar" earlier in this chapter.

Non-Document Discussions

To discuss a dashboard, web part, or other SharePoint Portal Server item that is not itself a document, you must discuss it using the discussion bar (which is my preferred method of discussing everything anyway). For more information about using the discussion bar, see the section "Discussion Bar" earlier in this chapter.

Additional Discussion Commands

There are additional discussion commands available from the discussion bar. They are described in the next three sections.

Refresh Discussions   Choosing Refresh Discussions will refresh the current discussion. This becomes necessary because a web page does not automatically refresh itself. Therefore a discussion could be ongoing, but your web page does not update in real-time. Therefore, to see current discussions, choose this option.

To refresh the discussion, follow these steps:

1. Open the discussion bar.

    Follow the procedures outlined earlier in this chapter to bring up the discussion bar.

2. Click Discussions.

    The Discussions menu is located on the discussion bar, on the left-hand side (see Figure 6-2).

3. Choose Refresh Discussions.

Filter Discussions   The Filter Discussions option allows you to limit the number of discussions that you see on the screen. This is necessary because if you have hundreds of responses to a discussion item, you don't want to see all of that. It would actually "drown out" your own text. Therefore, you can filter the display to see only what you want. Note that if you filter discussions, that does not actually remove them from the web storage system, it only limits what is displayed on the screen.

To filter the discussion, follow these steps:

1. Open the discussion bar.

    Follow the procedures outlined earlier in this chapter to bring up the discussion bar.

2. Click Discussions.

   The Discussions menu is located on the discussion bar, on the left-hand side (see Figure 6-2).

3. Choose Filter Discussions.

   Choosing this menu brings up the following dialog box:

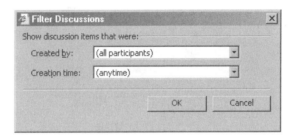

4. Choose the filtering criteria.

   You can choose to limit the discussion text by these fields:

   ■ **Created by**   This drop-down list shows the names of all participants in the discussion.

   ■ **Creation time**   This drop-down list shows time frames where discussions must have taken place to display. You can choose from the anytime, the last 24 hours, 2 days, 7 days, 30 days, 2 months, and 6 months.

   To turn off criteria, select the option to display all in both fields.

5. Click OK.

   Clicking OK applies the filter criteria and displays only the appropriate discussion items.

Discussion Options   Choosing Discussion Options allows configuration of where the discussions take place (what server) and what fields you see on the screen for the discussion.
   To change the discussion options, follow these steps:

1. Open the discussion bar.

   Follow the procedures outlined earlier in this chapter to bring up the discussion bar.

2. Click Discussions.

The Discussions menu is located on the discussion bar, on the left-hand side (see Figure 6-2).

3. Choose Discussion Options.

    Choosing this menu brings up the dialog box shown here:

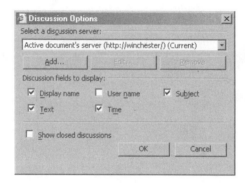

4. Select the discussion server.

    By default the current SharePoint Portal Server is displayed in this field. However, you can opt to have another server handle the discussions. If you want to do this, you can click Add to bring up this dialog box:

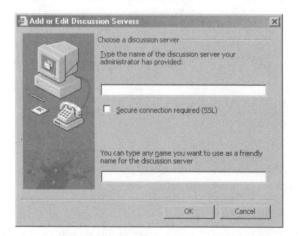

    Type in the name of the discussion server to add. This is the only required field. However, you can opt to have secure discussions on the server by selecting the SSL option. Keep in mind, if you choose the SSL option, your discussion server must have a valid security certificate installed to communicate using SSL. Additionally, you can give your server a friendly name. I usually opt to leave this blank, as I like explicit names.

Additionally, you can edit or remove a server (by clicking the respective buttons), as long as it is not the current discussion server.

5. Select the discussion fields.

    You can choose from the following fields to be displayed in the discussion:

    ■ **Display Name**   Name registered with Microsoft Office.

    ■ **User Name**   User logon name in the operating system domain. This is the only field that is not checked by default. If you check this option, the user logon name will be shown next to the display name in parenthesis.

    ■ **Subject**   Discussion subject.

    ■ **Text**   Discussion text.

    ■ **Time**   Time the discussion text was entered.

    Most of the time, you will use the default fields in your discussions.

6. Select Closed.

    If you wish to include closed discussions, check Show Closed Discussions. Since this can lead to clutter, it is not checked by default.

7. Click OK.

    Clicking OK applies the criteria and displays only the appropriate discussion fields from the selected server.

DISCUSSION SECURITY

Not all commands are available at all times to all people. That's where security comes into play. However, it is not just SharePoint Portal Server security that is involved. Windows 2000 or Windows NT domain security plays a part as well. Use Table 6-1 to decipher the actions that are available based on security permissions assigned to a user. Note in the table that SPS stands for SharePoint Portal Server.

To understand how to use Table 6-1, let's use an example. If you are a member of the Windows 2000 Domain Admins group, you can edit the discussion text of anyone in the workspace in that domain. As another example, according to Table 6-1, if you are not a member of the Domain Admins Windows 2000 group and you are a SharePoint Portal Server Reader, you can edit your own discussion text only.

Security Level/Group	Command	Available in Menu	Current User Only?
SPS Reader	Reply	Yes	No
SPS Reader	Edit	Yes	Yes
SPS Reader	Delete	Yes	Yes
SPS Reader	Close	No	No
SPS Reader	Close Item and Replies	No	No
SPS Reader	Activate	No	No
SPS Author	Reply	Yes	No
SPS Author	Edit	Yes	Yes
SPS Author	Delete	Yes	Yes
SPS Author	Close	No	No
SPS Author	Close Item and Replies	No	No
SPS Author	Activate	No	No
SPS Coordinator	Reply	Yes	No
SPS Coordinator	Edit	Yes	No
SPS Coordinator	Delete	Yes	No
SPS Coordinator	Close	No	No
SPS Coordinator	Close Item and Replies	No	No
SPS Coordinator	Activate	No	No
Domain Admins domain group	Reply	Yes	No
Domain Admins domain group	Edit	Yes	No
Domain Admins domain group	Delete	Yes	No
Domain Admins domain group	Close	Yes	No
Domain Admins domain group	Close Item and Replies	Yes	No
Domain Admins domain group	Activate	Yes	No

Table 6-1. Discussion Actions And Security Required.

CHAPTER SUMMARY

Discussions in SharePoint Portal Server are a great way to collaborate on a document, folder, link, dashboard, or web part. The discussions are stored in the web storage system. Peers that work on a discussion can respond to text entered by a user using an unlimited amount of space. This discussion is stored along with the document so that it is always available.

In this chapter, you learned how to participate in discussions. You also learned about the security requirements to participate in discussions and how to configure them from a user's perspective. If you want to learn more about configuring the server itself for discussions, proceed to Chapter 7.

PART III

General Administration

CHAPTER 7

Server Administration

Tbere is more to discuss about general server administration than there is about any other topic in SharePoint Portal Server. General server administration is a term that I use to describe things that all SharePoint Portal Server administrators need to know about. This includes things like how to layout the content of your dashboards, setup approval routing, setting up enhanced folders, and many more topics. Stay tuned and get ready for an information-packed chapter.

TIP: To perform most actions in this chapter, you must be assigned to the Coordinator role at the workspace level, except where noted.

CONFIGURATION USING SHAREPOINT PORTAL SERVER ADMINISTRATOR OR A NETWORK PLACE

As the name implies, this entire section is dedicated to using the SharePoint Portal Server Administrator or by using a network place to configure general administration aspects of the product. In all cases under this heading, you will first open the SharePoint Portal Server Administrator. To open the SharePoint Portal Server Administrator, choose Start | Programs | Administrative Tools | SharePoint Portal Server Administrator on the SharePoint Portal Server computer itself. Network places are opened by double-clicking the My Network Places icon on the Windows desktop. For information about creating network places, see Chapter 4.

Workspaces

A workspace is the basic container in which you will perform actions within SharePoint Portal Server. Each workspace has its own set of resources, such as disk space, security settings, configuration, and documents. More information on workspaces can be found in Chapters 1, 2, 3 and 8. The actions that you can perform on a workspace are add, rename, and remove. Each is described in the next three sections.

Adding Workspaces

Adding workspaces is covered in detail in Chapter 3. However, for the sake of continuity, just know that you can add a workspace that can be accessed as a portal, or a specialized index workspace which is used for the sole purpose of crawling content for indexing. This index is then propagated to the portal workspace where it can be searched. Indexes and index workspaces are covered in Chapter 8. Please refer to these two chapters for more information about adding workspaces.

NOTE: You can only create a maximum of 15 workspaces on a single server.

Renaming Workspaces

You cannot rename a workspace once it has been created. If you wish to rename a workspace, you must delete the workspace and recreate it. Because of this fact, you can opt to recreate documents, folder structures, and other resources within the workspace. On the other hand, you can implement a strategy of backup and restore. However, the MSDMBack utility that is described in Chapter 12 will not perform this functionality. You must use a third party utility, or check with Microsoft about a fix for this issue. The best solution, actually, is to name your workspaces correctly the first time.

Removing Workspaces

Removing, or deleting workspaces is very easy. Removing a workspace is permanent. This action will delete all data contained in the Web Storage System for the workspace, including folder structures, security permissions, content sources, and settings. Even though the workspace is deleted, you can restore it from a backup, which is covered in Chapter 12.

Removing a workspace cannot be done with a web browser. It must be done with the SharePoint Portal Server Administrator. To remove a workspace, follow these steps:

1. Open the SharePoint Portal Server Administrator.

   On the SharePoint Portal Server computer, choose Start | Programs | Administrative Tools | SharePoint Portal Server Administration.

2. Navigate to the desired workspace.

3. Right-click the desired workspace and choose All Tasks | Delete Workspace.

   You are prompted to confirm deletion of the workspace with this message:

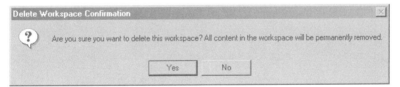

4. Click Yes.

   It may take several minutes for the workspace to become deleted.

Subscription Limitations

Due to limitation of server resources (memory, disk space, processor speed, etc), you most likely want to limit the number of subscriptions that a user can subscribe to. This only applies to portal workspaces, not index workspaces since subscriptions aren't allowed on index workspaces. SharePoint Portal Server needs to monitor for changes in documents, folder, categories, and searches that would result in a subscription notification. Therefore, this takes resources on the server. If you have only five people using the server, this becomes less of an issue. However, if you have two hundred people using the server, this becomes much more of an issue. As with most things, it's a judgment call that you have to make. Microsoft has made this decision a little easier with the defaults that they have set. These are the possible subscription limitation areas:

▼ **Maximum subscriptions for this workspace** The maximum number of subscriptions allowed in the workspace for all users. This number is set by default at 5,000.

■ **Maximum subscriptions per user** The maximum number of subscriptions that an individual user can subscribe to. This number is valid only until the maximum subscriptions for the workspace has been reached. This number is set by default at 20.

▲ **Maximum results per subscription** The maximum number of results that will be returned for an individual subscription. For example, if a subscription to a search yields 500 records, then that number will be limited to the value entered in this field. This number is set by default at 20.

Changing subscription limitations can be done with either the SharePoint Portal Server Administrator or a network place.

Using the SharePoint Portal Server Administrator

To use the SharePoint Portal Server Administrator to change subscription limitations, do this:

1. Open the SharePoint Portal Server Administrator.

   On the SharePoint Portal Server computer, choose Start | Programs | Administrative Tools | SharePoint Portal Server Administration.

2. Navigate to the desired workspace.

3. Right-click the desired workspace and choose Properties.

Which Results Are Returned?

You may be wondering how SharePoint Portal Server determines which results will be excluded from the subscription if you have it limited. Well, you'll be glad to know that it isn't arbitrary. For search subscriptions, the lowest-ranked results are excluded. These are the least relevant records in the results and therefore are eliminated. Only the highest, most pertinent results are returned, up to the maximum. For category, folder, and document subscriptions, only the newest (based on date and time) records are returned, up to the maximum.

4. Click Subscriptions/Discussions.

Clicking this tab brings up the following screen:

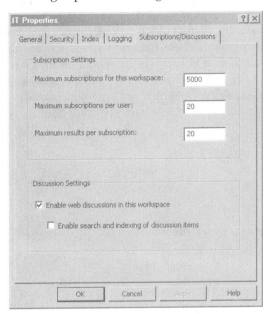

5. Change any of the three desired settings.
6. Click OK to save your changes and close the dialog box.

Using a Network Place

To use a network place to change subscription limitations, do this:

1. Open the network place that points to your workspace.
2. Double-click Management.
3. Double-click Workspace Settings.
4. Click Subscriptions/Discussions.

    This screen looks exactly the same as it does in the illustration shown under the prior heading, "Using the SharePoint Portal Server Administrator."

5. Change any of the three desired settings.
6. Click OK to save your changes and close the dialog box.

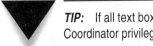

TIP: If all text boxes on the Subscriptions/Discussions tab appear disabled, then you do not have Coordinator privileges at the workspace level.

Folders

Folders are the basic unit of organization for your documents within SharePoint Portal Server. This is not a new concept. You've been doing this for years in Windows. If you didn't organize your operating system files into logical folders, you would have thousands of files in the root folder on your C: drive. Because you already have lots of experience doing this, I don't think I need to give you any examples. Instead, I'll focus on the mechanics and concepts that make SharePoint Portal Server folders unique.

There are two types of folders (in which you will store your documents) in SharePoint Portal Server: standard and enhanced. A standard folder allows for:

▼ Role-based security

■ Document profiles

■ Indexing

▲ Categories

However, an enhanced folder allows for all the above aspects, plus:

▼ Check-in

■ Check-out

■ Approval routing

▲ Versioning

So, why not just use enhanced folders all the time? There are two main reasons. The first is that an enhanced folder *requires* documents to be checked-in and checked-out. This can be cumbersome if you don't desire that activity. For example, if you are the only person who publishes documents to the portal, you don't necessarily want to be required to check in and check out the documents. It's not that this is difficult, but why perform some extra steps on every document if you don't need it? The second reason you don't want to always use enhanced folders is that multi-part documents are supported only in standard folders. A multi-part document is just what it sounds like. It's a document that is not complete in its entirety. An example of this type of document is a Microsoft PowerPoint presentation that grabs content from an Excel spreadsheet. In other words, one document has a dependency on another to be displayed. After having described the reasons why you might want to use a standard folder to store documents, you'll have to decide which is right for you and your organization.

As within Windows, you create a hierarchy of folders within SharePoint Portal Server. The top-most level of the hierarchy is the Documents folder, which cannot be deleted. This can be thought of as the root folder. Below the root folder, you create a hierarchy of folders and subfolders that make sense for your document organization. You set four sets of folder properties; the folder type (standard or enhanced), security roles, profiles, and approval routing. In addition, you can opt to inherit these properties from the parent folder. Inheriting properties means that all values set for these properties are used by a folder directly lower in the hierarchy. This "lower" folder is known as a *child folder*. Figure 7-1 shows this relationship.

As an example, if you set properties on the Documents folder, any folder below in the hierarchy can (and will by default) inherit those property settings. On the other hand, you can opt to have a folder *not* inherit the properties from the parent folder and instead, explicitly define its own properties. This new set of properties can then be inherited by its child folders, and so on.

The next few sections outline how you perform some administration on folders, but you should know that security roles are covered in Chapter 10, profiles are covered in Chapter 9, and approval routing is covered later in this chapter under the heading, "Document Approval Routing."

TIP: In addition to a Coordinator, an Author of a folder can create subfolders. Additionally, an Author can rename or delete folders which he/she owns.

Creating Folders

Creating a folder can be done by using a web browser or by using a network place. Each is discussed in the next two sections.

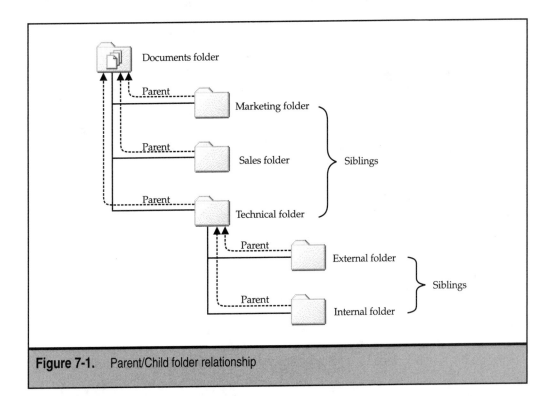

Figure 7-1.   Parent/Child folder relationship

Using a Web Browser   Using a web browser, such as Internet Explorer, to create a folder takes only a few steps, like this:

1. Open the desired workspace using a web browser.

   For example, to open the IT workspace on the winchester server, type:

   ```
   http://winchester/IT
   ```

2. Navigate to the Document Library dashboard.

3. Navigate to the Documents folder.

4. Continue to navigate to the desired folder under which you will create a new folder.

   As an example, look at Figure 7-2. It shows a folder named Scanned that contains a single document. If you wish to add a subfolder under the Scanned folder, then this is the correct folder level to be in when you create the new folder.

5. Click Add Sub-Folder.

6. Enter the desired name of the new folder.

7. Click Create.

   You will automatically be returned to the parent folder, where you can view your newly created folder.

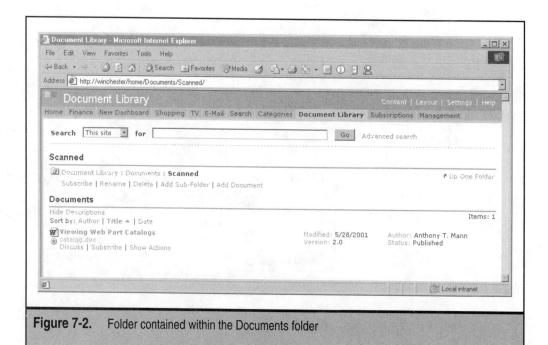

Figure 7-2.   Folder contained within the Documents folder

Using a Network Place   Creating a folder by using a network place in SharePoint Portal Server is done much like it is in Windows. You navigate to the parent folder, and then create the child folder within the parent folder. You can repeat the process as many times as you would like. Here's how you create a folder:

1. Open the network place that points to your workspace.

2. Double-click Documents.

3. Navigate to the desired parent folder in which you will create a child folder.

4. Right-click any open space in the parent folder and choose New | Folder.

    The new folder is created with the name New Folder and is in edit mode waiting for a new name.

5. Type the name of the desired folder and press ENTER.

6. Change properties, as desired.

    For information on which chapters in this book to reference for changing folder properties, refer to the earlier section, "Folders."

Renaming Folders

Renaming a folder can be also be done by using a web browser or by using a network place. See the next two sections for instructions on how to do this.

Using a Web Browser   Using a web browser to rename a folder is also quite simple. It's done with these few steps:

1. Open the desired workspace using a web browser.

    For example, to open the IT workspace on the winchester server, type:

    ```
    http://winchester/IT
    ```

2. Navigate to the Document Library dashboard.

3. Navigate to the Documents folder.

4. Continue to navigate to the desired folder that you wish to rename.

5. Click Rename.

6. Enter the desired new name of the folder.

7. Click Save.

Using a Network Place   Renaming a folder using a network place is also just as easy in SharePoint Portal Server as it is in Windows. Here's how you rename a folder:

1. Open the network place that points to your workspace.

2. Double-click Documents.

3. Navigate to the desired folder to rename.

4. Right-click the desired folder and choose Rename.

5. Type the new name of the desired folder and press ENTER.

Deleting Folders

Just like adding and renaming folders, deleting a folder can be also be done by using a web browser or by using a network place. The next two sections describe this.

Using a Web Browser   Using a web browser to delete a folder is also quite simple. It's done with these few steps:

1. Open the desired workspace using a web browser.

   For example, to open the IT workspace on the winchester server, type:

   ```
   http://winchester/IT
   ```

2. Navigate to the Document Library dashboard.

3. Navigate to the Documents folder.

4. Continue to navigate to the desired folder that you wish to delete.

5. Click Delete.

6. At the prompt, confirm that you want to delete the folder.

   Note that all of the contents in the folder will be deleted along with the folder.

Using a Network Place   Again, deleting a folder by using a network place is also quite easy. Follow these simple steps:

1. Open the network place that points to your workspace.

2. Double-click Documents.

3. Navigate to the desired folder to delete.

4. Right-click the desired folder and choose Delete.

5. Confirm deletion at the prompt by clicking Yes.

Changing Folder Types

To change a folder type (from standard to enhanced or vice-versa), you use a network place (which is discussed in Chapter 4), like this:

1. Open the network place that points to your workspace.

2. Double-click Documents.

3. Navigate to the desired folder on which you will change types.

4. Right-click the desired folder and click Properties.

5. Ensure General is selected (as it is by default).

Clicking this tab brings up the following dialog box:

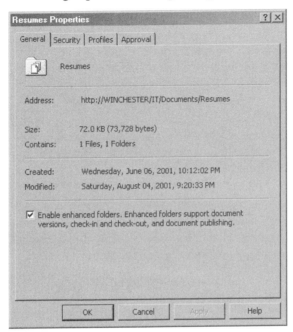

6. Check the desired option.

Check Enable Enhanced Folders to make the folder enhanced (which is actually selected by default) and uncheck this check box if you want the folder to be standard.

NOTE: The folder *must* be empty or SharePoint Portal Server will not allow you to change the folder type.

Document Approval Routing

One of the most important features of SharePoint Portal Server is its ability to route your documents for approval. In fact, your document doesn't physically get routed anywhere, but notifications are sent to approvers. In this section, I show you how to configure your folders for approval routing.

CAUTION: Your folders must be configured as enhanced folders to allow for approval routing. For more information about configuring enhanced folders, see the section in this chapter, called "Changing Folder Types."

Although this is mentioned in a blueprint in the center of this book, there are three types of approval routing:

▼ **Serial** Approvals must be made by approvers in a specific, predetermined order. This situation is likely when signoffs must begin at the lowest level. Such a document could include a signoff sheet for software that is ready to be released to manufacturing (RTM). The approval can begin with the developer, followed by a QA tester, the QA manager, the Sales Manager, the IT Manager, then by the CIO.

■ **Parallel (one vote)** Only a single approval is necessary by any of the specified approvers. This situation can be used for low dollar value expense reports where you only need a manager's approval. The advantage in this scenario is if your direct manager is on vacation, processing is not held-up.

▲ **Parallel (many votes)** Approvals must be made by each and every approver, but in no specific order. This situation can be needed when, for example, two approvals are necessary for a purchase order above $100,000. In this case, the approvals are not necessary to be serial, but you do need both approvals.

The opposite of approving is, of course, rejecting. An approver can reject a document for any reason. In addition, a workspace coordinator can bypass approval for a document, which means that the document does not have to go through the approval process. There may be times when this is necessary, but it is not recommended. Your company has determined that documents in a specific folder need approval for a reason. Therefore, you should use caution when bypassing approval.

Refer to Chapter 5 for information on how to actually perform approvals or rejections from a client perspective. This section is dedicated to setting up approvals from the server perspective. This includes designating that an enhanced folder needs approvals, as well as designating the approvers and routing.

Approval routing is configured by using a network place and is quite easy. Just follow these steps:

1. Open the network place that points to your workspace.
2. Double-click Documents.
3. Navigate to the desired folder requiring approval.
4. Right-click the desired folder and choose Properties.
5. Click Approval.

Clicking the Approval tab brings up this dialog box that allows you to configure approvals (with sample approvals shown):

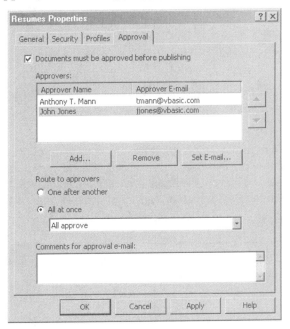

6. Click Documents Must Be Approved Before Publishing.

7. Select the desired approvers.

    The desired approvers are added by clicking Add. Clicking Add brings up a dialog box to allow you to select users from either the local server or a Windows 2000 or Windows.NET Server Active Directory or Windows NT domain. You can also remove approvers by selecting the approver and clicking Remove.

    If the e-mail address of the approver is contained within the domain, it will be placed in the Approver E-mail column. On the other hand, if it is not contained within the domain, or you wish to change the current entry, simply select the desired approver to change and click Set E-mail. Doing so brings up a simple dialog box allowing you to specify the e-mail address.

    One final, and very important option, is the up and down arrows, just to the right of the Approvers list box. These arrows set the order in which approvers must approve documents contained within the folder. This is only relevant if you opt for a serial approval.

8. Select the approval type.

   Although the options are not labeled as such, select the desired approval type as follows:

   - **Serial** Select One After Another.
   - **Parallel (one vote)** Select All At Once, then Only One Approval Required from the drop-down list.
   - **Parallel (many votes)** Select All At Once, then All Approve from the drop-down list.

9. Enter e-mail comments, if desired.

   Although not required, it is a good idea to enter comments that will be seen in the e-mail sent to approvers notifying them that an approval is pending. Such comments could be simply the name of the folder, such as Software Development, or any other comments which are germane to information about the approval.

10. Click OK to save your changes and close the dialog box.

CAUTION: Only documents that have not yet entered the approval stage will be affected by changes that you make. Any other documents that are pending approval are not changed.

CONFIGURATION USING A WEB BROWSER

The rest of this chapter shows you how to administer your SharePoint Portal Server by accessing features through a web browser. As always within this book, it is assumed that you are using Internet Explorer, not Netscape Navigator.

Dashboards

Dashboards are the high-level container unit that makes up the graphical web interface within SharePoint Portal Server. A dashboard is a way to categorize and classify web parts. Using dashboards is discussed in Chapter 4. This section is dedicated to learning how to add dashboards and subdashboards, as well as renaming and removing them. All these actions are performed by using a web browser. Before diving into the nitty-gritty of how to manage your dashboards, it is important to understand the concept of dashboard configuration and subdashboards.

First of all, the Home dashboard is the highest level of all dashboards. Everything under this is considered to be a subdashboard. Figure 7-3 shows what a default workspace looks like with all default dashboards.

In Figure 7-3, it looks like the Search, Categories, Document Library, Subscriptions, and Management dashboards are at the same level of the Home dashboard, but they are not. They are only presented at the same level. Therefore, Search is a subdashboard of

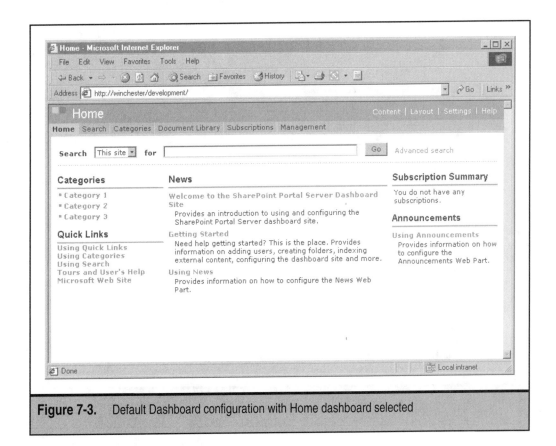

Figure 7-3. Default Dashboard configuration with Home dashboard selected

Home, and so on. If you wanted to create a new dashboard, called Sales, next to the Home dashboard, you would create a subdashboard in the Home dashboard.

The next thing to know is that all other subdashboards (besides Home) are displayed underneath the parent dashboard. As an example, look at Figure 7-4. It shows three subdashboards—Marketing, Sales, and Technical—all having a parent dashboard of Document Library. Notice how these subdashboards are laid out differently than the subdashboards shown in Figure 7-3 (where they are all next to the Home dashboard).

All subdashboards are, by default, organized automatically by SharePoint Portal Server to be displayed in alphabetical order. This is echoed in Figure 7-3. Marketing comes before Sales, which comes before Technical. These subdashboards were not created in this order. The same is true of subdashboards of the Home dashboard. This order can be changed by altering the settings for a dashboard. However, here comes the weird part.

The Home subdashboards only appear between the Home and Search dashboards. Even if you change the order of the subdashboards, they will only be placed between the Home and Search dashboards.

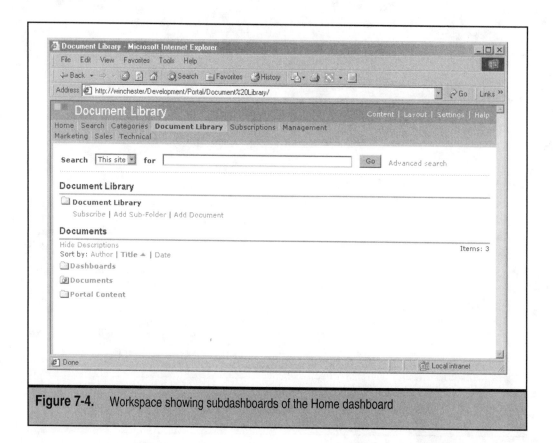

Figure 7-4. Workspace showing subdashboards of the Home dashboard

Adding Dashboards

Adding dashboards can be broken down into two different categories: *portal* and *personal* dashboards. Each is described and defined in the next two sections.

Portal Dashboards   Technically, you cannot add a dashboard to a portal. You can only add a subdashboard. If this is unclear, reread the earlier section, "Dashboards." Before you can add a subdashboard, you need to know where to add it. Are you adding it adjacent to the Home dashboard, or under another dashboard, or both? You must add your subdashboards one at a time. For example, if you add a subdashboard called Sales adjacent to the Home dashboard, you can add additional subdashboards like Tools and Documents under the Sales dashboard. Because this type of dashboard displays a tab in the portal, I call it a *portal dashboard*.

To add a subdashboard, perform the following:

1. Open the desired workspace using a web browser.

   For example, to open the IT workspace on the winchester server, type:

   ```
   http://winchester/IT
   ```

2. Navigate to the desired dashboard, under which you will create a subdashboard.

   If you wish to create a subdashboard adjacent to the Home dashboard, click Home. If you wish to create a subdashboard under a different dashboard, such as Document Library, click that dashboard.

3. Click Content.

   More details about dashboard content is discussed later in this chapter, under the section "Content."

4. Click Create A Subdashboard.

   You are automatically navigated to the Settings screen, which allow you to configure settings for the new dashboard. Settings are discussed later in this chapter, under the section, "Settings."

5. Change the name of your new subdashboard.

6. Click Save.

   Your new subdashboard now appears within the portal and you are free to add content (web parts) to your subdashboard. Figure 7-5 shows how the browser

Figure 7-5.   Web browser after creating a new subdashboard

looks after creating a subdashboard Sales under the Home dashboard. You can add content according to the instructions shown later in this chapter, under the section, "Content."

Personal Dashboards　Portal dashboards and subdashboards display themselves as tabs within the portal. In contrast, a *personal dashboard* has no "advertisement." It is accessed by URL only. Therefore, a user must know the URL to be able to access the personal dashboard. A personal dashboard allows you to create a dashboard that individuals can use to display web parts that others can access. Such dashboards can include web parts that are not germane to a corporate dashboard, but can provide some value to individuals. For example, an individual who is a member of a soccer club can publish his personal schedule on his own personal dashboard. The behavior of a personal dashboard, besides how it is accessed (by URL) is exactly the same as portal dashboards. However, creating them is slightly different. To create a personal dashboard, follow these steps:

1. Open the desired workspace using a web browser.
2. Click Management.

   Clicking Management brings up the screen shown in Figure 7-6.
3. Click Create A New Personal Dashboard.
4. Give the new dashboard a name.

   This dashboard name will be included in the name that you will use to access the dashboard via URL. For example, a dashboard named amann (that's me), would be accessed with this URL on the winchester server in the IT workspace:

   ```
   http://winchester/IT/Dashboards/amann/
   ```

   You can also change other settings for the dashboard at this time. For more information about settings, see section "Settings" later in this chapter.
5. Click Save.

TIP:　You must be assigned to the Coordinator or Author role at the workspace level to be able to save a personal dashboard.

All other actions that can be performed on portal dashboards can also be performed on personal dashboards. The only difference is that you must enter the dashboard by entering the URL instead of clicking the dashboard or subdashboard tab.

Renaming Dashboards

Dashboards are displayed by either clicking the dashboard link in your web browser, or by including the dashboard name in the URL of the web browser. Knowing this, it becomes obvious that your web site creates virtual directory within Internet Information Services (IIS) to "serve up" your dashboard. The point in mentioning all this is to tell you that you

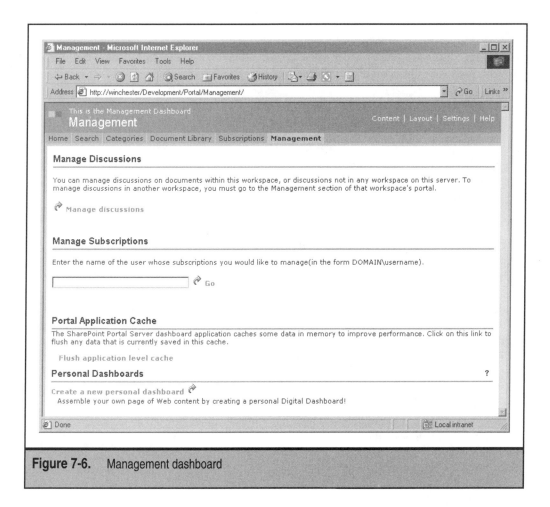

Figure 7-6. Management dashboard

can rename your dashboards, but it does not change the name within IIS. It only changes the name that is displayed on the tab. To rename your dashboards, follow these very simple steps:

1. Open the desired workspace using a web browser.
2. Navigate to the desired dashboard or subdashboard that you wish to rename.
3. Click Settings.
4. Change the name of the dashboard or subdashboard.
5. Click Save.

Removing Dashboards

You can remove, or delete, any dashboard or subdashboard, except Home. To remove a dashboard, follow these very simple steps:

1. Open the desired workspace using a web browser.
2. Navigate to the desired dashboard or subdashboard that you wish to remove.
3. Click Settings.
4. Click Delete Dashboard.

    You are prompted to confirm deletion before the dashboard is actually deleted.

Content

As you have probably gathered by reading this book so far, SharePoint Portal Server is completely flexible in the way you can configure your dashboards and the content on those dashboards. Content on dashboards generally refers to web parts that are displayed within the dashboard. This section assumes that you have already created a dashboard or subdashboard. Therefore, the concepts and procedures shown here will apply to any of the dashboards that you create. If you need more information about creating dashboards, see the prior section in this chapter, "Dashboards."

Adding content (i.e. web parts) that is already available is quite simple. It's a matter of instructing SharePoint Portal Server to where to grab the content. This can be from an XML or script file that exists on your corporate network or from a catalog of available web parts over the Internet. On the other hand, if the content does not already exist, it is a little more time-consuming because you must create the content. Chapter 4 covers the basics of grabbing web parts and the options that you specify when you create your own web parts. However, Chapter 4 shows how to grab data from a web part catalog—it doesn't show how to create a web part catalog from which you can make content available. Creating a web part catalog is outside the scope of this book, but you should know that you can create your own corporate web part gallery using the Digital Dashboard Resource Kit and the Microsoft whitepaper located at **http://www.microsoft.com/Sharepoint/techinfo/ administration/CreateWebPart.asp.**

Layout

Once you have added content (web parts) to your dashboard, you can configure the physical layout of that content. However, you must work within predefined positions on the dashboard. In other words, you cannot move a web part 15 pixels to the right. You can position your web parts within these predefined areas:

▼   **Top**   Web parts are positioned horizontally at the top of the page across all left, middle, and right columns, as you would see in the header of a Microsoft Word document.

■   **Left**   Web parts are placed within the left-most column, vertically between the top and bottom positions. Multiple web parts can be placed and positioned vertically within the left position.

■   **Middle**   Web parts are placed within the middle column, between the top and bottom positions vertically, and between the left and right positions horizontally. Multiple web parts can be placed and positioned vertically within the middle position.

■   **Right**   Web parts are placed within the right-most column, vertically between the top and bottom positions. Multiple web parts can be placed and positioned vertically within the right position.

▲   **Bottom**   Web parts are positioned horizontally at the bottom of the page across all left, middle, and right columns, as you would see in the footer of a Microsoft Word document.

Microsoft has come up with a very nice drag-and-drop interface for graphically positioning the web parts within a dashboard. Here's how you use it:

1. Open the desired workspace using a web browser.

2. Navigate to the desired dashboard or subdashboard on which you will change the layout.

3. Click Layout.

    Clicking this link will bring up the screen shown in Figure 7-7 which is showing the Home dashboard.

4. Configure your layout, as desired.

    To configure the layout of your web parts, you simply drag-and-drop the content into the area where you would like it to be displayed. For example, if you don't want the Search web part to be displayed on the top, you can drag-and-drop to its new location, such as the bottom. On the other hand, if you want to place it or any other web part in the left, middle, or right positions,

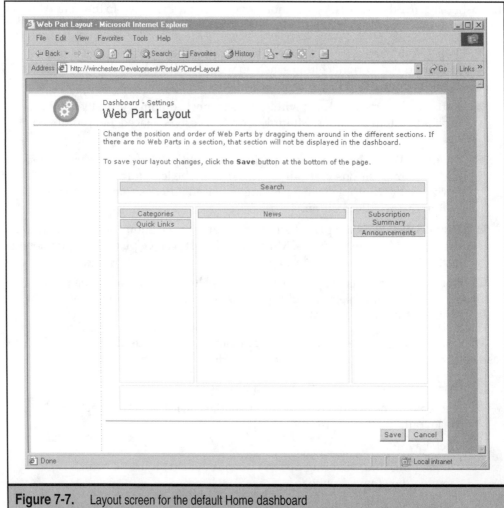

Figure 7-7. Layout screen for the default Home dashboard

drop it into the desired pane, but also drop it in the correct position vertically. For example, you can place the Search web part above the Categories web part, between Categories and Quick Links, or below Quick Links. Figure 7-8 shows what the screen looks like after moving the search Web Part to from the top position to the bottom position.

5. Click Save.

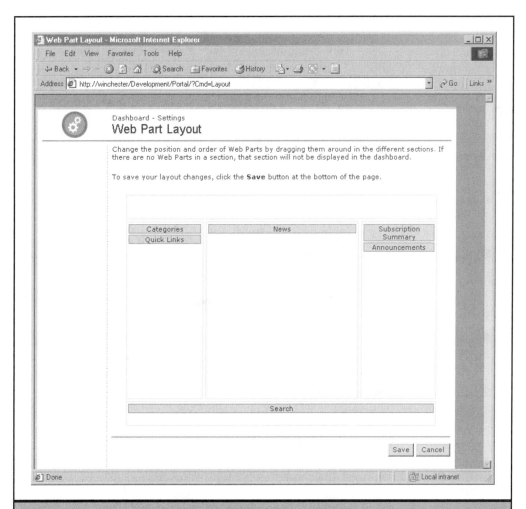

Figure 7-8. Layout screen for the default Home dashboard, showing repositioned Search web part

Settings

Dashboard settings relate to configuration options that you can change to define or alter the appearance of a dashboard. This configuration includes things like icons, style sheets, etc. The following highlights the settings that can be configured:

NOTE: The list shown here does not necessarily represent the names of the settings as they are actually shown on the screen. Some have been shortened to save space in this book, but convey the general idea as to which property on the screen is available for configuration changes. Only the first five options are displayed by default. To display all other options, click Show Advanced Settings.

▼ **Name** The name as it should appear to the users when they click on the dashboard. See the earlier note under the section "Renaming Dashboards" for information about the name of the virtual directory created in IIS.

■ **Caption** Displays a label that will always appear above the dashboard name. Refer to Figure 7-6. Notice how there is a caption that shows Welcome To The Management Dashboard. This is the caption. You can enter any text that adds value to the dashboard. This could be your company or department name, for example.

■ **Description** Describes the dashboard when an administrator views settings. This is not displayed on the dashboard for general users. If it is obvious what the dashboard is used for, you can leave this box blank.

■ **Refresh** If your dashboard contains web parts that need to be refreshed periodically, such as stock or news information, you need to adjust this setting. Click Yes and enter the refresh interval in seconds. If you do not need the dashboard to be refreshed automatically, click No. No is the default value.

■ **Stylesheet** Specifies the look and feel of the dashboard. You can choose from one of the twelve "out-of-the-box" style sheets, or create one of your own. Creating style sheets is beyond the scope of this book. If you do want to use one of your own, select Custom from the drop-down list and enter the name of your stylesheet. By default, the spsdash.css stylesheet is used.

■ **Apply custom styles** Allows you to specify custom styles for a dashboard. More information about custom styles can be obtained in the SharePoint Portal Server SDK. For information on where to get this SDK, see Chapter 2.

■ **Header image** Allows you to place an image or logo in the dashboard header. If you wish to use this, simply click the checkbox and enter the name of the image.

■ **Dashboard image** Allows you to place a 16 by 16 pixel image (or smaller) onto the tab next to the name of the dashboard. This allows your users to click the images to navigate between dashboards.

- **Order** Allows you to configure the physical placement of your dashboards or subdashboards. A number of 0 displays the dashboards alphabetically; 1 is always on the left-hand side; whereas a higher number, such as 60, will always display the dashboard on the right-hand side.

- **Show subdashboards** Check this box if you want to allow subdashboards to be shown. Subdashboards are discussed in the earlier section "Dashboards." To see what subdashboards look like, see Figure 7-4.

- **Check master versions** Automatically checks to see if there are new versions of web parts contained on the dashboard. This option is not checked by default, as it can be time-consuming to check for new versions every time the dashboard is loaded.

- **Help file** Allows you to specify an HTML help file for help with the dashboard. For more information on help, see the section, "Help" later in this chapter.

- ▲ **Store data** Allows you to store data that will be used by one or more web parts. If you are familiar with programming, this data is similar to parameters being passed into a function. More information about storing data can be obtained in the SharePoint Portal Server SDK. For information on where to get this SDK, see Chapter 2.

To change any of the settings for a dashboard, follow these steps:

1. Open the desired workspace using a web browser.
2. Navigate to the desired dashboard or subdashboard on which you will change the settings.
3. Click Settings.

   Clicking this link will bring up the screen shown in Figure 7-9. Note that Figure 7-9 shows advanced options, but cannot show the full screen due to space limitations.

4. Configure the desired settings.
5. Click Save.

Help

As long as you are the coordinator of the workspace, HTML-based help is available if you are not sure how to perform some action on pre-installed dashboards. For your own dashboards, you can create a help file that is used to provide additional help for users of your dashboard. This book does not show you how to create help files, since it is not a book on teaching HTML. Help files are assigned when you configure the settings for a dashboard. For more information on changing settings, refer to the section "Settings" earlier in this chapter.

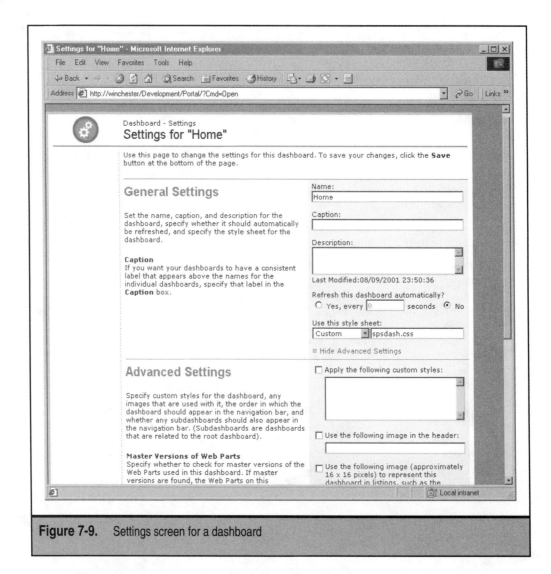

Figure 7-9. Settings screen for a dashboard

Bringing up help couldn't be easier. Here's how:

1. Open the desired workspace using a web browser.
2. Navigate to the desired dashboard.
3. Click Help.

   The help file that is invoked when you click Help is context-sensitive. In other words, the help that is shown depends on which dashboard is currently active. For example, Figure 7-10 shows the help file for the Home dashboard.

SharePoint Portal Server: A Beginner's Guide Blueprints

Table of Contents

SharePoint Portal Server Architecture

This illustration shows the architecture of a SharePoint Portal Server and the components that are used from the different client programs. Notice that when you use a browser for an Internet or Extranet scenario, the requests come through the Internet (and probably a firewall). On the other hand, an intranet browser, Windows Explorer, or Office application does not go through the Internet. Also, external content sources are crawled by going through the Internet.

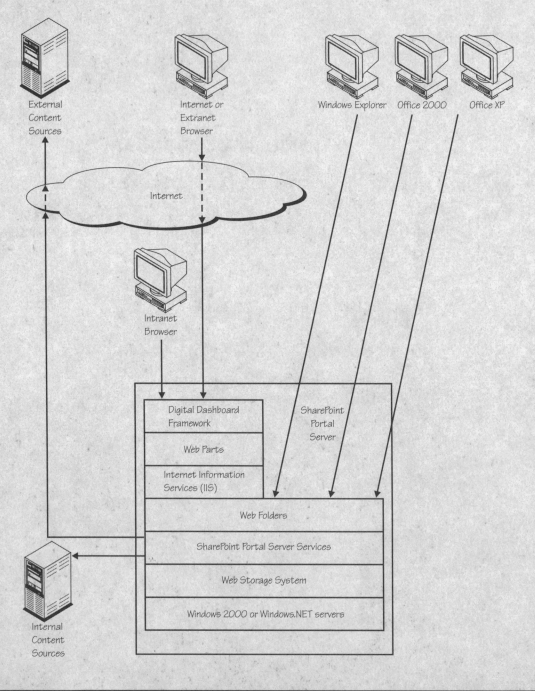

Installation Diagram

In this diagram, notice that you must install client components for use with Windows Explorer or Office 2000 or Office XP. You do not need to install any components for use with a web browser. You also need to install the SharePoint Portal Server components on any server that will be used on your network, regardless of the server's purpose.

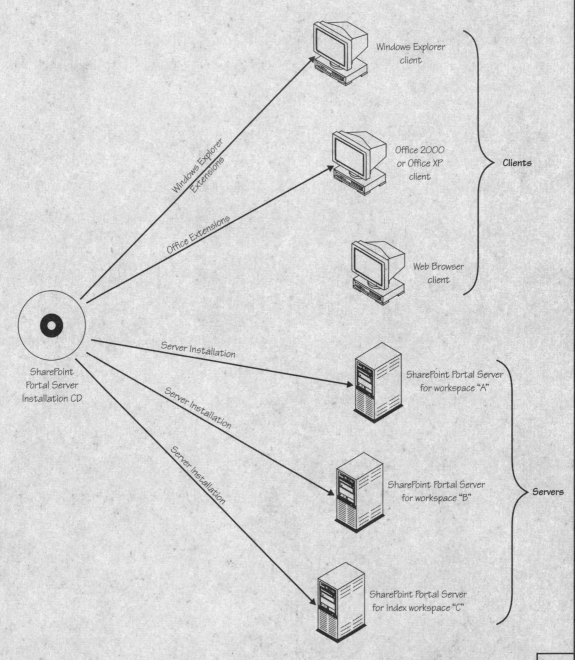

Approval Routing Process

This complex diagram shows four different scenarios of the roles of the author, approver, and reader. Once the author publishes a document, the type of folder that contains the document and the approval routing that has been set up dictates the process that a document goes through.

Case 1: Enhanced folders not configured for approvals or standard folders

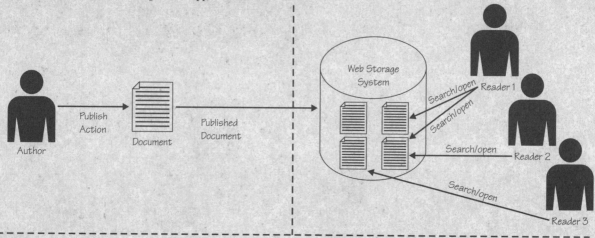

Case 2: Enhanced folders configured for approvals (Parallel-One vote)

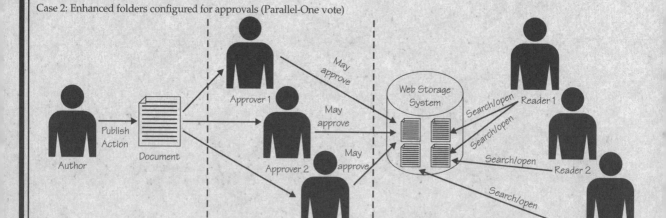

Case 3: Enhanced folders configured for approvals (Parallel-Many votes)

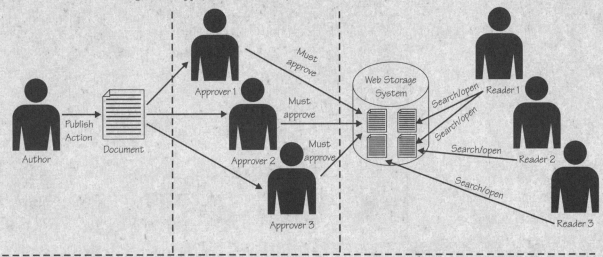

Case 4: Enhanced folders configured for approvals (Serial)

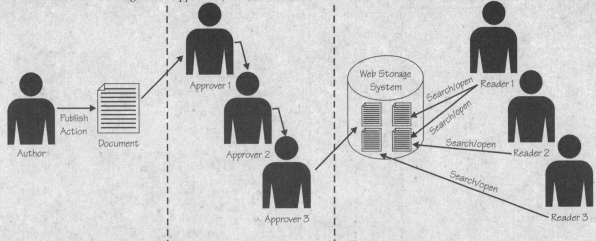

5

Portal Content Sources

This diagram shows the role of the crawler within a SharePoint Portal Server to grab (or crawl) content from the six predefined content sources. Notice that for a web site or SharePoint Portal Server content sources, content can be accessed either internally or over the Internet. Once content is crawled, one or more indexes are created for use by the search engine when a browser requests a search.

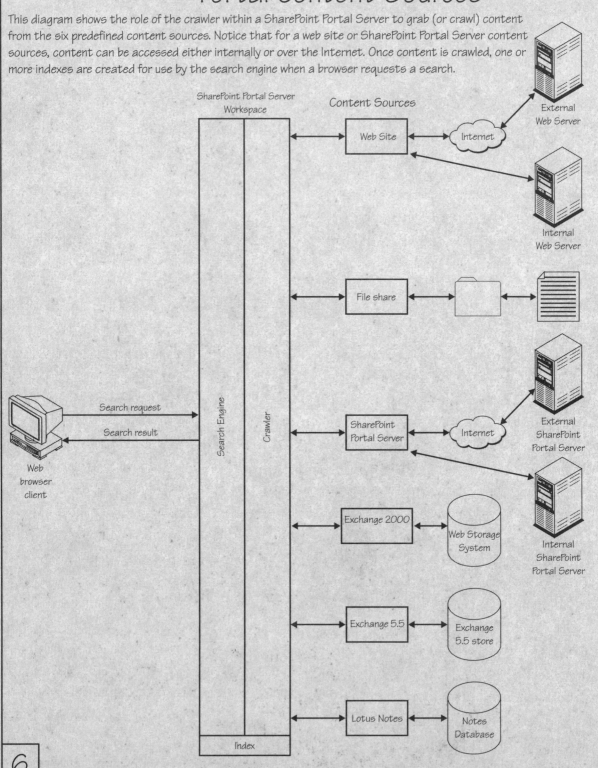

Indexing Scenarios

This blueprint shows the role of the crawler and search engines when using one, two, or more than two servers. As shown in scenario 1, when one server is involved, it must do all crawling and searching, which can bring down server performance. In scenario 2, two servers are used. One is used for searching content and one is used for crawling content. Once content is crawled, the index that is created is propagated to the search server. In scenario 3, three servers are shown, but there can be any number of servers used. One or more servers is used for searching content, and one or more servers is used for crawling content. If more than one server is used for searching content, each must be configured with a different workspace. If more than one server is used for crawling content, the index(es) created on that server must be propagated to the appropriate search server.

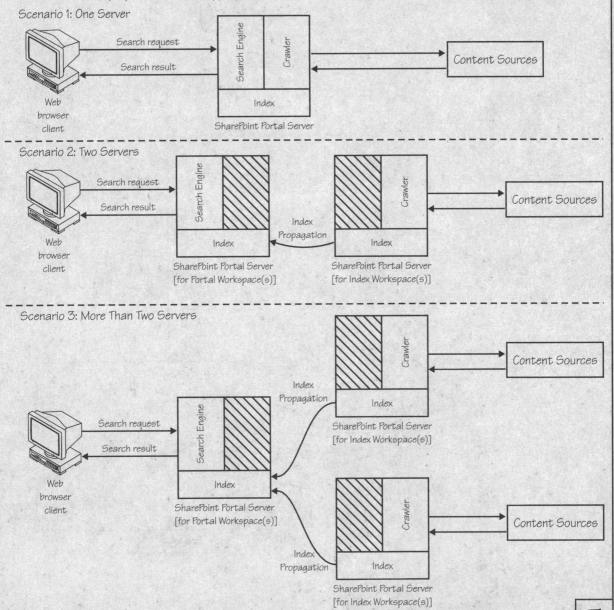

Security Roles Diagram

This diagram shows how users and groups are used when configuring security roles within SharePoint Portal Server. When a user logs into a Windows NT domain or a Windows 2000 Active Directory, a security identifier (or SID) is returned back to the client. Then, when a request is made to SharePoint Portal Server, the SID is checked against the assigned security role to determine if the requested action is allowed.

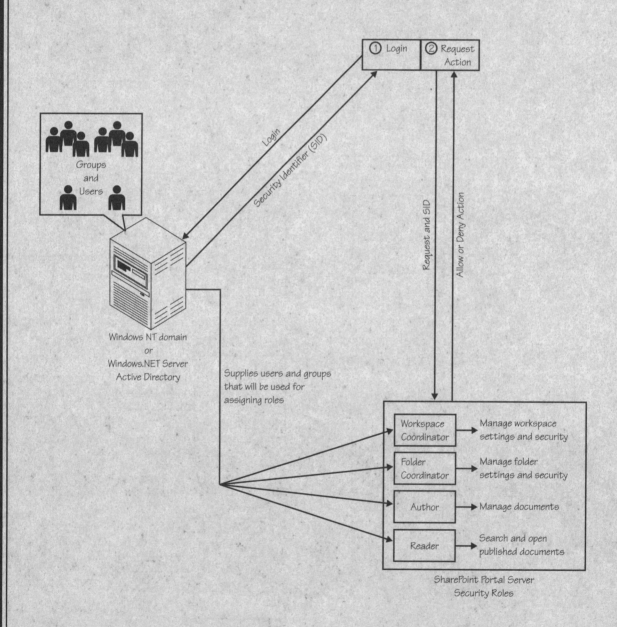

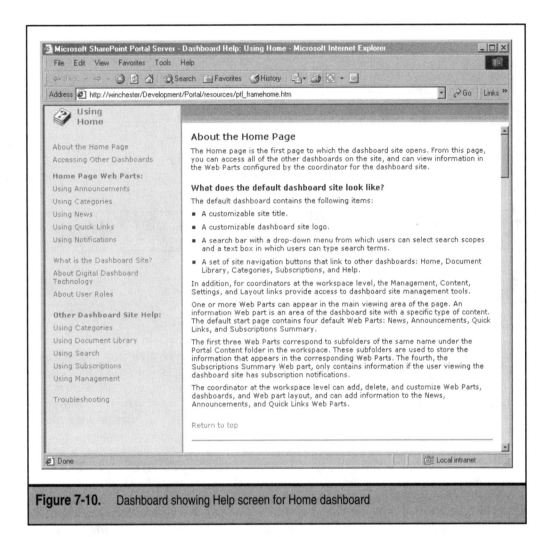

Figure 7-10.   Dashboard showing Help screen for Home dashboard

The default dashboards that are installed automatically each have a help file associated with that dashboard, which of course, you can customize if you wish. Table 7-1 shows a listing of help files for each dashboard.

If you configure your own dashboards to have help files, then the Help link will appear for a coordinator. Otherwise, this link will not appear.

Dashboard	Help File Name
Home	ptl_framehome.htm
Search	ptl_framesearch.htm
Categories	ptl_framecats.htm
Document Library	ptl_framedocs.htm
Subscriptions	ptl_framesubs.htm
Management	ptl_framemgmt.htm

Table 7-1.   Dashboard Help Files

CHAPTER SUMMARY

As you have seen in this chapter, there are many configurations that an administrator must make on the server. Without these configurations, your site would not be customized. You would only have the functionality of a default workspace after it is created. The customizations that you can make are virtually limitless because you can add as many subdashboards and web parts as your site requires. In addition, you can change the layout of the web parts within a subdashboard. You also learned how dashboards and web parts exist within a workspace. Therefore, I showed you how to create and manage workspaces on a server.

Additionally, you learned all about folders, both standard and enhanced. You saw that configuration and organization of those folders is as easy as it is using the Windows Explorer, using concepts and techniques that you are already familiar with.

Most of the administrative options discussed in this and other chapters are quite simple. Probably the most difficult aspect of administering SharePoint Portal Server is when you need a web part that doesn't exist. As a SharePoint Portal Server administrator, you may not have the knowledge on how to create web parts using XML or scripting languages, so you have to rely on developers. This might be an opportunity to learn those technologies ☺.

CHAPTER 8

Indexing

One of the major reasons that you purchase SharePoint Portal Server is for its indexing and searching capabilities. SharePoint Portal Server automatically maintains an index for documents that are stored within the Web Storage System. However, if you wish to create indexes for content outside the Web Storage System, or in another workspace, you must instruct SharePoint Portal Server how to do that. Although SharePoint Portal Server gives you easy ways to configure indexing, this chapter will help you out a lot. This chapter discusses how to configure all aspects of indexing in SharePoint Portal Server, including content sources, search scopes, and file types. If that isn't enough, you'll learn how to manage your index updates.

If, while going through this chapter, you encounter any problems with your indexes, you might take a gander at Chapter 13, which deals with troubleshooting. Also, check out the blueprint in the center of this book for more details on the architecture and scenarios for indexing.

OVERVIEW

Before you can search on a document or content that is contained *outside* the current workspace, you must tell SharePoint Portal Server how to do that. Once you define where this content is located, SharePoint Portal Server accesses that content and creates an index, which is stored on the SharePoint Portal Server computer. The act of grabbing that content and storing it in an index is known as *crawling*. This is known as crawling because the indexing can take quite a long time, depending on the following factors:

▼ LAN/Connection speed

■ Type of content

■ Location of content

▲ Type of updating that index must perform

TIP: To configure any of the indexing scenarios presented in this chapter, you must have coordinator privileges for the workspace.

INDEXING CONFIGURATION

Configuring indexing is done mostly by using a network place. However, there are some configurations that are done on the SharePoint Portal Server in the SharePoint Portal Server Administrator. These configurations are discussed on the next few pages.

CONTENT SOURCES

A content source is a way to indicate to the SharePoint Indexing Engine where content is stored that will be indexed. If you are familiar with database technologies, this is quite analogous to an ODBC data source. With a content source, you can index data that is stored within the following locations:

▼ Current SharePoint Workspace

■ Another SharePoint Portal Server Workspace

▲ Content not stored in a SharePoint Portal Server Workspace

Standard Content Sources

To enable the indexing of data from these locations, SharePoint Portal Server provides you with six standard, "out-of-the-box" content sources. These content sources allow SharePoint to know how and where to grab data to be indexed. SharePoint Portal Server allows for these built-in content sources:

▼ **Web Site**   Indexes content displayed on web pages

■ **File Share**   Indexes files located in a file share on your network

■ **SharePoint Portal Server**   Indexes a SharePoint Portal Server workspace

■ **Exchange 2000**   Indexes of public folders on an Exchange 2000 Server

■ **Exchange 5.5**   Indexes of public folders on an Exchange 5.5 Server

▲ **Lotus Notes**   Indexes Lotus Notes or Domino databases, but they must be version 4.6a or higher. There is a special configuration that you must perform when using Lotus Notes as a content source. This is shown in the next section, "Configuring for Lotus Notes."

SQL Server Support

You'll notice that support for SQL Server databases or Full-text catalogs is conspicuously missing from the list of content sources. For some unknown reason, Microsoft did not include SQL Server support in version 1 of SharePoint Portal Server. However, you have two work-around options:

1. You can create a web page that accesses data from SQL Server, then crawl content using a web site as your content source. This is not an ideal solution, but it is the one that Microsoft recommends at the time of this writing.

2. Write your own custom protocol handler that accesses SQL Server data directly. Protocol handlers are described later in this chapter, under the heading "Protocol Handlers".

Configuring for Lotus Notes   Before you can connect to a Lotus Notes database, you have to use the Lotus Notes Index Setup Wizard. This wizard configures settings that connect SharePoint Portal Server to a Lotus Notes database. To use the wizard, follow these steps:

1. Open the SharePoint Portal Server Administrator.

    On the SharePoint Portal Server computer, choose Start | Programs | Administrative Tools | SharePoint Portal Server Administration.

2. Right-click the name of your server and choose Properties.

3. Click Other.

    Clicking Other brings up this dialog box:

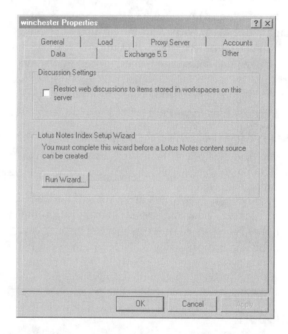

4. Click Run Wizard.

    Clicking Run Wizard starts the wizard, showing the welcome screen seen in Figure 8-1.

5. Click Next.

    Clicking Next brings up the screen shown in Figure 8-2, which allows you to specify the location of the Lotus Notes database and initialization file.

Figure 8-1. Index Setup Wizard welcome screen

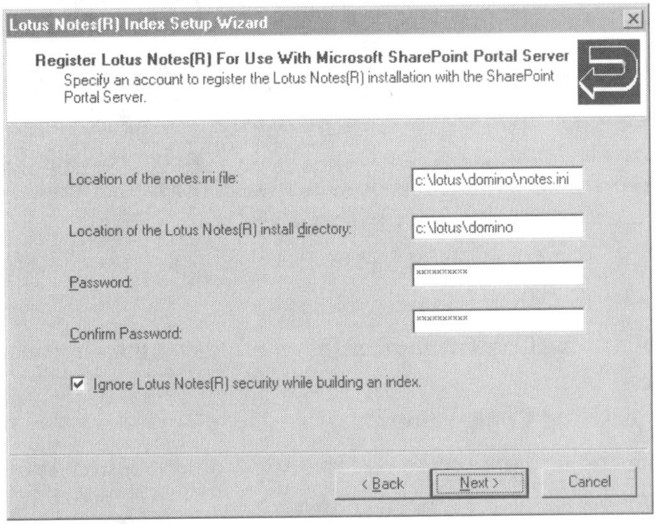

Figure 8-2. Specify the location of the Lotus Notes database and initialization file.

6. Fill in all fields.

    The fields that you must fill in or select are:

    - **Location of the notes.ini file**   File path that contains the notes.ini file. A typical location might be C:\Lotus\Domino.

    - **Location of the Lotus Notes(R) install directory**   Location where SharePoint Portal Server can find installation files.

    - **Password**   Password of the Lotus Notes server

    - **Confirm Password**   Confirmation of the Lotus Notes password

    - **Ignore Lotus Notes(R) security while building an index**   Check this box if you don't want to specify an account to use to access the Notes database. If you uncheck this box, you will have to fill-in fields for another step in which you specify security and database information. For specific information on how to configure specific security settings, refer to the Microsoft "Q" article at **http://support.microsoft.com/support/kb/articles/ Q288/8/16.ASP**.

7. Click Finish.

    You are now ready to add or edit a Lotus Notes content source.

Adding a Content Source   Content Sources are added using a wizard in SharePoint Portal Server by using a network place. It's (not surprisingly) called the Add Content Source Wizard. It's exceptionally simple to use, as you'll see with these instructions:

1. Open the network place that represents the workspace on your portal.

    In my example, I open the network place for a workspace called IT (for information technology) on the SharePoint Portal Server called winchester. This network place is called IT on winchester. For more information about creating a network place, see Chapter 4.

2. Navigate to the Management folder.

3. Navigate to the Content Sources folder.

    Navigating to the Content Sources folder brings up the screen shown in Figure 8-3.

4. Double-click Add Content Source.

    This brings up welcome screen for the Add Content Source Wizard shown in Figure 8-4.

5. Click Next.

    Clicking Next brings up the Content Source Type screen shown in Figure 8-5. Notice that this screen shows the content sources discussed earlier.

6. Click the desired content source in the Types list.

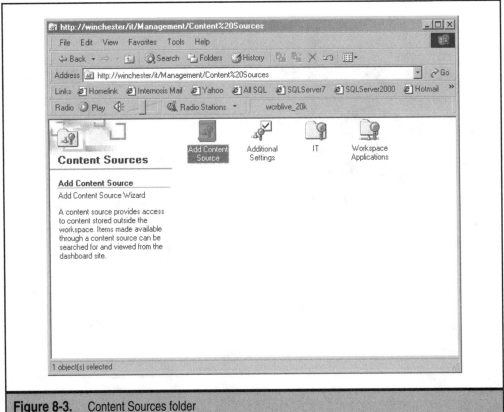

Figure 8-3.   Content Sources folder

7. Click Next.

   Clicking Next brings up the Content Source screen shown in Figure 8-6.

8. Fill in the content source data.

   Enter the requested data. The data requested depends on the content source type that you chose earlier. Table 8-1 shows the data that you must specify for each content source type.

9. Select the desired option.

   Choose the desired option of whether to create an index of This Folder And All Subfolders, or Only This Folder. In other words, if you choose to create an index based on subfolders, data will be crawled from the point specified and lower in the hierarchy. For example, when you specify a web site address, all directories and folders below that point are also crawled.

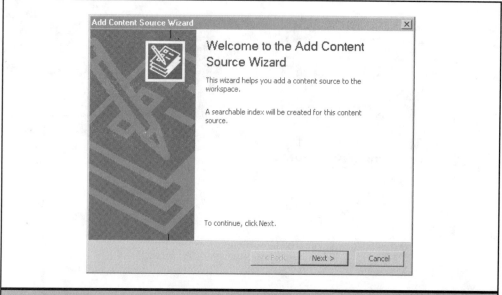

Figure 8-4. Add Content Source Wizard welcome screen

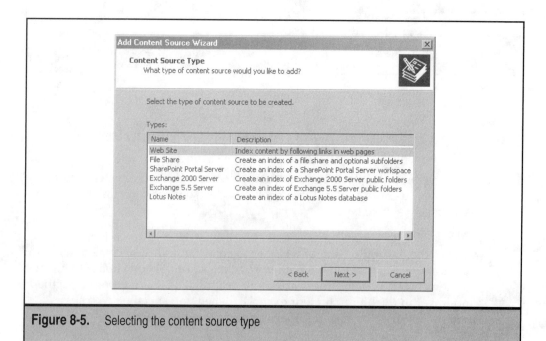

Figure 8-5. Selecting the content source type

Content Source Type	Required Information
Web Site	Base web address of the web site. For example, to crawl all content in the xyzcorp.com web site, type: `http://xyzcorp.com`
File Share	UNC path of a folder in a file share. For example, to search all content contained within the Resumes folder in the Documents share on the Winchester server, type: `\\winchester\documents\resumes`
SharePoint Portal Server	Base web address of the SharePoint Portal Server workspace. For example, to crawl all content in documents folder in the IT workspace on the portal server called winchester, type: `http://winchester/IT/documents`
Exchange 2000	Base web address of the Exchange 2000 Server public folders. For example, to crawl all content in all public folders on the Exch01 server, type: `http://Exch01/Public`

Exchange 5.5	Base folder path of the Exchange 5.5 public folders. For example, to crawl all content in all public folders on the Exch02 server, type:
	
	`exch://Exch02/Public Folders/`
	`All Public Folders`
	
	Note: You must configure SharePoint Portal Server to use Exchange 5.5 for this content source to work. Otherwise, you'll receive an error at this point. For more information about configuring Exchange 5.5, see the related section in this chapter.

Lotus Notes	Lotus Notes server and database to crawl for content. However, before you can configure a Lotus Notes Content Source, you must configure your SharePoint Portal Server. See earlier section in this chapter, "Configuring for Lotus Notes."

Table 8-1.   Required Content Source Data, Based On Content Source Type Chosen

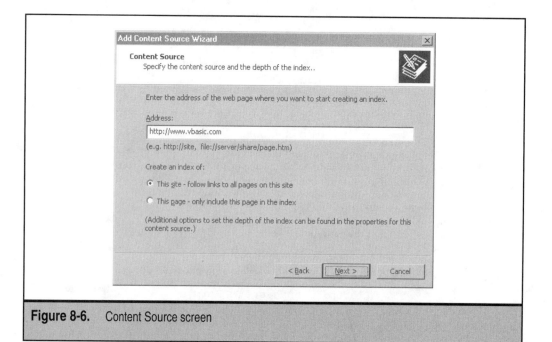

Figure 8-6.   Content Source screen

NOTE: If you choose a web site as a content source, the above explanation still holds true, but the options are labeled This Site and This Page, respectively, instead of This Folder and all Subfolders and Only this Folder.

10. Click Next.

    Clicking Next brings up the Name screen shown in Figure 8-7. Enter a name for your content source.

11. Click Next.

    Clicking Next brings up the final screen , as shown in Figure 8-8.

12. Check the desired index option.

    You can choose to create an index for the new content source upon completion of the wizard. To do so, ensure that the Start Creating an Index option is checked, which is the default value. If you wish not to create the index at the completion of the wizard, ensure that this option is unchecked.

13. Click Finish.

    Clicking Finish creates your new content source.

    Once you create a content source, you'll notice that the content source is now shown in the Content Sources folder in the network place.

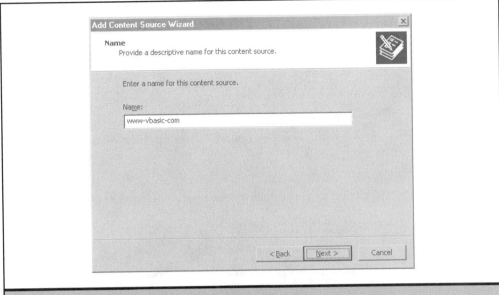

Figure 8-7.   Specifying a name for your new content source

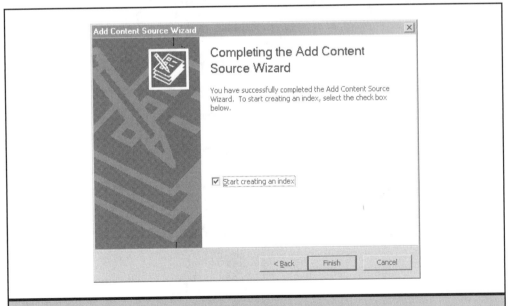

Figure 8-8.   Completing the configuration of your new content source

Editing a Content Source   Like adding a content source, modifying a content source is also done by using a network place. Here's how:

1. Open the network place that represents the workspace on your portal.
2. Navigate to the Management folder.
3. Navigate to the Content Sources folder.
4. Double-click the desired content source.

   Double-clicking the desired content source brings up the properties dialog for that content source.
5. Click Configuration.

   Here's how the dialog looks for the content source we created earlier:

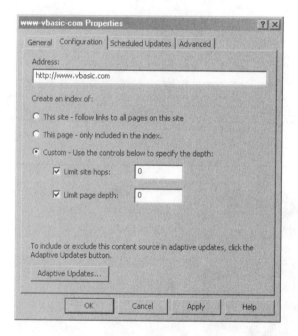

6. Select or change the desired option.

   Depending on the type of content source you are editing, the information that is available to change varies. This is discussed in the next six sections.
7. Click OK to save your changes and close the screen.

Web Sites   If you want to edit a web site content source, you'll notice that you have most of the same options to configure your content source as you did when you created the source. There is one major exception, however. It is the Custom option. When you create the content source, you can only configure it to crawl content at the current level only or the current level and all subfolders. With the Custom option, you can configure the content source to crawl content somewhere in between the two.

When you click Custom, two more options become enabled:

▼ **Limit site hops**   If checked, the number of site hops will be limited to the number entered. If 0 is entered (or the option is unchecked), the number of hops is unlimited. If non-zero, hops will be limited to the number entered. A *site hop* is when, during the process of crawling a web site, a link to another site or web page is encountered. Because this can include unlimited crawling, it can slow down or halt the server indefinitely. Therefore, you must configure site path rules for site hops. This is covered later in this chapter in the section "Site Path Rules."

▲ **Limit page depth**   If checked, the page depth will be limited to the number entered. If 0 is entered (or the option is unchecked), the depth will not be limited. If non-zero, the depth will be limited to the number entered. A *page depth* is the number of folder or virtual directory levels that will be scanned during the crawl.

File Share   If you want to edit a file share content source, you have almost the same options available as you did when you created the content source. However, there is one difference. This difference is that you can specify update methods for the index. Although updating the index is discussed later in this chapter, it is important to know that you can choose from these two additional index update options:

▼ **Automatically using notifications**   When selected, will update the index automatically and immediately when a change occurs. If many changes are being made to your site, selecting this option can bring performance down.

▲ **Only when updates are scheduled or started manually**   When selected (as it is by default), will update the index the next time SharePoint Portal Server updates the index. This can be by either a manual command or a scheduled update. This option is beneficial for nightly batch updates.

SharePoint Portal Server   There are no additional options available when you edit a SharePoint Portal Server content source. You can only change whether the index crawls content from the current folder or the current folder and subfolders. This is discussed under the earlier section on adding content sources.

Exchange 2000 and Exchange 5.5 There are also no additional options available when you edit Exchange 2000 or Exchange 5.5 content sources. You can only change whether the index crawls content from the current folder or the current folder and subfolders. This also is discussed under the earlier section, "Adding a Content Source."

Lotus Notes There are no additional options available when you edit a Lotus Notes content source. You can only change server and database-related information.

Deleting a Content Source Like adding and modifying a content source, deleting a content source is also done by using a network place. Here's how:

1. Open the network place that represents the workspace on your portal.
2. Navigate to the Management folder.
3. Navigate to the Content Sources folder.
4. Right-click the desired content source.
5. Click Delete.

You are prompted to confirm before deletion will occur.

Protocol Handlers

If you don't see an "out-of-the-box" content source that you need, this does not mean that you can't crawl content from that source. It only means that Microsoft didn't provide the ability to crawl this content source by default. You can write a custom protocol handler yourself or obtain one from a third party. A *protocol handler* allows you to crawl custom data sources. Writing a protocol handler is well beyond the scope of this book, but I wanted to mention that it can be done. More information about writing protocol handlers is available from the SharePoint Portal Server SDK (briefly discussed in Chapter 2).

iFilter Interface

The types of files that can be crawled (like HTML or DOC files) are implemented by using an iFilter interface. Although there is no directory of available iFilters at the time of this writing, there is at least one that I know about. It is from Adobe. This iFilter interface allows you to crawl content contained within PDF (Portable Document Format) files.

The Adobe iFilter is called PDF IFilter 4.1 (which is the version available at the time of this writing). It is available for download at:

```
http://www.adobe.com/support/downloads/8122.htm
```

As writing an iFilter interface is well beyond the scope of this book, more information is available in the SharePoint Portal Server SDK and on the Microsoft web site at:

```
http://msdn.microsoft.com/library/psdk/indexsrv/ixrefint_9sfm.htm
```

SITE PATH RULES

A *site path rule* is a specific configuration of either a file share path or an HTTP web site address. The site path rule allows you to configure:

▼ **Path Location**   Location of the file share path or web site address.

■ **Security Accounts**   Account used to access resources for the site path.

■ **Inclusion or Exclusion of the path**   Specifies whether the site path is included or excluded from the index.

▲ **Link Properties (for certain types of site path rules)**   Specifies options for site hops.

Site path rules are very useful for excluding specific paths from index crawling. For example, suppose that you have a file share for which you crawl the current folder and all subfolders. However, there is a specific folder within that hierarchy that contains confidential information, like Salaries. Therefore, you want to exclude this from being crawled. You would create a site path rule for this.

TIP   You must be a workspace Coordinator to configure site path rules.

To change (add, edit, or delete) site path rules, you must use a network place. Follow these instructions to configure site paths:

1. Open the network place that represents the workspace on your portal.

2. Navigate to the Management folder.

3. Navigate to the Content Sources folder.

4. Double-click the Additional Settings icon.

Double-clicking this option brings up this dialog box:

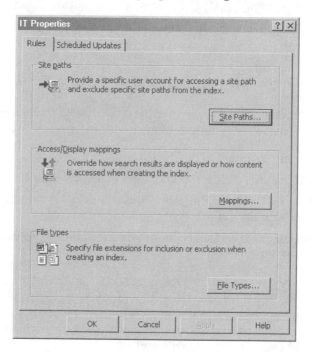

5. Click Site Paths.

   Clicking Site Paths brings up the dialog box shown in Figure 8-9.

NOTE: Notice in the above illustration the icon next to the only site path listed. It indicates that the site path displayed is excluded so that the Shadow folder is not indexed.

Choose any of the desired options in the following sections:

Adding a New Site Path Rule

Following the prior steps, add a new site path rule by doing this:

1. Click New.

   Clicking New brings up the dialog box shown in Figure 8-10.

2. Enter the path for the rule in the Path text box.

   This path is used for the inclusion or exclusion of the rule. Therefore, if you followed my previous example (about the salaries,) you could type something like:

   ```
   http://www.vbasic.com/salaries
   ```

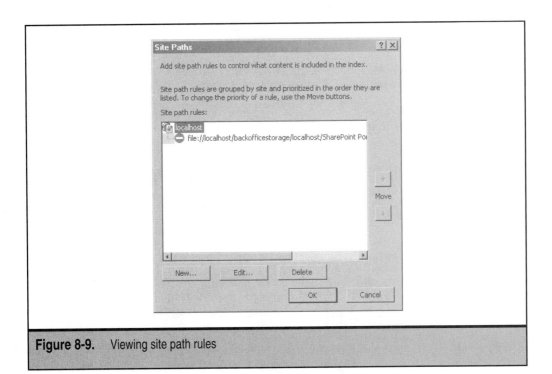

Figure 8-9.   Viewing site path rules

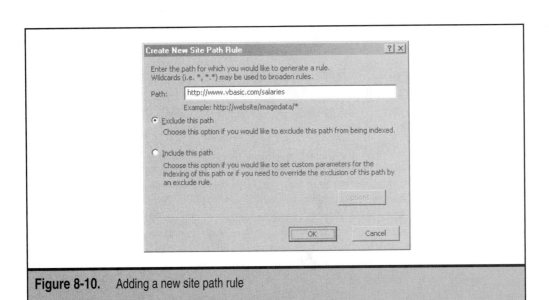

Figure 8-10.   Adding a new site path rule

3. Select whether to include or exclude the path.

   If you wish this rule to not be used in this index, click Exclude This Path. If you wish this path to be used while creating the index, click Include This Path. If the latter option is chosen, Options becomes enabled.

4. Click Options.

   Options is only enabled if you choose Include This Path. Clicking this button brings up this screen:

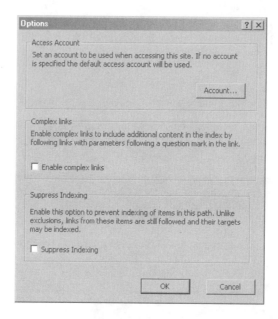

5. Click Account.

   Clicking Account allows you to specify a security account that has network privileges to the path chosen earlier. Clicking Account brings up the screen shown in Figure 8-11.

6. Enter security information.

   If you have been working in any version of Windows, you are familiar with entering a domain, user name, password, and confirmation password. Additionally, choose the authentication type. Integrated Windows authentication is the default type and is secure. The other option, Basic authentication, is less secure because it sends data in clear text. Basic authentication might need to be used if authentication is going through a firewall. If you use Basic authentication, you may want to consider using Secure Sockets Layer (SSL) to encrypt data going to and from your web server.

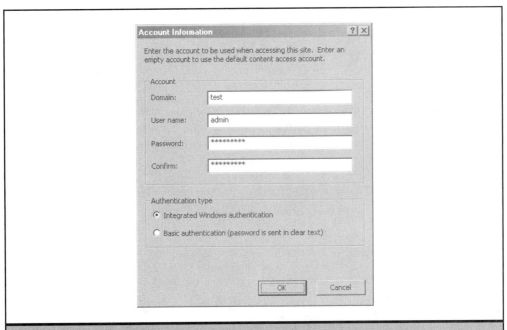

Figure 8-11. Entering account information for a site path rule

7. Click OK to save and close the Account Information screen.

8. Select desired options.

   You can choose from these options:

   ■ **Enable complex links**   This check box will force the indexing engine to crawl content of pages that are linked into higher-level pages of a hierarchy.

   ■ **Suppress indexing**   This is similar to an exclusion rule because this path is not indexed. However, the difference is that any links on pages contained in this path are still indexed.

NOTE: The Enable Complex links and Suppress Indexing options are only enabled if your path contains a fully qualified path, including a starting folder. In other words, the path *http://www.xyzcorp.com* is not enough. These options will be disabled if you use a path like this. However, the path *http://www.xyzcorp.com/** will enable the options.

Editing an Existing Site Path Rule

Edit an existing site path rule by following these steps:

1. Click Edit.
2. Change the desired options.

   The options for editing the site path rules are exactly the same as when you added a new site path rule, except that the path cannot be changed. If you need to change the actual path in the site path rule, you must delete and recreate the rule.

Deleting an Existing Site Path Rule

To delete an existing site path rule, simply click Delete. You are prompted to confirm before deletion occurs.

DISPLAY MAPPINGS

Display mappings give you a way to map one path to another path. The reason that you might need to do this is mainly because a reference to a local file on one server might not work on another. For example, suppose you reference a file path c:\inetpub\wwwroot\vbasic. Because the reference is to a local file on one machine, it may not physically reside in the same path on another machine. Therefore, you can map it to:

```
http://www.vbasic.com/
```

It may not be obvious, but notice in the example that we are mapping a file on the network to a web site reference.

To add a display mapping, follow these steps:

1. Open the network place that represents the workspace on your portal.
2. Navigate to the Management folder.
3. Navigate to the Content Sources folder.
4. Double-click Additional Settings.
5. Click Mappings.

   Clicking Mappings brings up the dialog box shown in Figure 8-12.
6. Enter the appropriate mapping data.

   In the Access Location text box, type the path that you wish to map *from*. In the preceding example, you would type c:\inetpub\wwwroot\vbasic. In the

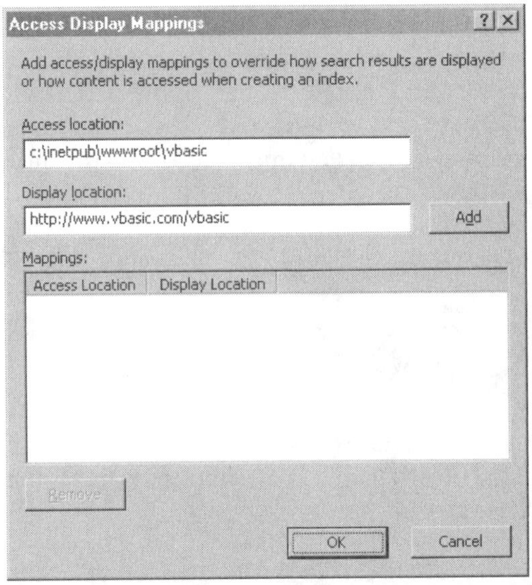

Figure 8-12. Access Display Mappings dialog

Display Location text box, type the path that you wish to map *to*. Again, using the preceding example, you would type **http://www.vbasic.com/vbasic**.

7. Click Add.

8. Click OK.

If you want to remove an existing mapping, simply select it and click Remove.

FILE TYPES

In any version of Windows, when you open a file, how does it know what program to use to open the file? For example, when you try to open a text file (with a TXT file extension), how does Windows know to open it with the Notepad application? That's simple. There is an association between a program and a file extension, which is also known as a *file type*.

The way SharePoint Portal Server deals with file types is somewhat similar. Although you don't specify which program is used to open a file with a specific file type, you do specify a list of file types. This list is either included or excluded from being indexed, depending on how SharePoint Portal Server is configured.

Let me give you an example. An EXE file is an executable file and does not contain text that would be placed into a SharePoint Portal Server index. Therefore, it is not included in the list of files to crawl. However, a CSV file (which stands for comma separated values) is a text file that might need to be crawled and placed into the index. By default, these file types are included in the index crawl:

HTM	XML	EML	TIF
EXCH	XLS	DOT	MHT
NSF	ODC	DOC	HTML
ASP	TIFF	PPT	TXT

The decision of whether to include or exclude files in the list is quite simple. Most often it is easier to add a list of the files that are to be included, so this is the default. To change any of the options, follow these steps:

1. Open the network place that represents the workspace on your portal.

2. Navigate to the Management folder.

3. Navigate to the Content Sources folder.

4. Double-click Additional Settings.

5. Click File Types.

   Clicking File Types brings up the dialog box shown in Figure 8-13.

6. Enter the appropriate file type data.

   First decide whether the list of file types will be included in the index crawl or excluded. Click Include File Types Listed Below; Exclude all Others or Exclude File Types Listed Below; Include all Others, respectively. Next, add or remove items in the list. To add an item, simply enter the file extension in the File Types text box and click Add. To remove an item, click the desired item to remove and click Remove.

7. Click OK.

SEARCH SCOPES

Do you know what a search scope is? If you answer, "No," then you probably don't realize that you use them all the time. For example, have you ever been to Microsoft's MSDN web site at **http://msdn.microsoft.com/library/default.asp** or Amazon.com's web site at **http://www.amazon.com/exec/obidos/subst/home/home.html**? Well, each of these sites allow you to type in a search word or phrase. Additionally, you can specify which catalog that search should apply to. This is known as a *search scope*. In the case of Microsoft, you

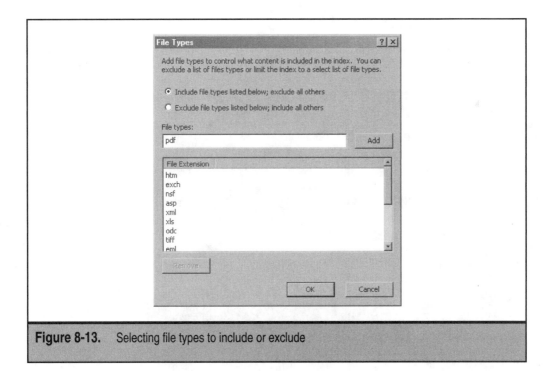

Figure 8-13.   Selecting file types to include or exclude

can specify that the search should apply to either all of MSDN or the Library only. In the case of Amazon.com, you can search all products, only books, only videos, and so on.

Limiting which catalogs, or indexes, that the search engine has to do can dramatically increase performance. Obviously, if you have 5 catalogs and you know that your data is in the first one, it would take more time to search all 5 than it would to search the desired one directly. You can set up your own search scopes in SharePoint Portal Server for each content source. If you need a refresher, content sources are covered earlier in this chapter, in the section, "Content Sources."

TIP: You must be a Coordinator of the workspace to configure a search scope.

To create a search scope that users can use to limit their searches, follow these steps:

1. Open the network place that represents the workspace on your portal.
2. Navigate to the Management folder.
3. Navigate to the Content Sources folder.
4. Double-click the desired content source.

   Double-clicking the desired content source brings up the properties dialog for that content source.

5. Click Advanced.

   Here's how the Advanced dialog box looks for a content source we
   created earlier:

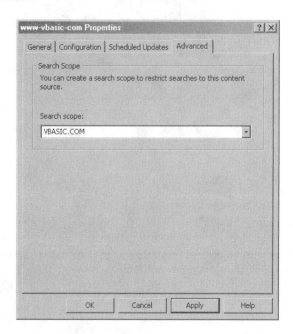

6. Enter the name of the search scope.

   In the Search Scope text box, enter the name of a new search scope or select an
   existing search scope from the drop-down list. If you wish to remove a search
   scope, simply clear the box. Use the name of a search scope that is easy to
   understand and is germane to the index that will be created or updated for the
   search scope. Remember, users are going to see this search scope in a drop-down
   listbox on the search dashboard. For example, if you have an index of executive
   documents, you might create a search scope called Executive Documents.

7. Click OK to save your changes and close the screen.

   You are prompted to rebuild the index before changes in search scope can be
   applied in the workspace.

WEB DISCUSSIONS

As you learn in Chapter 6, web discussions are text that you type when you are collabo-
rating on documents with others. You might be very interested to know that you can have

SharePoint Portal Server index the text of those discussions. This is very useful if, for example, you want to find out who said, "This software stinks," in a web discussion.

Enabling the searching of web discussions couldn't be simpler. However, it is not configured by using a network place (as most things are in this chapter). It is enabled by using the SharePoint Portal Server Administrator on the server computer itself. To configure SharePoint Portal Server to index web discussions, do this:

1. Open the SharePoint Portal Server Administrator.

   On the SharePoint Portal Server computer, choose Start | Programs | Administrative Tools | SharePoint Portal Server Administration.

2. Navigate to the desired workspace.

3. Right-click the desired workspace and choose Properties.

4. Click Subscriptions/Discussions.

   Clicking Subscriptions/Discussions brings up this dialog box:

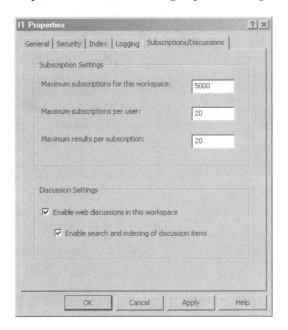

5. Check Enable Web Discussions In This Workspace if it is not checked.

6. Check Enable Search And Indexing Of Discussion Items.

   This option is only enabled if the Enable Web Discussions in this Workspace box is checked.

TIP: The indexing of web discussions is not secure, but the documents that the index points to are secure. Therefore, if you index web discussions, a user might see that a discussion is going on, even if he/she cannot view the document(s) referenced in the discussion. If this is a necessity, you may consider creating a separate workspace for this discussion or enabling SSL on the web server.

CONFIGURING EXCHANGE 5.5

If you intend to use Exchange 5.5 as a content source, you must configure SharePoint Portal Server first. It is an explicit step that you must take. Before you begin, you can only crawl Exchange 5.5 content if you have installed Outlook Web Access (OWA) and configured it to have access to Exchange public folders.

NOTE: If you want to use Exchange 2000 as a content source, you do not need to perform these steps. This is because Exchange 2000 is integrated with Active Directory so all configurations are already known by SharePoint.

To configure SharePoint Portal Server to use Exchange 5.5, you use the SharePoint Portal Server Administrator program. Just follow these steps:

1. Open the SharePoint Portal Server Administrator.

    On the SharePoint Portal Server computer, choose Start | Programs | Administrative Tools | SharePoint Portal Server Administration.

2. Navigate to the name of the server.

3. Right-click the name of the server and choose Properties.

4. Click Exchange 5.5.

    Clicking Exchange 5.5 brings up the dialog box shown in Figure 8-14.

5. Select the Enable Exchange 5.5 Crawl check box.

    Clicking this option enables all other fields on the form.

6. Fill in the Exchange Server Name text box.

    This is the Exchange 5.5 server that contains the content that will be crawled.

7. Fill in the Outlook Web Access Server Name text box.

    By default, this value is the same as the Exchange server name text box. SharePoint Portal Server assumes that OWA is installed on the Exchange 5.5 server box. If you wish to change this, simply type-in the new value.

8. Fill in the Exchange Server Site Name box.

    As your Exchange 5.5 server can have multiple sites, fill-in the name of the site you wish to crawl.

9. Fill in the Exchange Server Organization Name box.

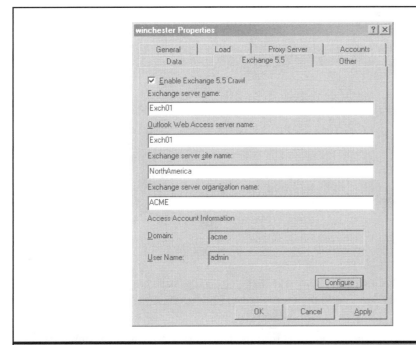

Figure 8-14.   Congifuring Exchange 5.5 server settings

As your Exchange 5.5 server can have multiple organizations within a site, fill in the name of the organization that contains the public folders you wish to crawl.

10. Click Configure to select user account information.

When you click Configure, a dialog box appears that allows you to select the domain account, user name, and password of the account that has access to crawl content in the Exchange public folders. It is likely that this account is an administrator account, or at least an account that has administrative access. When you are finished with this dialog box, click OK.

11. Click OK to save your changes and close the dialog box.

A Note About Validation

When you configure SharePoint Portal Server to use an Exchange 5.5 server, the data entered is not actually validated. You can type anything. However, if all parameters are not correct, the Indexing engine cannot crawl your data from the Exchange 5.5 public folders.

UPDATING INDEXES

Suppose you have the indexing engine crawl content from a web site and create an index of those documents. Then, the web site changes, but your index never gets updated. The consequences of this could be:

- ▼ Searching on a term results in a hit of a document that doesn't actually contain the term
- ▲ Searching on a term does not produce a hit when a document from the web site really does contain the term.

Therefore, to avoid either of these situations, you must have the indexing engine update its indexes. To allow for the updating of indexes, SharePoint Portal Server provides for a few different options. In fact, there are three types of index updates:

- ▼ **Full**   Crawls all content in the content source. This option is the most complete, but takes the most time.
- ■ **Incremental**   Crawls content and makes updates to the index only for documents that have actually changed in content. This option is not as complete as a full update, but it can take considerably less time.
- ▲ **Adaptive**   Like the incremental update, crawls content that has changed. However, instead of making updates to the index based on documents that actually have changed, updates are made to documents that are likely to have changed. SharePoint Portal Server uses a clever analysis of historical changes to documents to determine what is likely to have changed. This is potentially the least efficient update (at least in the beginning), but is the fastest. Over time, this becomes a very efficient way of updating indexes.

If your SharePoint Portal Server contains lots of documents, it is the recommended practice that you perform an incremental update in short intervals and a full update in longer intervals. For example, you could create an incremental update at 2:00 A.M. Monday through Saturday and a full update at 2:00 A.M. on Sunday.

Performing full, incremental, or adaptive updates of indexes can be initiated from either a network place or the SharePoint Portal Server Administrator. The next few sections show how to setup and configure each of these types of indexes.

Full Updates

A full update scans all content in the content source and creates a full index. This type of index can take quite a bit of time if the content source contains a lot of documents. You will need to perform a full update under these circumstances:

- ▼ When a content source is altered in any way (created or updated)
- ■ Category is altered in any way (created, updated, or deleted)

- The noise file is changed (which is covered later in this chapter)
- If you notice that documents are missing from adaptive updates
▲ If the index is reset

Performing the Full Update Immediately

You can perform the update immediately by using either a network place on a client machine or the SharePoint Portal Server Administrator on the SharePoint Portal Server machine. The next two sections outline how to perform the update immediately using these methods.

Using a Network Place   To perform a full update immediately using a network place, follow these steps:

1. Open the network place that represents the workspace on your portal.
2. Navigate to the Management folder.
3. Navigate to the Content Sources folder.
4. Right-click the desired content source and select Start Full Update.

    Additionally, you can right-click the Content Sources folder and select Start Full Update without navigating to the desired content source. This starts a full update immediately for all content sources.

Using the SharePoint Portal Server Administrator   To perform a full update immediately using the SharePoint Portal Server Administrator on the server computer, follow these steps:

1. Open the SharePoint Portal Server Administrator.

    On the SharePoint Portal Server computer, choose Start | Programs | Administrative Tools | SharePoint Portal Server Administration.

2. Navigate to the desired workspace.
3. Right-click the desired workspace and choose All Tasks | Start Full Update.

    This option will start a full update for all content sources in the workspace.

Scheduling the Full Update

If you wish for a full index update to be performed upon a specific schedule, you can do that. As mentioned earlier, it might be a good idea to perform a full index update at least once a week. If your content doesn't take too long to update, consider performing a full index update every night. To schedule a full update, follow these steps:

1. Open the network place that represents the workspace on your portal.
2. Navigate to the Management folder.

3. Navigate to the Content Sources folder.

4. Right-click the desired content source and select Properties.

5. Click Scheduled Updates.

   Clicking Scheduled Updates shows this dialog box:

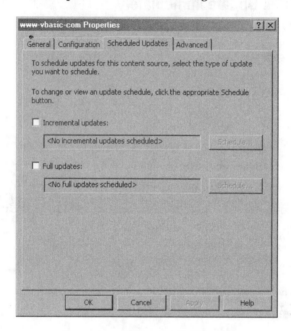

6. Click Full Updates.

   Clicking this check box enables the adjacent Schedule button and automatically selects the button for you so that the scheduling screen comes up as shown in Figure 8-15.

7. Select Schedule Task.

   Select from the Schedule Task drop-down list of frequencies, which can be Daily, Weekly, Monthly, Once, At System Startup, At Logon, or When Idle.

8. Select the start time.

   The Start Time box is only enabled if you chose Daily, Weekly, Monthly, or Once.

9. Select the schedule task parameters.

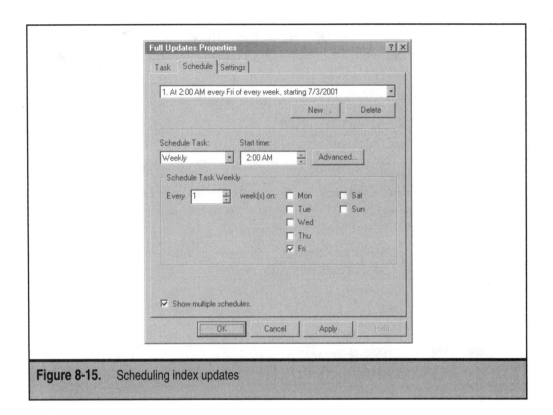

Figure 8-15. Scheduling index updates

Depending on the value that you choose for the schedule task option, this section changes. You can make the appropriate selections. For example, if you choose the Weekly option, you must instruct the scheduler as to which weeks and days to use in the schedule.

10. Click OK to save your schedule changes and close that dialog box.

11. Click OK again to save your changes to the full index properties dialog and close the dialog box.

Incremental Updates

As mentioned earlier, incremental updates to indexes are faster than full updates because only changed documents are updated. This includes deleted or updated documents. If you don't change a document, it will not be updated in the index. That's what makes incremental updates faster than full updates.

Performing the Incremental Update Immediately

Using a Network Place   To perform an incremental update immediately using a network place, follow these steps:

1. Open the network place that represents the workspace on your portal.
2. Navigate to the Management folder.
3. Navigate to the Content Sources folder.
4. Right-click the desired content source and select Start Incremental Update.

Additionally, you can right-click the Content Sources folder and select Start Incremental Update without navigating to the desired content source. This starts an incremental update immediately for all content sources.

Using the SharePoint Portal Server Administrator   To perform an incremental update immediately using the SharePoint Portal Server Administrator on the server computer, follow these steps:

1. Open the SharePoint Portal Server Administrator.

   On the SharePoint Portal Server computer, choose Start | Programs | Administrative Tools | SharePoint Portal Server Administration.

2. Navigate to the desired workspace.
3. Right-click the desired workspace and choose All Tasks | Start Incremental Update.

   This option will start an incremental update for all content sources in the workspace.

Scheduling the Incremental Update

To schedule an incremental update, follow exactly the same procedure as listed under the earlier section, "Scheduling the Full Update."

Adaptive Updates

An adaptive update is an innovative concept. The adaptive update is very similar in concept to the incremental update, except that the adaptive update does not update the index for every document that has actually changed. Instead, it updates the index for documents that are likely to have changed. It does this using statistics that are generated when incremental updates are performed. That way, every incremental update "fine-tunes" the statistics so that over time, the adaptive update will become more accurate. Therefore, it is the recommended practice to do the following:

▼ Create your workspace.

■ Perform a full update to populate the index.

■ Perform incremental updates nightly for one to two weeks.

▲ After that time, you can perform adaptive updates, as statistics should be accurate for the index at that time.

Performing the Adaptive Update Immediately

Using a Network Place   To perform an adaptive update immediately using a network place, follow these steps:

1. Open the network place that represents the workspace on your portal.

2. Navigate to the Management folder.

3. Right-click the Content Sources folder and select Start Adaptive Update.

   This option will start an adaptive update for all content sources in the workspace.

Using the SharePoint Portal Server Administrator   To perform a full update immediately using the SharePoint Portal Server Administrator on the server computer, follow these steps:

1. Open the SharePoint Portal Server Administrator.

   On the SharePoint Portal Server computer, choose Start | Programs | Administrative Tools | SharePoint Portal Server Administration.

2. Navigate to the desired workspace.

3. Right-click the desired workspace and choose All Tasks | Start Adaptive Update.

Scheduling the Adaptive Update

To schedule an adaptive update, follow exactly the same procedure as listed under the earlier section, "Scheduling the Full Update," with one exception. In step 4, Right-click the Additional Settings folder and select Open. Everything else is exactly the same when you apply the concept to the Adaptive Updates section of the dialog, as shown in this dialog:

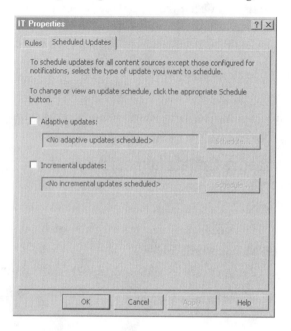

OPTIMIZING INDEXING

There are two ways to optimize the indexing in your SharePoint Portal Server(s). The first is to create one or more workspaces for the sole purpose of crawling content and creating indexes. These workspaces, called *index workspaces*, are not used to service client requests at all. This way, you can have one or more workspaces dedicated for searching and one or more workspaces for creating indexes.

CAUTION: An index workspace must be located on a different server than the one used to service client search requests. This is because the whole purpose of the index workspace is to conserve workspace resources by distributing the load across multiple servers.

The second way to optimize your indexes is to adopt a strategy for updating your indexes. This concept was shown earlier in this chapter, so this section will be dedicated to creating index workspaces.

Creating an Index Workspace

Creating an index workspace is done just like creating any other workspace, with one exception that you'll see shortly. Create the workspace on a SharePoint Portal Server computer just as you normally would. This is shown in Chapter 3 and discussed more in Chapter 7. However, when using the new workspace wizard, on the workspace definition tab, perform these steps:

1. Click Advanced. This brings up the Advanced Workspace Definition dialog box, like this:

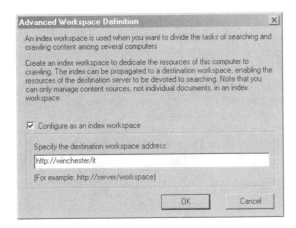

2. Click the Configure As An Index Workspace check box.

   Checking this box enables the text box to allow you to specify a workspace address.

3. Enter the workspace address.

   The workspace address that you enter in this box is the "regular" or "portal" workspace that will be used to receive the index after it is created in the index workspace. This is known as propagation, which is covered in the next section.

4. Continue with the rest of the workspace definition, as shown in Chapter 3.

A Note About Index Workspaces

Even though the creation of an index workspace is virtually the same as a "regular" or "portal" workspace, I wanted to at least mention here that there are a couple of differences when you open the workspace in a browser:

1. You cannot add documents to an index workspace.

2. The Management dashboard is opened automatically, instead of the Home dashboard, as in a "regular" workspace.

Propagating the Index

If you use an index workspace to create or update an index, you must transfer the created index to the workspace that will be used for searching by a client computer. After all, it is the index that is used to return an accurate list of documents from a search or browse. Therefore, the act of transferring the index from an index workspace to a "regular" or "portal" workspace is known as *propagation*.

Mostly, propagation takes place automatically when an index is created or updated. The index workspace knows where to propagate the index to because you configure that when you create the index workspace. See the prior section for more information on this.

Because propagation automatically takes place, you normally don't need to propagate the index manually. However, if automatic propagation fails, you probably don't want to wait for the next update of the index to propagate the index. Therefore, to manually propagate the index, follow these steps:

1. Open the SharePoint Portal Server Administrator.

   On the SharePoint Portal Server computer, choose Start | Programs | Administrative Tools | SharePoint Portal Server Administration.

2. Navigate to the desired index workspace.

3. Right-click the desired workspace and choose All Tasks | Propagate Index menu.

NOTE: This menu is only available if you right-click an index workspace.

RESETTING THE INDEXING

Resetting an index deletes the data from that index, but it does not affect statistics for the index. Remember from the earlier discussion in this chapter, statistics are used to determine which documents are likely to change in an adaptive update.

Normally, you don't need to reset the index, but if the index becomes corrupted, you may need to reset it. Once reset, the next full, incremental, or adaptive update will actually result in a full update anyway. To reset an index, you can use a network place or the SharePoint Portal Server Administrator. These are discussed in the next two sections.

Using a Network Place   To use a network place to reset an index, follow these steps:

1. Open the network place that represents the workspace on your portal.

2. Navigate to the Management folder.

3. Right-click the Content Sources folder and select Reset Index.

Using the SharePoint Portal Server Administrator   To perform an incremental update immediately using the SharePoint Portal Server Administrator on the server computer, follow these steps:

1. Open the SharePoint Portal Server Administrator.

   On the SharePoint Portal Server computer, choose Start | Programs | Administrative Tools | SharePoint Portal Server Administration.

2. Navigate to the desired workspace.

3. Right-click the desired workspace and choose All Tasks | Reset Index.

   This option will reset the index for all content sources in the workspace.

NOISE WORD FILES

A *noise word file* is a text file that contains a list of words that are insignificant enough so that they are not considered for indexing purposes. For example, without this file, if a user searches on the word *an*, probably every document in the portal will be returned. Therefore, you want to exclude this word when the index is created. How does SharePoint Portal Server do this? Simple, it checks the noise word file and excludes all words that are considered to be "noise" from the index.

The noise word file is located on the SharePoint Portal Server computer(s) in the C:\Program Files\SharePoint Portal Server\Data\FTData\SharePointPortalServer\ Config folder (unless you installed SharePoint Portal Server elsewhere). There is one file for each language and a default file that is used if a specific language file is not found. The default (also known as a neutral file) version of the file is named noiseneu.txt. The English version of the file is named noiseenu.txt. The file names appear to be the same, but if you look closely, they are not. As these text files simply contain a listing of words, they are too long to list here, but to give you an idea, here are the first five entries in the noiseenu.txt file:

▼   about
■   1
■   after
■   2
▲   all

If you want to add (or remove) words from this or any other noise word file, simply open it in a text editor, such as Notepad, and make the change.

CHAPTER SUMMARY

This chapter contained much information about the indexing operations of SharePoint Portal Server. It focused on configuration of indexing and indexing-related options from the perspective of the administrator on the server's side. It contained no information about how to perform searches. This is covered in Chapter 5.

What you did learn in this chapter is how to setup content sources for crawling content, site path rules, display mappings, file types, search scopes, and web discussion configuration. As if you weren't thrilled with all of that, this chapter goes further to discuss updating your SharePoint Portal Server indexes. It includes how and when to use full, incremental, and adaptive updates.

CHAPTER 9

Document Management

ocument Management is one of the major parts of SharePoint Portal Server (along with the portal and searching capabilities). Although I explain how a user navigates and uses document management in Chapter 5, this chapter focuses on the configuration of document management from an administrative perspective. This perspective includes considerations for setting up properties, folders, profiles, etc. In this chapter I explain many concepts around managing your documents. I also show you step-by-step how to perform specific actions. Therefore, if you glance at this chapter, it appears that it is loaded with steps, but they are all broken down into specific tasks.

OVERVIEW

The structure and concept of how one organizes documents, folders, properties, and profiles is called a *taxonomy*, or a *storage taxonomy*. Most likely, you'll hear a lot of buzz about this word, if you haven't already. This may seem like no big deal, as you are already used to storing your documents in a structure called a folder in the operating system. However, it really *is* a big deal, as you see within this chapter. The choices you make in your storage taxonomy have pros and cons. If you're curious about this, read on.

By the way, there are many sections in this chapter where I refer you to creating a network place. Refer to Chapter 4 for a discussion on how to do this.

FOLDERS

The traditional way for you to organize your documents and information is in folders in the operating system. For example, suppose you have these documents:

▼ 2000_Financials.xls

■ 2001_Financials.xls

■ AnthonyMann_Resume.doc

■ UpgradeProject_TechSpec.doc

■ UpgradeProject_ProjectPlan.mpp

▲ DataWarehouse_TechSpec.doc

It might make sense to organize these documents into logical folders, like:

▼ Financials

■ Resumes

■ UpgradeProject

▲ DataWarehouse

On the other hand, it might make sense to organize these documents into these logical folders:

▼   2000

■   2001

■   Resumes

■   TechSpecs

▲   ProjectPlans

You see, the point is that many people organize documents into folders that make sense to them. The nice thing about taxonomies in SharePoint Portal Server is that these decisions become easier. Which of the aforementioned folders is correct? The answer is that they both are. In SharePoint Portal Server, what the folder structure should look like is more related to security.

I discuss security in Chapter 10, but for now, know that security settings are set at the folder level. Therefore, it is important for you to organize your folders keeping in mind the security requirements for the documents contained within the folders.

PROPERTIES

If you have done any programming at all, you are likely familiar with the concept of properties. In fact, if you have used Office 2000 or Office XP at all, you most likely know of the concept of properties. For the rest of you, quite simply, a property describes an object. For example, suppose I'm writing a document (as I'm doing for this chapter). I automatically become the author of that document. Therefore, the property called Author is set to a value of Anthony T. Mann by the Office product.

Now, does the Author property alone describe the document? Most likely not! To further describe the document, you might need additional properties, like Subject, Category, Keywords, Page Count, etc. In fact, these are the default properties that describe an Office 2000 or XP document, as shown in Figure 9-1.

It is difficult to tell in Figure 9-1, but some of the properties are required to be filled in. These are called mandatory properties. In fact, some of these mandatory properties are automatically populated by the product, like Last Saved By. You cannot change this property. It is automatically updated.

Why does all this matter? Because if you understand the concept of these properties, you can easily translate that knowledge to SharePoint Portal Server properties. You can specify properties for documents. These properties help to describe documents that are contained within folders. You want to define properties so that you can effectively search for documents that contain values associated with properties.

When you define a property, you also define what type of data is represented by the values that will be assigned to the property. This is known as a *datatype*. For example, if a

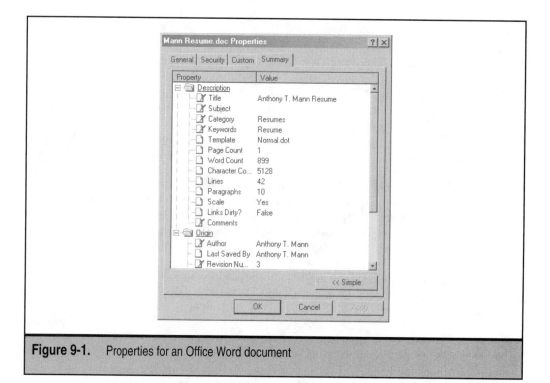

Figure 9-1. Properties for an Office Word document

property called Suggested By contains a name value, you cannot define it as holding a currency value. If you do, letter characters will never be accepted in the field. SharePoint Portal Server allows these possible datatypes:

▼ **Text** Useful for storing single-line alphanumeric values, such as a user's name

■ **Number** Useful for storing single-line numeric values only, such as a currency value

■ **List** Stores a listing of values, but allows the selection of only one value by the user

■ **Multivalue list** Stores a listing of values, but allows the selection of multiple values by the user

■ **Comment box** Useful for storing multi-line alphanumeric values, such as comments or free-form text

▲ **Date** Stores date fields, such as a last updated date

Profile Properties

If you create your own properties, make sure that these names don't contain any spaces or you will have trouble writing those values into the Web Storage System.

In addition to assigning the datatype to a property, you can also choose whether or not the property is mandatory. If it is mandatory, SharePoint Portal Server will not allow you to save a document without filling in this property.

Even though I cover searching and indexing in Chapter 8, you're probably already forming questions about this topic. My guess is that you are asking yourself, "Why don't I just create mandatory properties for all eventualities, so I can search on everything?" The answer, quite honestly, is that you could. However, as with all things, the right solution is probably somewhere in the middle. If you add too many mandatory properties, you'll get a lot of complaints from users that they have to fill in lots of properties before SharePoint Portal Server will allow them to save a document. It also becomes more difficult to manage. Therefore, there are pros and cons to be considered when defining properties, as shown in Figure 9-2.

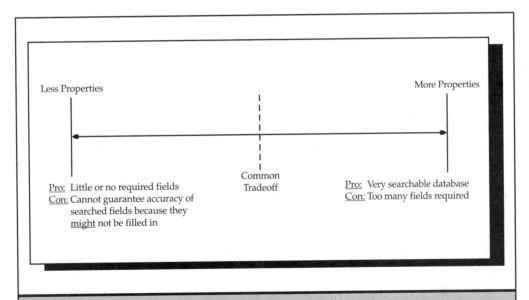

Figure 9-2. Pros and cons of defining many properties

PROFILES

A *profile* is quite simply, a collection of properties. A profile can be useful when you want to ensure that like documents contain the same properties. These like documents do not have to be stored in the same folder. They can be stored in any number of folders. To illustrate this point, when you install SharePoint Portal Server, a default profile called Base Document is also installed. This default profile contains the following system properties:

- ▼ **Title**   Title of the document
- ■ **Author**   Person who writes the document originally
- ■ **Keywords**   Specific keywords that help in searching for the document
- ▲ **Description**   Description of the document, as the file name is not usually enough to identify a document

These properties are known as system properties because they install automatically when you install SharePoint Portal Server. In addition to the above system properties, profiles can be created with these system properties:

- ▼ **Categories**   Allows the selection of categories that are associated with a document
- ■ **Company**   Company that the author works for
- ■ **Link**   Link to the storage location of the document
- ■ **Manager**   Manager that the author reports to
- ▲ **Subject**   Subject of the document

In addition to the above system properties, you can create your own properties. This is shown later in this chapter, under the heading "Creating a Profile."

Profiles are a convenient way to allow you to reuse sets of properties without needing to remember which properties you assigned to a previous document. This is similar to the reason why you create groups in a Windows NT domain or a Windows 2000 Active Directory. Allow me to illustrate the point.

Suppose you have three users: Sandra, Dave, and Brian. You want each of them to have administrative access on a local machine. Instead of giving them each administrative privileges, it is probably easier to use the built-in Administrators group and add Sandra, Dave, and Brian to that group. This way, you only need to manage permissions in one place instead of three.

Carry this concept one step further. If you create a SharePoint Portal Server profile called TechDocs, you can configure all of the properties necessary for technical documents and store them in this once centralized, convenient place. If you remember from the earlier section, called "Properties," you can define a datatype and some other aspects of the properties. Since these are specified at the same time you define the property, they are also included in the profiles. The "glue" that ties all of this together into something meaningful is that a profile is associated with a folder. In fact, more than one profile can be associated with a folder. This way, when a document is saved into that folder, the author of the document is prompted for the associated profile to use (if there's more than one), as shown here:

Once you choose a profile, the set of properties that define the profile "magically" appears and is available to have values entered. If you determine in the future that you need to capture more or less information in the profile, that's no problem. Simply edit the profile.

So, why not create lots of profiles to cover every situation? The answer to this is the same as it was for properties. It's all about trade-offs. Figure 9-3 shows the pros and cons of defining profiles.

Editing Profiles

Editing a profile does not affect existing documents that use that profile unless the document is checked-out and then checked-in again. In other words, SharePoint Portal Server does not automatically "re-profile" all documents.

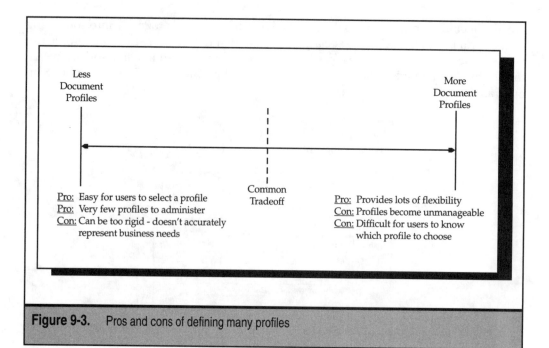

Figure 9-3. Pros and cons of defining many profiles

Creating a Profile

You create a profile from a network place. Therefore, you can do the following:

▼ Create a network place on the client computer

■ Create a network place on the server computer and physically log in at the server computer

▲ Create a network place on the server computer and use terminal services to log into the server computer.

Open your new network place and follow these steps to create a profile:

1. Navigate to the Management | Document Profiles folder.

   Navigating to the Document Profiles folder shows a list of all existing profiles, plus one additional icon, Add Document Profile.acc. This is shown in Figure 9-4.

2. Double-click Add Document Profile.acc to bring up the Add Document Profile Wizard (see Figure 9-5).

3. Click Next.

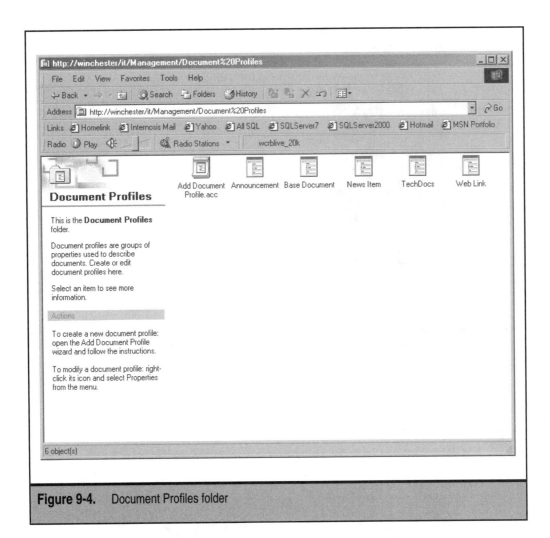

Figure 9-4.   Document Profiles folder

4.   Give the new profile a name and select a template.

Figure 9-6 shows the field that allows you to enter a name for the new profile, as well as the existing template that you will use to base your new profile, known as a template. The template is used to help you easily create new profiles without having to add a lot of properties at once. You can change any of the properties that are present in the template if you don't want them in the new profile. Likewise, you can add properties that didn't exist in the template.

For example, if you want to create a new profile named TechDocs, enter that name in the Name field and select Base Document as the template name.

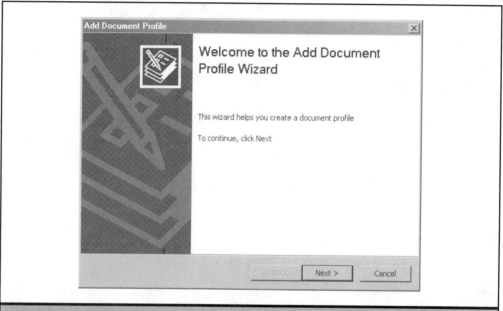

Figure 9-5. Welcome screen for the Add Document Profile Wizard.

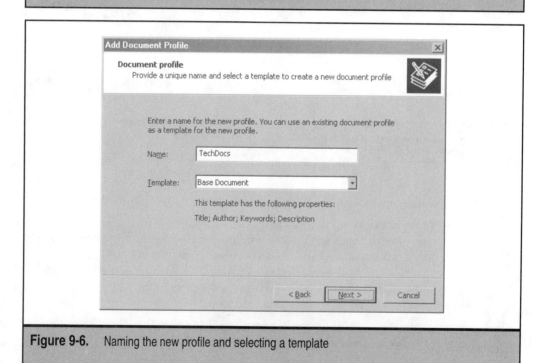

Figure 9-6. Naming the new profile and selecting a template

5. Click Next.

6. Select the properties for the profile.

   To select the desired properties for the new profile, simply ensure that there is a check mark next to the property name. You'll notice that the properties contained in the profile template are checked by default. You can uncheck these if you like or add your own. This is all shown in Figure 9-7.

   If you want to add new properties that aren't shown in the list, simply click New. Doing so brings up this dialog box:

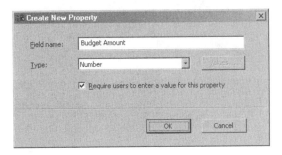

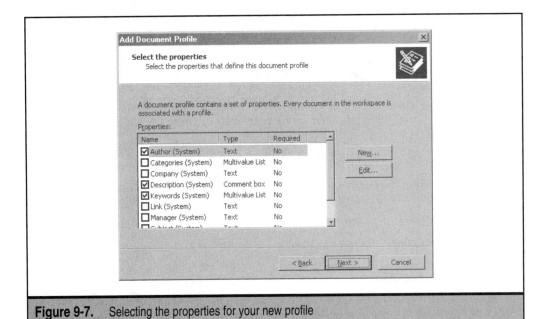

Figure 9-7.   Selecting the properties for your new profile

Enter the name of the new property in the Field Name text box. Also select the datatype from the Type drop-down list. For example, if you have a property named Budget Amount, type this in the Field Name box and select Number from the Type drop-down list.

If the datatype of your new property is either List or Multivalue List, then you have an additional option, which is to add items to the list. For example, if your list contains values Yes and No, you must add these items into the list. This is done by clicking Values. Doing so brings up this dialog box:

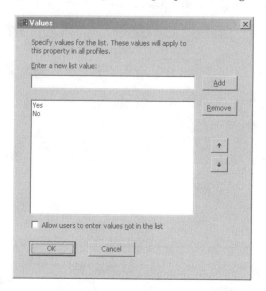

To add items to the list, simply type the name of the item into the Enter A New List Value text box and press Enter or clicking Add. Likewise, you can remove an item by selecting the value and then clicking Remove. You can also change the order in which the values are displayed by clicking the value, followed by the up or down buttons to relocate the item in the list. Finally, if you want to allow users to type in their own values, click Allow Users To Enter Values Not In The List. In the earlier example, you most likely don't want people to enter a value of Maybe if they don't like the Yes and No values in the list. Therefore, in this case, you would ensure that the check box is *not* checked.

7. Click Next.

8. Select the order of the properties for the profile.

   Shown in Figure 9-8, choose the order in which the properties are displayed to the user when documents are created or edited. To change the order, simply click the property and then the up and down arrows respectively. This moves the current selection up or down.

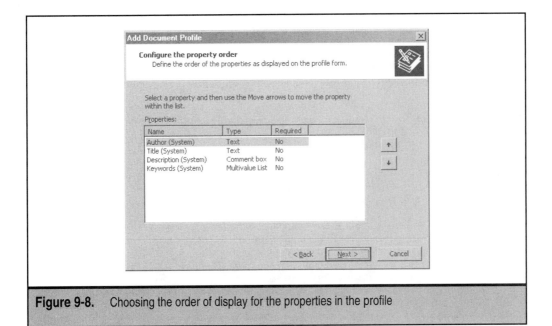

Figure 9-8.   Choosing the order of display for the properties in the profile

9. Click Next.

10. Review your choices.

    Figure 9-9 shows the final screen that allows you to review your choices.

11. Click Finish.

    Clicking Finish creates your profile with the choices that you've made.

Editing a Profile

Editing a profile follows basically the same steps as creating a profile, except that there is no wizard to guide you through the process. If you've added a profile, then you are already familiar with all screens, topics, and concepts. Therefore, you simply need to follow these steps to edit a profile:

1. Navigate to the Management | Document Profiles folder.

    Navigating to the Document Profiles folder shows a list of all existing profiles. This is shown in Figure 9-4.

2. Double-click the icon of the profile you wish to edit.

    Double clicking the icon brings up the properties page (showing the General Tab) for the profile to edit. The tab is shown in Figure 9-10.

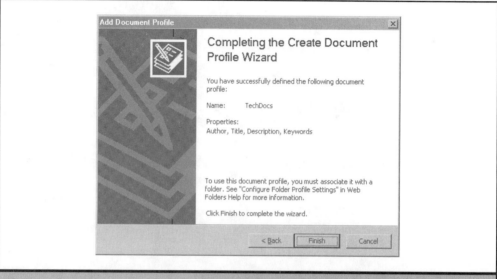

Figure 9-9. Reviewing your choices for the new profile

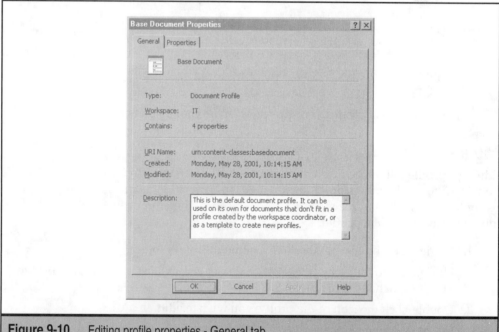

Figure 9-10. Editing profile properties - General tab

3. Edit Fields on the General tab.

The only thing that you can edit on this tab is Description.

4. Click the Properties tab.

Clicking the Properties tab allows you to edit the properties associated with the profile, as shown in Figure 9-11.

5. Edit Fields on the Properties tab.

There are three things that you can do on this tab. You can edit the currently selected property (by clicking Edit); add or remove properties from the profile (by clicking Select Properties); or change the order of the properties (by clicking the up and down arrows). If you are going to edit or change the order of a property, you must first select the desired property.

Clicking Edit brings up the screen:

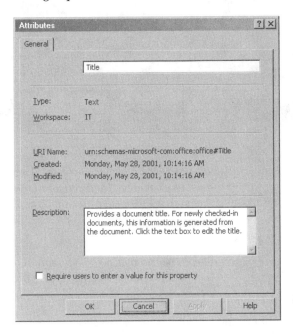

Clicking Select Properties brings up a screen *similar* to the screen shown in earlier Figure 9-7.

There are not many attributes that you can edit for a property. However, you can change its name and description by filling in the respective fields. Additionally, you can make this property mandatory. In other words, the

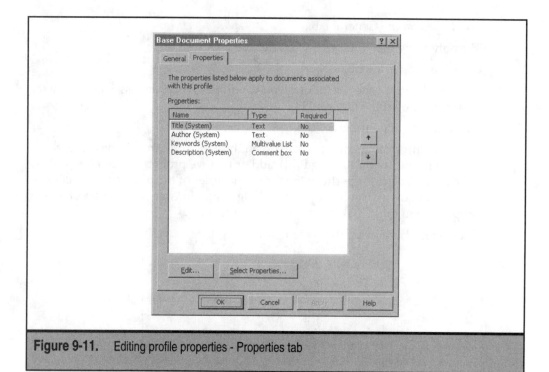

Figure 9-11.   Editing profile properties - Properties tab

user must enter or select a value for the property or SharePoint Portal Server will not allow a user to check-in the document. To make the property mandatory, simply check Require Users To Enter A Value For This Property.

6. Click OK to save changes to the property attributes.

7. Click OK to save your changes to the profile.

Deleting a Profile

Deleting a profile in SharePoint Portal Server is just as easy as it is to delete a folder in Windows NT or Windows 2000. Therefore, here's how you do it:

1. Navigate to the Management | Document Profiles folder.

2. Right-click the icon of the profile you wish to delete.

3. Click Delete.

4. Click Yes at the confirmation prompt if you wish to delete the profile.

Renaming a Profile

Just like deleting a profile, renaming a profile in SharePoint Portal Server is just as simple. Here's how you do it:

1. Navigate to the Management I Document Profiles folder.

2. Right-click the icon of the profile you wish to rename.

3. Click Rename.

4. Type the new desired name.

5. Press Enter when you are finished.

Associating a Profile

To be able to use a profile, you must associate it to a folder. If you never associate the profile with a folder, it becomes useless. Also, this goes without saying, but I'll say it anyway. You must create the profile before it can be associated to a folder.

Associating a profile is done with a network place. Open your network place for the workspace and follow these steps to create a profile:

1. Navigate to the Documents folder.

   Navigating to the Documents folder shows a list of all existing documents and folders.

2. Drill down to the desired folder.

3. Right-click the desired folder and select Properties.

4. Click Profiles, which brings up the dialog box shown in Figure 9-12.

5. Check all profiles that you want to make available to documents in the folder.

   If you have more than one profile checked, the user checking in a document will make a choice of which profile to associate to a document in that folder. If you want to force the use of a specific profile, check only that profile. For example, if you create a profile called TechDocs and your folder name is TechDocs, most likely this is the only type of document that is contained in the folder. Therefore, it probably makes sense that all documents in this folder will conform to a specific profile. Make TechDocs the only profile checked in the TechDocs folder.

6. Select the default profile to use.

   If you have more than one profile, select from the drop-down list of checked profiles that you wish to use by default. If you only have one profile checked, you cannot change the default profile.

7. Click OK to save your changes.

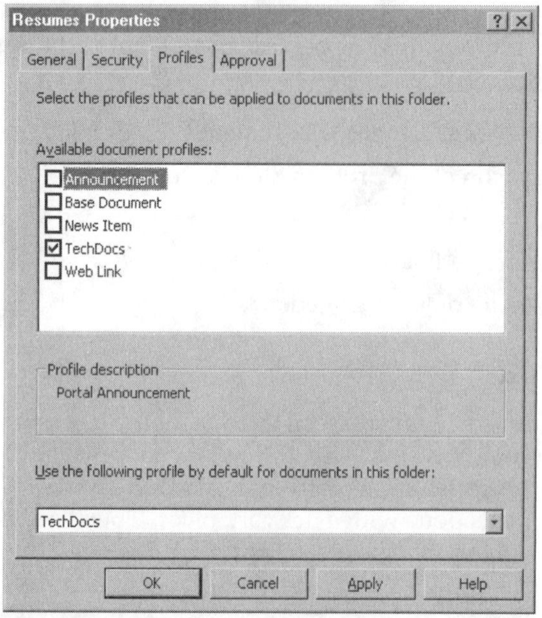

Figure 9-12. Associating profiles to a folder

CATEGORIES

Categories are a way to logically group documents without needing to physically store the documents in the same structure. For example, suppose you have documents in this folder structure:

▼ Resumes

■ Resumes/Technical

■ Resumes/Administrative

▲ Resumes/Executive

It would be almost impossible to list the résumés in these folders based on skills. For example, it doesn't make sense to organize résumés into this folder structure:

▼ Resumes

■ Resumes/Technical

- Resumes/Technical/Visual Basic
- Resumes/Technical/Visual InterDev
- Resumes/Technical/SharePoint Portal Server
- Resumes/Administrative
- Resumes/Administrative/Typing
- Resumes/Administrative/Good Communication
- Resumes/Executive
- Resumes/Executive/Managerial
- Resumes/Executive/Business Development
- ▲ Resumes/Executive/Mergers

The easiest way to illustrate why this structure doesn't make sense is by example. Suppose John Smith had experience using Visual Basic. Therefore, you place his résumé into the Resumes/Technical/Visual Basic folder. However, this person has great communication skills. Would you actually copy the résumé into the Resumes/ Administrative/Good Communication folder? Not very likely. You'd probably be fired on the spot! It would also be impossible to search for a person with a combination of skills.

Categories take care of this for you. A category lets you organize your documents into logical groupings, regardless of the physical underlying folder structure. Therefore, it might make sense to create these categories:

- ▼ Technical
- Administrative
- ▲ Executive

Then, instead of creating sub-categories like Visual Basic and Visual InterDev, it makes more sense to simply add a Keyword property that allows you to specify these skills.

Creating a Category

Creating a category can be done in two ways. It can be done by using a network place or by using the portal and a web browser. Both are created in exactly the same way once you navigate to the Categories folder.

Open your new network place and follow these steps to create a category:

1. Navigate to the Categories folder.

   Navigating to the Categories folder shows a list of all existing categories. This is shown in Figure 9-13.

2. Right-click in any white space on the screen and click New | Category.

   Clicking this menu creates a new category (which is actually a folder), called New Category. Type the desired name. Bear in mind that this category is a created at the highest level. If you wanted to create a folder at another level, drill down to the level where you wish to create the new category within.

3. Edit the properties of the new category.

   Right-click the icon and choose Properties. Doing so brings up this screen:

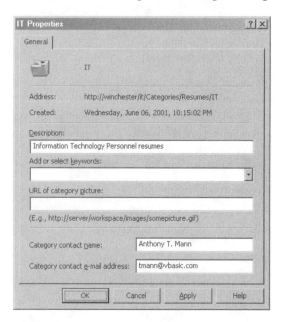

Enter a description for the category. This helps make the purpose of the category more understandable. For example, if you have a category called Resumes and another category under Resumes, called IT, you might want to note that this category is for Information Technology Personnel résumés.

Then, add or select keywords associated with the category. These keywords are not mandatory, but they aid in using the Category Assistant (shown later in this chapter). For example keywords related to IT résumés might include these:

■ Development

■ IT

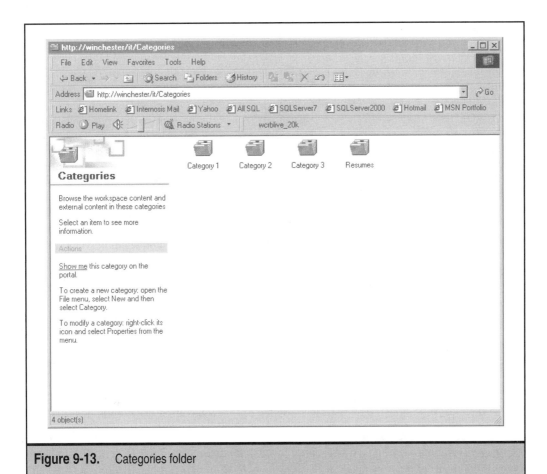

Figure 9-13.   Categories folder

- Computer
- Server
- Systems
- Software
- Engineering

To use this field, simply ensure there is a check mark next to the desired keywords. If the keywords don't exist, simply type them into the space provided and press ENTER. Here's what the expanded keywords drop-down list looks like:

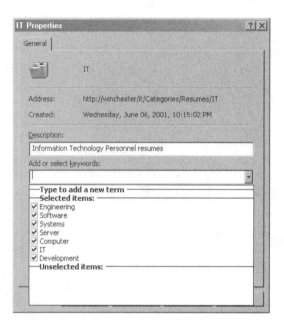

If you wish for an icon to be displayed next to the category name for users, specify the URL of that icon in the URL Of Category Picture field.

Specify a contact name and e-mail address in the fields provided. This name will appear as a link on the Category dashboard.

4. Click OK to save your changes.

Editing a Category

Editing a category is done basically the same way as creating a category. If you've added a category, then you are already familiar with all screens, topics, and concepts. Editing a category is done with a network place, just like adding a category. Therefore, you simply need to follow these steps to edit a category:

1. Navigate to the Categories folder.

   Navigating to the Categories folder shows a list of all existing categories. This is shown in earlier Figure 9-13.

2. Right-click the icon of the category you wish to edit and select Properties.

   Double clicking the icon brings up the properties page (showing the General Tab) for the profile to edit. This is shown in an earlier illustration under the section, "Creating a Profile."

3. Edit the desired properties.

   The instructions for filling in the properties is listed in the section, "Creating a Category" earlier in this chapter.

4. Click OK to save your changes.

Deleting a Category

Deleting a category in SharePoint Portal Server is quite simple, just as it was for deleting a profile. Here's how:

1. Navigate to the Categories folder.
2. If necessary, drill down to the sub-category you wish to delete.
3. Right-click the icon of the category you wish to delete.
4. Click Delete.
5. Click Yes at the confirmation prompt if you wish to delete the category.

Renaming a Category

Again, to rename a category

1. Navigate to the Categories folder.
2. Drill-down to the appropriate sub-category, if necessary.
3. Right-click the icon of the category you wish to rename.
4. Click Rename.
5. Type the new desired name.
6. Press Enter when you are finished.

Associating a Document with a Category and Best Bets

Just as you must associate a profile with a web folder, you must also associate a category with a document. I'll bet you can guess how to do it by now, but I'm going to outline the steps anyway. In addition to associating a document with a category, you can follow this same procedure to assign a best bet to one or more documents.

Renaming Categories

If you rename a category, you must retrain the category assistant. Training the category assistant is shown later in this chapter, under the heading "Using the Category Assistant."

To associate a category with a document, you do this with a network place. Additionally, you must have the document checked out to change any of its properties or attributes. Therefore, follow these steps carefully:

1. Navigate to the Documents folder.

   Navigating to the Documents folder shows a list of all existing documents and folders.

2. Drill down to the desired folder containing the desired document(s).

   You can alter the properties of multiple documents at once by selecting them all before going to the next step.

3. Right-click the desired document(s) and select Check-Out.

4. Right-click the desired document(s) and select Properties.

5. Click Search And Categories, as shown here:

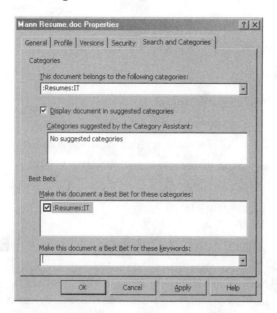

6. Select the desired categories.

   Select any or all of the existing categories, which are displayed in the Categories drop-down list. A category is selected when a check mark appears to the left of the category name. If you have trained the Category Assistant, suggestions will appear in the corresponding text box.

7. Select the best bet categories, if desired.

From the list of categories that you have selected, you can also select "best bets." Every selected category will appear in the list of best bets, from which you check the categories that you consider to be a best bet. Refer to Chapter 1 to find out what best bets are.

8. Right-click the desired document(s) and select Check-In.

9. Right-click the desired document(s) and select Publish.

Selecting Publish makes the document available to all users. If you are the administrator, you can bypass approval routing (by selecting the corresponding right-click menu) if approval routing is enabled for this folder.

10. Click OK to save your changes.

Using the Category Assistant

Using the Category Assistant is another way to create categories. The Category Assistant is included in SharePoint Portal Server to automatically sample manually configured categories on existing documents. This sampling "teaches" SharePoint Portal Server how you categorize your documents. Once this is "learned," SharePoint Portal Server can automatically categorize your documents. This can help to save you lots of time because you don't have to manually categorize documents.

To use the Category Assistant, once again, you must open a network place that points to the workspace on the SharePoint Portal Server. Then follow these steps:

1. Navigate to the root folder of the workspace.

Navigating to the root folder for the workspace shows a list of folders and objects that are available in the portal, as shown in Figure 9-14.

2. Right-click on the Categories folder and click Properties.

Clicking this menu brings up the properties for the root categories. This is the only place where you can get to the Category Assistant.

3. Click Category Assistant.

Clicking Category Assistant brings up the screen shown in Figure 9-15.

Using the Category Assistant

Before you use the Category Assistant, it is recommended that you first manually assign categories to at least ten documents. This gives enough of a sampling for the Category Assistant to accurately learn how to categorize.

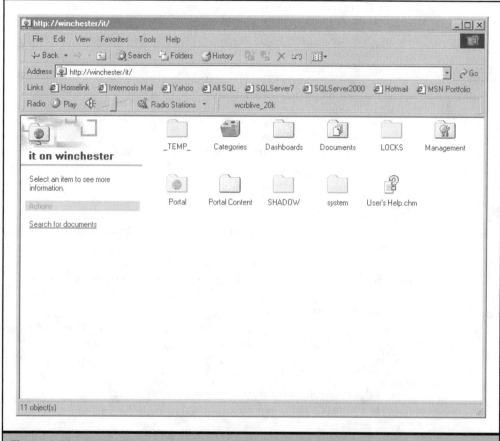

Figure 9-14. Root of the portal

4. Click Train Now.

Clicking Train Now begins the process of training the Category Assistant. This process looks at all documents that have been manually categorized. For more information on manually categorizing documents, see section "Associating a Document with a Category and Best Bets," earlier in this chapter. Clicking this button brings up this dialog box:

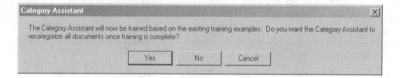

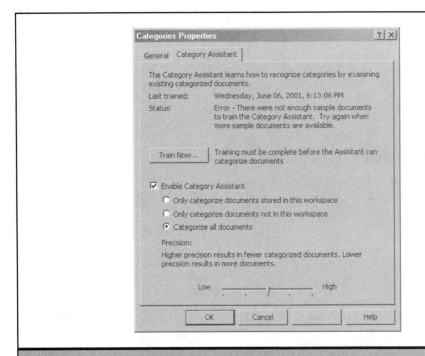

Figure 9-15. Using the Category Assistant

NOTE: If you choose not to recategorize all of your documents, this will be done anyway the next time the index is updated. See Chapter 8 for information on indexes.

By default, the Category Assistant will be enabled once your documents are trained. If you wish to disable the Category Assistant, simply uncheck Enable Category Assistant. However, if it is enabled, you have a couple of additional options:

■ **Only categorize documents stored in this workspace**   Use this setting if you only want documents to be categorized from this workspace. You may want this option if you cannot guarantee the accuracy of how documents were trained in other workspaces.

■ **Only categorize documents not in this workspace**   Use this setting if you want only documents that are stored in another workspace to be categorized.

■ **Categorize all documents**   This is the default setting and will categorize any and all documents.

Additionally, you can specify the precision of your training. You may think that you want the training to be most precise all of the time. However, the higher the precision, the longer it takes to train and will actually result in fewer categorized documents. The lower the precision, the faster it is to train and will result in more categorized documents. By default, precision is set in the middle.

5. Click OK to save your changes.

SERVER-WIDE SUBSCRIPTIONS

A user can create subscriptions to any of the following:

▼ Folders

■ Search Results

■ Categories

▲ Documents

OK, so what happens if a user leaves the company? You would need to edit the subscriptions for that user. This can also be true for a user that is having some trouble with subscriptions. The term *server-wide subscriptions* is used to describe the management of subscriptions for a user other than the one currently logged on. The next few sections describe how to modify subscriptions for other users.

Creating and Editing Subscriptions

You cannot create or edit a subscription for another user by either a web browser or a network place. You can only delete a subscription (which is described in the next section). You can, however, write a program using the object model and the SharePoint SDK to accomplish this task. Using the SDK is outside the scope of this book, as it is a programming topic. If you wish to create subscriptions for yourself, see Chapter 5 for more information.

Deleting Subscriptions or Notifications

As the workspace coordinator, you can delete either subscriptions or notifications for subscriptions for another user. This is done by using a combination of the Subscriptions and Management dashboards from a web browser. To delete a subscription or a notification, follow these steps:

1. Open the web browser on the client's computer.

    On the client's computer, open the web browser. If you are using Internet Explorer, go to Start | Programs | Internet Explorer.

2. Click the Management dashboard.

    Clicking the Management dashboard brings up the screen shown in Figure 9-16.

3. Enter the user name for which you will manage subscriptions.

    Subscription management starts with the Manage Subscriptions web part on the Management dashboard. Enter the user name in the form of:

    `DOMAIN\USER`

    For example, my domain is VBASIC and my user name is amann. Therefore, I type:

    `VBASIC\amann`

    Then click Go. Doing so will jump to the Subscriptions dashboard for the desired user. If the domain or user name is invalid, an error will occur.

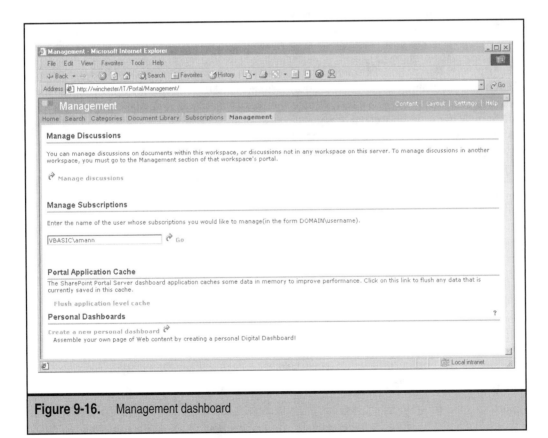

Figure 9-16.   Management dashboard

4. Click the desired option for subscriptions.

   You have three possible links that you can click for the desired user:

   - **Delete all subscriptions**   Click this link if all subscriptions and notifications are to be removed for the user. If someone has left the company, most likely this is the option to choose.

   - **Clear all notifications**   Click this link if you want to clear the notifications that you've received for an individual subscription. Note that if you subscribe to a folder, search, or category, more than one document can appear, but it would be considered a single subscription. Clearing notifications is useful to remove clutter from the screen, especially if you have multiple subscriptions.

   - **Delete subscription**   Click this link if you want to delete only the subscription and notifications represented by the link. This allows you to delete subscriptions and notifications individually.

CHAPTER SUMMARY

This chapter contained lots of information. You learned how, from an administrative perspective, you can manage folders, properties, profiles, categories, and subscriptions. In addition, you learned how to train SharePoint Portal Server to learn how you categorize documents to use the Category Assistant.

You can also manage subscriptions for other users. These are all very handy ways to help administer your SharePoint Portal Server.

PART IV

Advanced Administration

CHAPTER 10

Securing your Server and Documents

Security is a very important concept to consider while using SharePoint Portal Server, or any other computer software. With SharePoint Portal Server specifically, you might be storing documents that are of a sensitive nature, such as salaries, promotions, contact information, and more. Therefore, steps have to be taken to protect that information.

Additionally, you might have set up workspaces for the express purpose of segregating content from specific people or groups. For example, a workspace called Executive should obviously only be used by executives. Therefore, this is a security-related topic and is covered in this chapter.

Throughout almost every chapter in this book, I have shown you areas of special security considerations for performing certain actions. For example, in Chapter 5, under the section "Adding Documents," you'll find this note:

TIP: You must be assigned to the Author or Coordinator security levels to add documents.

This note is a special indication of the security levels required to add documents, but it doesn't show you *how* to configure the security. You'll learn that in this chapter.

This chapter is divided into two main parts, as the title suggests. The first part covers security of the server itself, such as workspaces, access issues, and the like. The second part of the chapter focuses on the security of documents within the server. This is an important chapter, so grab a cup of coffee (perhaps with a touch of Bailey's) and read on.

SERVER SECURITY

Server security relates to access to a server and permissions on workspaces contained within that server. SharePoint Portal Server uses a concept called *role-based security*. That is, permissions to perform certain actions are grouped into responsibilities called roles. A specific individual can be assigned to only one role within a workspace on any given object (workspace or folder). There are three possible roles that can be assigned to a user or group:

▼ **Reader**   Users or groups that are assigned this role can only read documents contained within the workspace or folder in which the role is assigned. They cannot modify them or create them.

■ **Author**   Users or groups that are assigned to this role can read, modify, or create documents that are contained within the workspace or folder in which the role is assigned.

▲ **Coordinator**   Users or groups that are assigned to this role have administrative privileges to update the portal in any way. This role can create, modify, or delete folders, documents, dashboards, content sources, categories, profiles, and more.

To be more precise, within the Coordinator role, a user or group can be assigned as a workspace coordinator or a folder coordinator. This is only an implicit distinction, not an explicit one. In other words, someone who is assigned to the Coordinator role at the workspace level is a workspace coordinator, whereas someone assigned to the Coordinator role on a folder is a folder coordinator. There is no "Workspace Coordinator" role, or "Folder Coordinator" role. A workspace coordinator can manage workspaces (add dashboards, etc), while a folder coordinator can manage folders and documents within those folders. Also, a user or group can be assigned to both workspace and folder coordinator roles because a workspace and a folder are different objects.

The aforementioned text indicates that users or groups can be assigned to roles. What groups? Simple! Windows NT, Windows 2000, or Windows .NET Server groups. Although this book is not about setting up your domain security, you should know that you can assign your domain groups, either built-in or user-defined, to roles. For example, there is a built-in Administrators group in Windows NT, Windows 2000, and Windows .NET Server domains. You can assign the Administrators group to the Coordinator role in SharePoint Portal Server. Configuring security in this way will allow any new individual that is assigned to the domain Administrators group to automatically have Coordinator privileges within the SharePoint Portal Server without needing to configure anything else. On the other hand, you may want to have the control over which individuals have Coordinator privileges within SharePoint Portal Server. For example, if you have John, Mary, Tim, Alison, and Tony as members of the Windows 2000 Administrators domain group, you may want only Alison and Tony to have Coordinator privileges within SharePoint Portal Server. Therefore, you would not assign the Administrators domain group to have Coordinator privileges or John, Mary, and Tim will also have Coordinator privileges. Instead, you would explicitly assign Alison and Tony to have Coordinator privileges. The next section, "Workspace Security," describes how to configure your workspaces to allow users access to workspaces.

It is possible for a user or group to be assigned multiple permissions on a resource. For example, suppose the Workspace_Coordinators group is assigned to the Coordinator role on a folder and the Workspace_Readers group is assigned to the Reader role on the same folder. Can you guess what level of permissions you'd have if you are a member of both groups? Will you have Coordinator or Reader privileges? The answer is Coordinator privileges. SharePoint Portal Server allows the most permissive (or least restrictive) of all of the permissions. The exception (as there is always one of those) is if one of the groups or your user name was explicitly denied access to a document within the folder. In this case the explicit denial takes precedence and you would not be able to read the document.

Workspace Security

Before a user can access a workspace, he or she must be explicitly granted access. SharePoint Portal Server does not allow anonymous access to its resources. However, when you create a workspace, the installation program allows access to the Everyone domain group using the Reader role. When a user connects to Internet Information Services (IIS), if he/she is not authenticated, he/she will automatically belong to the Everyone domain group. If your SharePoint Portal Server is configured for intranet access only, there is no danger of people outside the company coming in over the Internet. On the other hand, if your SharePoint Portal Server is configured (by way of network/router restrictions) for Internet access, there is a real danger of any user being able to access the server because the Everyone domain group can read and search on documents. In this case, you probably want to do one of the following:

▼ Explicitly configure security using known groups or users, such as Administrators, Executives, Programmers, etc.

▲ Allow read access to the Authenticated Users built-in domain group. Only members that log-in to the server correctly will be members of the Authenticated Users group. Bear in mind, though, that this is a "catch-all" group and perhaps should be used with caution. The first option might be the best bet in most cases.

NOTE: Remember, it is better to be more restrictive with your security policies than to allow more access than what is required. The latter could cause a security breach and you'd be to blame. I'm sure you don't want that.

If you are not logged into the network or your login does not allow for access to SharePoint Portal Server, you will be prompted with a dialog box to log in.

Configuring workspace security is exceedingly simple. It is configured using the SharePoint Portal Server Administrator on the server computer. The next few pages show you how to add, modify, and delete users and domain groups from accessing the SharePoint Portal Server.

Allowing Access

To allow access to a SharePoint Portal Server workspace, follow these instructions:

1. Open the SharePoint Portal Server Administrator.

   On the SharePoint Portal Server computer, choose Start | Programs | Administrative Tools | SharePoint Portal Server Administration.

2. Navigate to the desired workspace.

3. Right-click the desired workspace and choose Properties.

4. Click the Security tab.

   Clicking the tab brings up the dialog box shown in Figure 10-1.

FYI: Notice in the dialog box shown in Figure 10-1 that there are two predefined groups: Everyone and Administrator. The Everyone group is assigned to the Reader role and the Administrator user is assigned to the Coordinator role.

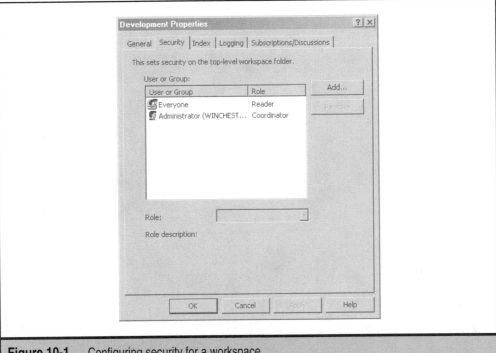

Figure 10-1.   Configuring security for a workspace

5. Click Add to add users or groups.

   Clicking Add brings up a dialog box to allow you to select users, local groups, or domain groups that will have access to the server. The dialog box looks like the one shown in Figure 10-2.

NOTE: The dialog box shown in Figure 10-2 is from Windows 2000. Although it performs the same function, it looks different under Windows XP and Windows .NET Servers. In these operating systems, you can further qualify your search for users and groups.

6. Select the desired users or groups.

   You can select multiple users or groups at once simply by holding the SHIFT (for contiguous selections) or CTRL (for non-contiguous selections) keys while clicking with the mouse. Additionally, you can select users or groups from different domains or local accounts by selecting the computer or domain in the Look In drop-down list. By default, the currently logged-in domain will be selected in the drop-down list.

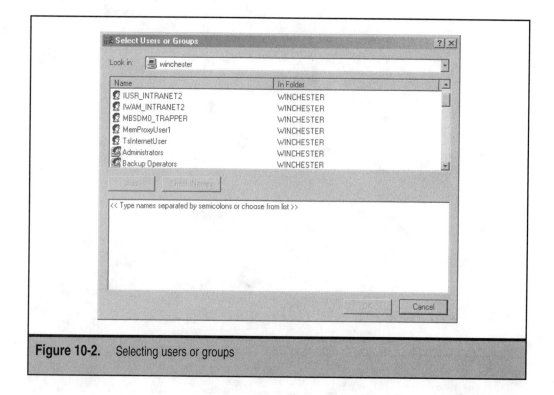

Figure 10-2. Selecting users or groups

7. Click OK.

    Clicking OK closes the dialog box and enters all selected users and groups into
    SharePoint Portal Server, assigning all added users and groups to the Reader role.

NOTE: The sheer fact that a user or group is in the list means that they have access to SharePoint
Portal Server in some capacity. That capacity is determined by the role assigned to them.

8. Modify roles, if required.

To find out how to modify roles for users or groups that have been given access to
SharePoint Portal Server, see the next section, "Modifying Roles."

Modifying Roles

Modifying roles refers to changing the role assigned to one or more users or groups once
they have already been given access to SharePoint Portal Server workspace. Note that
even if you modify a role for a user or group, they will still have access to the workspace.
You will only be changing the permissions for the user or group within that workspace.

To modify roles for a SharePoint Portal Server workspace, follow these steps:

1. Open the SharePoint Portal Server Administrator.

    On the SharePoint Portal Server computer, choose Start | Programs | Administrative Tools | SharePoint Portal Server Administration.

2. Navigate to the desired workspace.

3. Right-click the desired workspace and choose Properties.

4. Click the Security tab.

5. Click the desired user or group to change in the User Or Group list box.

    You can select one or more users and groups to change at once.

6. Select the desired role.

    Roles are selected from the Role drop-down list. Roles are changed for all selected users or groups. You can choose from Reader, Author, or Coordinator. You may only choose one role for a given user or group in a workspace. However, in a different workspace, that user or group can be assigned to a different role.

7. Click OK or Apply to save your changes.

    You will not be prompted to confirm removing users or groups.

Revoking Access

If you want to prevent access to a SharePoint Portal Server workspace, you must make sure that the desired user or group is not in the Users Or Group list box in the Security tab in the workspace properties dialog box. Remember that the only roles you can assign a user or group to are Reader, Author, or Coordinator. There is no privilege such as Deny Access or Not Allowed. You also cannot (within SharePoint Portal Server) make an account inactive or expired. Therefore, the only thing you can do to restrict access to a workspace is make sure that a user or group is not listed for access.

CAUTION: If you do not want a user to have access to a workspace, make sure that the user is not a member of a group that has access to the workspace. If they do, your desired intent will not be achieved.

To revoke access to a SharePoint Portal Server workspace, follow these steps:

1. Open the SharePoint Portal Server Administrator.

    On the SharePoint Portal Server computer, choose Start | Programs | Administrative Tools | SharePoint Portal Server Administration.

2. Navigate to the desired workspace.

3. Right-click the desired workspace and choose Properties.

4. Click the Security tab.

5. Click the desired user or group for which you will revoke access in the User Or Group list box.

    You can select one or more users and groups to revoke at once.

6. Click Remove.

    The selected users or groups are removed from the list, but your changes are not yet saved.

7. Click OK or Apply to save your changes.

Proxy Configuration

Many times a corporation will use a proxy server, which issues Internet requests on your behalf. By using a proxy server, you are not allowed direct access to the Internet. One reason for using a proxy server is security. Not only can the company monitor the Internet activity from inside the corporation to the outside world, but it can also prevent access from the outside to corporate resources. A proxy server is also sometimes known as a firewall because it can be configured to block access. However, a firewall is not necessarily a proxy server.

Microsoft has a few proxy server products available. First, Proxy Server (version 2.0 being the latest) is available as a proxy server. However, most recently, Microsoft released its Internet Security and Acceleration (ISA) Server. It is an outstanding proxy and firewall product that protects your corporate resources. Also, in Windows 2000, Window XP, and Windows.NET Servers, Routing and Remote Access can be configured to act as a proxy and firewall. If you are using one of these, or another proxy server, you must configure SharePoint Portal Server to work with these products.

Have you ever noticed a request for configuring proxy and Internet connection settings when you ran Internet Explorer for the first time? If you have, you'd remember that a wizard comes up allowing you to specify how you will access the Internet. One of the options is to indicate if you will access the Internet through a proxy [server]. SharePoint Portal Server works exactly the same way.

Portal Configuration

If you are using a proxy server within your organization, you must configure SharePoint Portal Server to use the proxy server from outside the corporate firewall. If you don't do this, you will not be able to access your workspaces externally. However, you will be able to access SharePoint Portal Server within the corporate intranet. Configuring SharePoint Portal Server for use with a proxy server can be done either graphically with the SharePoint Portal Server Administrator on the server itself, or by using a command-line utility, called proxycfg.exe. Both methods are shown in the next few pages.

Using SharePoint Portal Server Administrator   To use the SharePoint Portal Server Administrator, you must be physically sitting at the server computer or use the Terminal Services

Client program with Terminal Services installed on the SharePoint Portal Server computer. In either case, follow these steps:

1. Open the SharePoint Portal Server Administrator.

   On the SharePoint Portal Server computer, choose Start | Programs | Administrative Tools | SharePoint Portal Server Administration.

2. Navigate to the name of your server (not a workspace).

3. Right-click the name of your server and choose Properties.

4. Click Proxy Server.

   Clicking this tab brings up this dialog box:

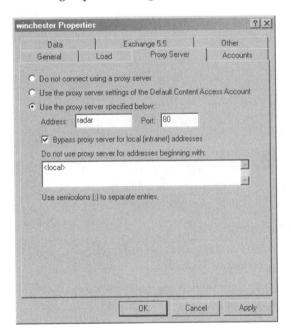

5. Choose the appropriate option.

   You can select from the following three options:

   ■ **Do not connect using a proxy server**   Select this option if you do not have a proxy server installed.

   ■ **Use the proxy server settings of the Default Content Access Account**   Select this option if you want SharePoint Portal Server to use the proxy server settings that have been specified for use with Internet Explorer (IE). The IE settings specified are those which have been set up for the user specified by the Default Content Access Account. Therefore, if you are having trouble using this account, log into Windows using this account and configure the IE settings. For more information about the Default Content Access Account, see the section called "Server Accounts" later in this chapter.

- ■ **Use the proxy server specified below** Select this option if you want to manually configure the settings of the proxy server. If you choose this option, you must enter the server name and port number. The prior illustration shows the proxy server name of Radar that communicates through TCP/IP port number 80. Additionally, you can opt to not use the proxy server for specific addresses. The above illustration bypasses all local addresses. This means that the proxy server is not used for HTTP traffic that uses servers on the local intranet. Selecting this option generally speeds up communications to internal servers, because the proxy server is not used under these specific cases. To bypass all local intranet traffic, enter <local>.

6. Click OK or Apply to save your changes.

Using proxycfg.exe In addition to using the graphical SharePoint Portal Server Administrator, you can use a command-line utility, called proxycfg.exe. Why would you do this? The simple answer is that you might have a script that performs configurations, such as in the case of setting up multiple SharePoint Portal servers. Therefore, you can use this utility within your scripts to configure the appropriate proxy settings. You can configure exactly the same options using proxycfg.exe as you can by using the SharePoint Portal Server Administrator.

To use this command-line utility, follow these steps:

1. Open the command prompt.

   On the SharePoint Portal Server computer, choose Start | Programs | Accessories | Command Prompt.

2. Change to the appropriate drive where the proxycfg.exe resides.

   By default the proxycfg.exe resides on the C: drive. Therefore, at the command prompt, type:

   ```
   C:
   ```

3. Press ENTER.

4. Change to the appropriate folder where the proxycfg.exe resides.

   By default the proxycfg.exe resides in the \Program Files\SharePoint Portal Server\Bin folder. Therefore, at the command prompt, type:

   ```
   CD \Program Files\SharePoint Portal Server\Bin
   ```

5. Press Enter.
6. Use the appropriate syntax for the proxycfg.exe utility.

   Following is the syntax for the proxycfg.exe utility:

   ```
   Proxycfg.exe [-?] [-d] [-u] [-p <server-name:port>
   [<bypass-list>]]
   ```

   In learning how to use this syntax, it might help to review the graphical way of configuring SharePoint Portal Server to use a proxy server, as shown earlier in this chapter under the heading, "Using SharePoint Portal Server Administrator." The following substitutions can be made with the above syntax:

   - *server_name*   The name of your proxy server. As an example, the name of my proxy server is Radar. This parameter is the same as entering a server name in the Address field while using the SharePoint Portal Server Administrator.

   - *port*   The port number that will be used to communicate with the proxy server. I have used the default port of 80. This parameter is the same as entering a port number in the Port field while using the SharePoint Portal Server Administrator.

   - *bypass-list*   The optional list of addresses that are not to be used with the proxy server that begin with the list that you specify. This is exactly analogous to the Do Not Use Proxy Server For Addresses Beginning With box when using the SharePoint Portal Server Administrator. Entering values for this parameter is also the command-line equivalent of checking Bypass Proxy Server For Local (Intranet) Addresses. If you have multiple addresses that should be bypassed, make sure to separate them by commas. As an example, I enter <local> to bypass all intranet addresses. The bypass list must be enclosed in quotes.

   Additionally, using the syntax above, you can specify these command-line switches:

   - **-?**   Displays syntactical help. If this switch is specified, all other settings are ignored.

   - **-d**   Specifies that the proxy server is direct, or not to use a proxy server. This switch takes no additional arguments and can be used with the -p switch. This is analogous to using the Do Not Connect Using A Proxy Server option in the SharePoint Portal Server Administrator.

   - **-u**   Specifies that Internet Explorer settings for the Default Content Access Account are used. This is analogous to using the Use The Proxy Server

Settings Of The Default Content Access Account option in the SharePoint Portal Server Administrator.

■ **-p** Specifies that the indicated proxy server settings should be used. This switch can be used with the -d switch. This is analogous to using the Use The Proxy Server Specified Below option in the SharePoint Portal Server Administrator and specifying the parameters after the proxy server name.

As an example, to mimic the options shown under the earlier section, "Using SharePoint Portal Server Administrator," you would type:

```
proxycfg -p radar:80 "<local>"
```

7. Press Enter.

Your configuration will be saved within SharePoint Portal Server, as shown here:

Web Part Configuration

Even if you don't use a proxy server, you must do some configuration for web parts to be downloaded for use with SharePoint Portal Server. Although adding web parts is covered in Chapter 4, I'm going to show you a specific example. Suppose you wanted to download the Content Viewer web part from the Microsoft Web Part Gallery. Without configuring any proxy settings after creating a workspace, you receive the error shown in Figure 10-3.

You must use the proxycfg.exe utility to fix this problem (not the SharePoint Portal Server Administrator). Even though you may not be using a proxy server, you must use this utility to "fake out" SharePoint Portal Server. To see how to bring up the proxycfg.exe utility, see the earlier section, "Using proxycfg.exe."

Under the scenario where you do not have a proxy server, proxycfg.exe is used with this syntax (which is slightly different than the earlier syntax):

```
proxycfg -d -p proxy_name:port "web_part_gallery;<local>"
```

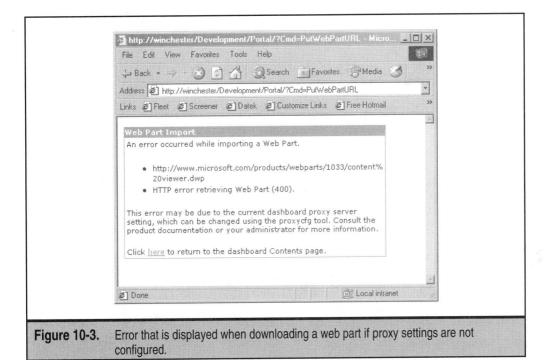

Figure 10-3.   Error that is displayed when downloading a web part if proxy settings are not configured.

The following substitutions can be made with the above syntax:

▼   *proxy_name*   The name that you give to a fake proxy server. This name can be any name that is not a real proxy server, such as fake_proxy.

■   *port*   The port number that will be used to transport the HTTP requests. This port is usually 80.

▲   *web_part_gallery*   The name of the web part gallery that you wish to configure access for. For example, if you wish to configure SharePoint Portal Server to access all web parts, regardless of where they are located on the internet, you can use the wildcard *. On the other hand, if you wanted to access the web parts only from the Microsoft web site, you can use *.microsoft.com. The <local> part of the syntax indicates that you can access web parts from your intranet. If you want to access web parts only on the internet, remove this part of the syntax. Note that you can string together multiple sites from which you will download web parts, but each web site must be separated by a semi colon.

As an example, if you want to configure SharePoint Portal Server to access any web part, either from the internet or your intranet over port 80, you could use the proxycfg.exe utility like this:

```
proxycfg -d -p fake_proxy:80 "*;<local>"
```

Even if you configure SharePoint Portal Server to access and download web parts from the internet, you might encounter a further problem, as shown in this dialog box:

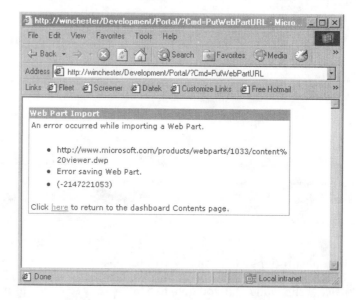

To get around this problem, simply make sure that you have Coordinator privileges within the workspace and this error will go away.

Server Accounts

As with most operations on any Windows platform, a process operates within a security context. A *security context* is an account that is used to gain access to resources on a server or within a domain. In SharePoint Portal Server, there are two accounts which must be configured if you plan to use any of the workspaces for indexing. Although indexing is covered in Chapter 8, I cover the security-related topics of indexing herein.

The two accounts which you can configure at the server level (regardless of the workspaces contained on the server) are:

▼ **Default Content Access Account**   The security account that has access to the resources to read, or crawl, content that will be indexed. Additionally, this is the account that is used to detect Internet Explorer settings for configuration with a proxy server. For more information about configuring a proxy server, see the section, "Proxy Configuration" earlier in this chapter.

▲ **Propagation Access Account**   The security account that has administrative access to the servers that will receive a propagated index from an index workspace.

To access the screen that allows you to change the security accounts associated with these items, you use the SharePoint Portal Server Administrator. Simply follow these steps:

1.   Open the SharePoint Portal Server Administrator.

     On the SharePoint Portal Server computer, choose Start | Programs | Administrative Tools | SharePoint Portal Server Administration.

2.   Navigate to the name of your server (not a workspace).

3.   Right-click the name of your server and choose Properties.

4.   Click Accounts.

     Clicking this tab brings up this dialog box:

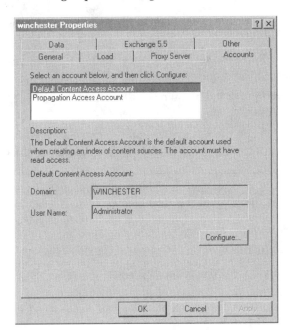

5.   Select the desired account to change.

6. Click Configure.

Clicking this button brings up this dialog box:

7. Fill in all fields.

You must fill in these fields:

- **Domain** Enter the domain or local server that contains the account which you will specify.
- **Account** Enter the security account within the domain or local server that has access to the required resources.
- **Password** Enter the password associated with the account in the domain or local server.
- **Confirm** Type the password again to make sure you typed it in correctly, as the account will not be validated when you close the dialog box.

NOTE: For some reason, Microsoft chose not to give the standard dialog box that allows you to select a domain/user combination, so you must enter the account information by hand, risking typographical errors.

8. Click OK to close the Account Information dialog box.
9. Click OK again to save your changes.

DOCUMENT SECURITY

Documents are contained at the lowest level of the hierarchy in SharePoint Portal Server. At the top-level is the workspace, which has been previously discussed in this chapter. A workspace contains many folders. One level down from the workspace is the folder-level. A folder contains many documents or other folders. This is exactly the same as it is when you store you documents on your hard drive. Security can be configured to inherit from or be redefined in this hierarchy, as depicted in Figure 10-4.

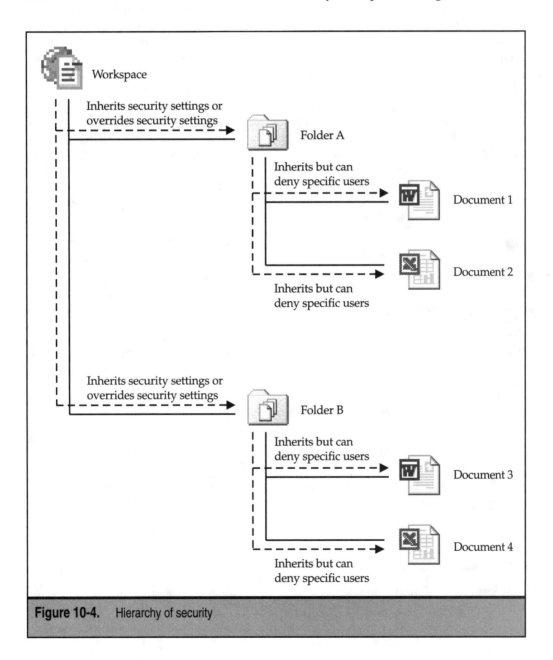

Figure 10-4. Hierarchy of security

When you give access to a user in the workspace, you configure his/her access level (i.e. role) within the workspace. If you do nothing else, that security role will be inherited from the workspace to all folders and subfolders and to all documents contained within the workspace. However, this may not always be the desired result. For example, if people from sales, marketing, and information technology (IT) all have access to a workspace, you probably don't want sales people or marketing folks modifying IT documents, such as software development plans and project plans. It might make sense, however, to allow them to have read-only access to those documents, in case they are curious. Likewise, you wouldn't want IT folks to modify sales-forecast documents. Let's take this example one step further. Even though you want the sales people to have read-only access to IT documents, suppose there is a specific document about special projects going on that you don't want them to see, called Special Projects.doc. At the document level, you can explicitly deny access to this group which lets the sales people see all documents except this one. This example is shown in Figure 10-5.

You've already seen how to configure workspace security throughout this entire chapter up to this point. Therefore, all you need to know how to configure are folders and documents. Each is described in the following sections.

NOTE: While you are reading about securing your documents, keep in mind the scenario described just above. It will help you to comprehend how folder and document security works.

Configuring Folder Security

Configuring folder security is much like configuring workspace access and security. In fact, the dialog box is almost identical. Folder security is configured by using a network place. For more information about creating network places, see Chapter 4. To configure folder security, follow these steps:

1. Open the network place that represents the workspace on your portal.

   In my example, I open the network place for a workspace called IT (for information technology) on the SharePoint Portal Server called winchester. This network place is called IT on winchester.

2. Review security for all documents by right-clicking the Documents folder and selecting Properties.

3. Click Security.

   Clicking the Security tab brings up the dialog box shown in Figure 10-6.

   Select from the following options:

   ■ **Use parent folder's security settings** If you check this option (which is actually checked by default), documents or folders will inherit the security settings from the parent. For the Documents folder, the parent is

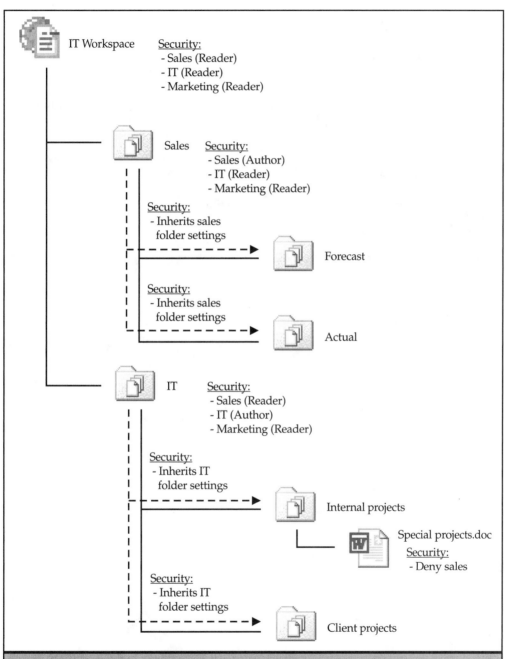

Figure 10-5. Example of how security might be configured on folders in a workspace

the workspace settings. For subfolders, the parent is the folder immediately above in the hierarchy.

■ **User or Group** This list box is only enabled if the Use Parent Folder's Security Settings is not selected. If it is enabled, you can add users, change roles, or remove users from accessing documents. For more information on adding users, changing permissions, or removing users, see the headings "Allowing Access," "Modifying Roles" and "Revoking Access" earlier in this chapter. Each of these is in the "Workspace Security" section.

■ **Reset all subfolders to use these security settings** Changing any security permissions at this level does not automatically reset any subfolder permissions that might be inheriting from this folder. Therefore, if you want to make sure that changes are reflected in subfolders, check this option.

4. Click OK to save your changes, apply the security settings that you have chosen, and close the dialog box.

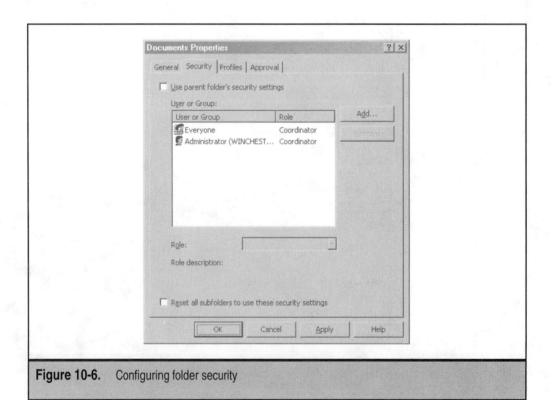

Figure 10-6. Configuring folder security

The above steps show how to apply security settings to the Documents folder. However, what if you want to change settings on some other folder lower in the document folder hierarchy? For example, what if you wanted to change security settings on the IT folder to assign members of the IT group to the Author role and members of the Sales and Marketing groups to the Reader role? Simple! Assuming you have folders already created like those shown in Figure 10-5, you follow these steps:

1. Navigate to the IT folder.

2. Click Security.

3. Uncheck Use Parent Folder's Security Settings.

4. Ensure that only the IT group is assigned to the Author role.

5. Ensure that the Sales and Marketing groups are assigned to the Reader role.

6. Ensure that no other groups or users appear in the list.

7. Check Reset All Subfolders To Use These Security Settings to ensure that all subfolders lower in the hierarchy have security settings reflect these changes.

8. Click OK.

NOTE: In addition to folder security for documents, you can also change the same security settings for the dashboards, portal, and portal content folders.

Configuring Document Security

The document is the lowest point in any hierarchy of folders and subfolders. This is known as the document level or also sometimes referred to as the leaf level. You cannot assign specific users or roles at the document level. The only thing that you can do at the document level (which is performed on the document itself) is to deny access to specific users or groups. By default access on documents is *not* denied to any user or group. Therefore, as long as a user or group has access to the document by using folder-level security, he/she can read or edit the document according to the role assigned on that folder. Likewise, if the folder is inheriting permissions, the roles assigned to the parent folder from which the subfolder is inheriting will take effect.

To configure document security, you use a network place. Again, network places are covered in Chapter 4. To configure folder security, follow these steps:

1. Open the network place that represents the workspace on your portal.

    In my example, I open the network place for a workspace called IT (for information technology) on the SharePoint Portal Server called winchester. This network place is called IT on winchester.

2. Navigate through the hierarchy until you reach the document for which security will be changed.

3. Right-click the desired document and click Properties.

Clicking Properties brings up this dialog box:

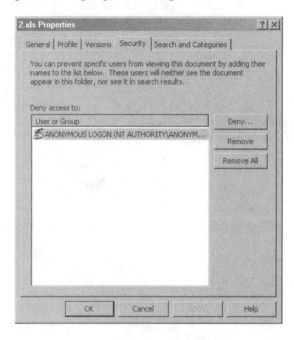

4. Select users or groups that are denied access.

To select users or groups who are not to be allowed to view or search for the selected document, click Deny and select the appropriate users or groups. These users will be shown in the Deny Access To list box. If you wish to remove one or more users or groups from the list, simply select those users or groups, followed by Remove. If you want to allow access to all users, simply click Remove All (which removes all users from the list of denied users, thereby allowing access).

CHAPTER SUMMARY

Security is a very important part of your SharePoint Portal Server installations. There are aspects of security that affect the server, workspaces, folders and documents. In this chapter, you learned about all of these aspects of security to enable you to apply the concepts to your own installations. I showed you an example of how security might be configured in a real-world scenario to aid in your understanding of security. Refer to this example in the future to further enhance your understanding security.

CHAPTER 11

Monitoring and Optimizing the Server

OK, so your SharePoint Portal Server installation is up and running. Everything is great. You are providing a portal for miscellaneous data to your organization and even some personalization aspects with web parts. In addition, you have enabled searching and search scopes to provide fast access to documents. However, you are not sure that your server installation is as optimal as it could be. This chapter is dedicated to helping you to determine if there are any problems and what you can do about them.

MONITORING

Before you can really optimize your system, you have to find out if there are any problems. However, this can be quite difficult to do if you are not familiar with using the Performance Monitor. The *Performance Monitor* is a tool that comes with all versions of Windows that allows you to monitor specific counters. A *counter* is a specific monitoring variable that is monitored by the Performance Monitor and sampled over a specific period of time. These counters are displayed in a standard Windows screen called the Microsoft Management Console, or MMC. The MMC is used to display information in a tree-like fashion. Also, the data selected for display within the MMC (the counters in this case) can be saved into a file so that you don't have to go through the selection process again in the future. You can save the state of the MMC and recall it in the future.

Normally, when you install an application on a Windows server (either NT or 2000), specific counters are also installed to allow you to monitor that application. Counters are normally grouped into categories, called *objects*. Additionally, some objects have a further categorization of an object, called an *instance*. An instance allows you to specify a qualifier for a given object. For example, there is a SharePoint Portal Server object called Microsoft Search Catalogs. Because this object is more of a grouping, the Performance Monitor needs to know which catalog to monitor, so the instance that you select is actually the specific catalog (or catalogs) to monitor. Furthermore, when you select the instance of the search catalog to monitor, you then select one or more counters to monitor. Such counters could be Queries, or Number of Documents. There are hundreds of counters available for the objects in SharePoint Portal Server. In fact, there are too many to mention here, but Table 11-1 shows a listing of the objects and descriptions of those objects available for the monitoring of SharePoint Portal Server.

Using the Performance Monitor

Using the Performance Monitor can be a little difficult if you've never used it before. In this section, I'll show you how to use it. Using the Performance Monitor is done on

Object	Description
SharePoint Portal Document Management Server	Monitors all aspects of the document management features of SharePoint Portal Server, like check-ins, check-outs, approvals, etc.
SharePoint Portal Server Subscriptions	Monitors all aspects of subscriptions that are made within SharePoint Portal Server. These aspects include total subscriptions, total notifications, total documents processed, and more.
Microsoft Gatherer	Monitors all aspects of SharePoint Portal Server operations, like idle time, the number of documents in memory, and performance levels.
Microsoft Gatherer Projects	Monitors specific aspects of SharePoint workspaces. Such aspects are the number of documents accessed by using HTTP, number of documents that are adaptively crawled, and the number of documents that have changed since the last crawl.
Microsoft Search	Provides counters for all aspects of the searching service, such as the number of concurrent connections, number of queries sent to the server, and the number of threads available for searching.
Microsoft Search Catalogs	Provides counters for specific workspaces (or catalogs), such as the number of documents in the catalog, the size of the catalog (in megabytes), and the number of failed queries for the catalog.
Microsoft Search Indexer Catalogs	Also provides counters for specific workspaces (or catalogs), but related to the indexing of catalogs. Such counters include the number of documents being added to the catalog, the percentage of merge complete for a merge process, and the number of persistent indexes.
MSExchange Oledb Resource	Provides counters related to the access of the Web Storage System. Such counters include the number of active sessions, number of transactions that are committed, and the total number of transactions that are aborted.
MSExchange Oledb Events	Provides counters that are related to events that are generated from the Web Storage System, such as the total number of events that are submitted and the total number of events that are completed.
MS Exchange Web Mail	Provides counters that are related to Exchange mail requests. Such counters include the number of message saves per second, attachments deleted per second, and the total number of authentications.

Table 11-1.   Performance Counter Objects Available On A SharePoint Portal Server Computer

the SharePoint Portal Server computer because that's where the objects and counters are installed. To use the Performance Monitor, follow these steps:

1. Open the Performance Monitor.

   On the SharePoint Portal Server computer, choose Start | Programs | Administrative Tools | Performance. This brings up the Performance Monitor, as shown in Figure 11-1.

2. Click System Monitor.

3. Click Add.

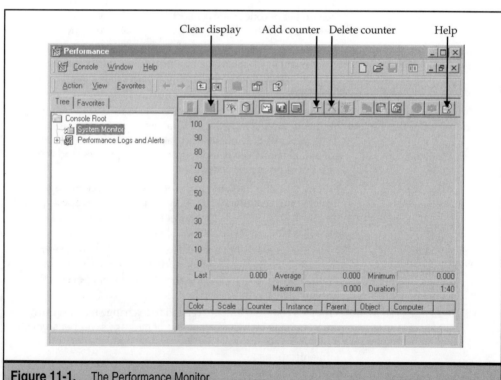

Figure 11-1. The Performance Monitor

Clicking this button, which looks like a plus sign, brings up the Add Counters dialog box, like this:

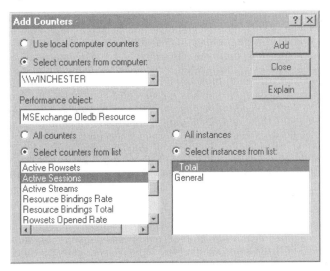

4. Select the desired computer.

   Choose Use Local Computer Counters if you want to select counters from the local computer. Choose Select Counters From Computer if you want to include counters from objects on another computer. Selecting the latter option will enable a drop-down list of servers. By default, the latter is selected, with the current computer name in the drop-down list. You can either select or type the desired computer name, using the UNC convention (starting with \\).

5. Select the desired performance object.

   Select from the list of objects shown in Table 11-1 the desired object to monitor. For example, if you wish to monitor the number of active sessions, select MSExchange Oledb Resource from the drop-down list. Doing so populates a list of counters and instances for this object.

6. Select the desired counter(s).

   If you wish to select all counters for the object, click All Counters. Alternatively, if you wish to select individual counters, select Select Counters From List, which is selected by default. As with any other list box in windows, you can multi-select items in the list by using the CTRL key while clicking the desired option. As an example, if you only wanted to select the number of active connections, since you already chose the MSExchange Oledb Resource object, click the Active Sessions counter.

7. Select the desired instance(s).

If you wish to select all instances for the object, click All Instances. Alternatively, if you wish to select individual counters, choose Select Instances From List, which is selected by default. Again, you can use the CTRL key while clicking the desired option to select multiple options. The instances shown are dependent upon which object you select to monitor. If you don't know which instance(s) to select, you might want to select All Instances. Additionally, if you want to get a brief explanation of what a counter monitors, click Explain.

8. Click Add.

   Clicking Add includes the selected counter to the MMC console.

9. Repeat the process for additional counters, if desired.

   If you want to monitor additional counters, perform the above steps again for the additional counters. Each counter is given its own color in the MMC to differentiate it from other counters.

10. Click Close to dismiss the dialog box.

    Closing the Add Counters dialog box reveals the counters that you have selected to monitor in the MMC. This is shown in Figure 11-2.

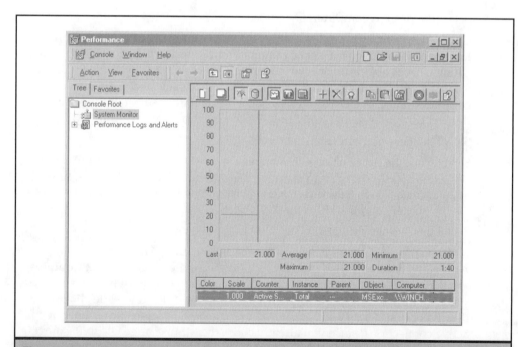

Figure 11-2.   The Performance Monitor showing selected counters

Reading the Performance Monitor

The performance monitor samples data from the selected objects, counters, and instances over time. As the vertical line passes across the screen, it leaves behind a trail of information for each counter that you've selected to monitor. This can be difficult to read, depending on the number of counters that you have chosen to monitor.

It is impossible for me to tell you all the possibilities that may occur in each of the available counters, but I can give you some pointers in what to look for. These pointers will help you to determine if your server is overloaded and needs to be optimized, which is covered throughout the rest of this chapter. Some things to look for are:

▼ Spikes that occur very often

■ Maxing-out of counter values

■ Memory-related counters that regularly consume more than 50% of available memory

▲ Processor-related counters that regularly consume more than 50% of available processor time

As an example, let's take two separate views of the Performance Monitor. These examples are very simplistic. If you have ever used the Performance Monitor to analyze many counters, you know that the screen can become quite cluttered. Therefore, I'll show a very simple example to get the point across. The example is shown in Figure 11-3.

In Figure 11-3, there is only one counter shown in the window. It is the % Processor Time counter, which belongs to the Processor object. Why is it maxed out (near 100%) for most of the time? The answer lies within the process that is occurring during that time. If you haven't guessed by now, it is crawling content. This is the exact reason why you want to have an index workspace dedicated to crawling content, while leaving the searching workspace free.

The second example is shown in Figure 11-4 where there are two counters in the window. One is the % Processor Time counter, which belongs to the Processor object, as shown in Figure 11-3. There is also another counter, called Query Rate, which belongs to the Microsoft Search object. These counters show perfectly normal operations. The Query Rate counter has values so small that they are difficult to see. This is because there are not too many queries per second that are issued to the server. At the same time, the processor is showing spikes. This is because the processor needs cycles to perform the query. This Performance Monitor example does not represent need to take any optimization actions.

OPTIMIZING

Once you determine that there are problems by using monitoring techniques discussed earlier in this chapter, (in the section "Monitoring,") you should correct those problems.

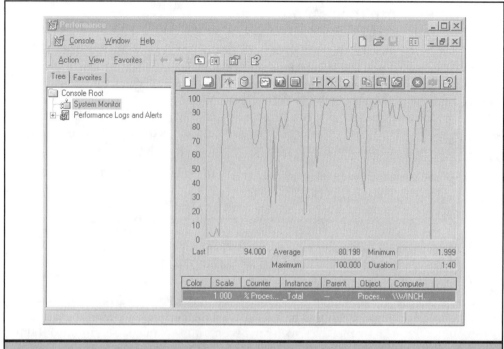

Figure 11-3. Performance Monitor example showing performance problems

There are five major areas in which you can optimize your SharePoint Portal Server installations. They are:

▼ **File Locations** Placement of SharePoint Portal Server, Web Storage System, and other files can have an impact on performance.

■ **Indexes** One of the greatest impacts on performance is the method you choose to update indexes.

■ **Resource Usage** Optimization can be achieved by setting resource values.

■ **Query Timeouts** Adjusting the time that queries can stay active.

▲ **Scalability** Either "beefing-up" a server computer or distributing processing will scale a SharePoint Portal Server installation, thereby optimizing the solution.

Each of these areas is discussed throughout the remainder of this chapter.

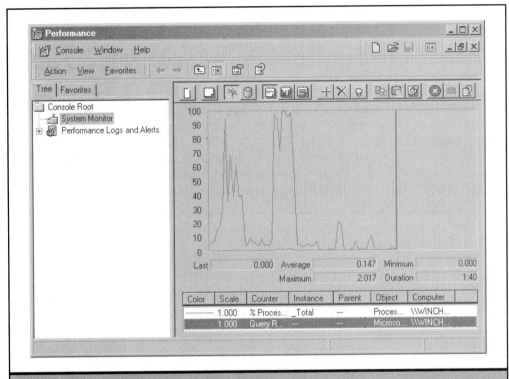

Figure 11-4.   Performance Monitor example showing normal operations

File Locations

For SharePoint Portal Server to function, files that are required for proper operation are placed into folders. Obviously, SharePoint Portal Server must know where these files are located. Most likely, when you installed SharePoint Portal Server, you accepted all of the default file locations. This may be fine for some installations, but for others, this can cause performance problems. Just as with most performance-related problems, there is usually a bottleneck that is causing the majority of issues. For example, if you have a server with a really fast Pentium IV 1.3GHz processor and four 60GB hard drives, but only have 64MB memory, the bottleneck will be the memory. In other words, you have a relatively great server, but it is not optimum because the memory is underpowered.

File locations can have the same impact on performance. If you have only one disk volume where all SharePoint Portal Server files are placed, performance can be slow (depending on the amount of data that you have). Therefore, you should consider implementing more than one volume. Additionally, performance is greatly increased if all volumes are formatted as NTFS (Windows NT File System).

If you are familiar with SQL Server optimization, you know that placing log files on a separate volume is a great idea. Well, SharePoint Portal Server is exactly the same way. The Web Storage System Database Log should be placed on its own dedicated volume. In addition, it is best to store the indexes on their own volumes. Doing so will minimize the impact of searching and writing data to the Web Storage System at the same time. Note that this is true even if you create dedicated index workspaces. Index workspaces, as shown in Chapter 8, benefit performance by crawling content and propagating the index to the search computer. However, that search computer is still used to modify content within the portal.

There are six separate file locations that you can alter. I refer to these individual file locations as data elements. Table 11-2 explains all about these file locations. Table 11-2 assumes that you have not altered any of the default installation paths.

TIP: You must be a domain or local administrator to change file locations for the server.

Changing file locations is done by using the SharePoint Portal Server Administrator on the Server computer. Here's how you change any of the file locations shown in Table 11-2:

1. Open the SharePoint Portal Server Administrator.

   On the SharePoint Portal Server computer, choose Start | Programs | Administrative Tools | SharePoint Portal Server Administrator.

2. Expand the tree until you see the name of your server.

3. Right-click the desired server.

   Do not right-click any of the workspaces themselves, just the name of the server.

4. Click Properties.

5. Click Data.

A Note About Changing WSS Locations...

If you installed SharePoint Portal Server on the same box as Microsoft Exchange 2000 (which you shouldn't do), you cannot change locations of the Web Storage System files by using the procedure outlined next. You must use the Exchange System Manager that comes with Exchange 2000.

Data Element	Description	Default Location
Search Indexes	Contains location of indexes that are generated from crawling content. The Projects folder contains subfolders for each workspace that you create.	C:\Program Files\SharePoint Portal Server\Data\FTData\ SharePointPortalServer\ Projects
Search Temporary Files	SharePoint Portal Server uses this location for temporary files to process indexes. This is similar to the way Windows uses page files.	C:\WINNT\TEMP or wherever the location of the TEMP environment variable points to.
Search Gatherer Logs	Contains location of log files that are generated when crawling content sources. The GatherLogs folder contains subfolders for each workspace that you create.	C:\Program Files\SharePoint Portal Server\Data\FTData\ SharePointPortalServer\ GatherLogs
WSS - Database	Contains the Web Storage System database, called WSS.MDB. Note that MDB is NOT the same MDB file extension used by Microsoft Access. If you change this location, SharePoint Portal Server will automatically move the existing database.	C:\Program Files\SharePoint Portal Server\Data\Web Storage System
WSS - Streaming Database	Contains the Web Storage System database specifically used for streaming media, called WSS.STM. If you change this location, SharePoint Portal Server will automatically move the existing database.	C:\Program Files\SharePoint Portal Server\Data\Web Storage System
WSS - Database Log	Contains location of log files that are generated during the course of using SharePoint Portal Server.	C:\Program Files\SharePoint Portal Server\Data\Web Storage System

Table 11-2.   SharePoint Portal Server File Locations

Clicking this tab brings up the dialog box shown here:

6. Select the desired log file to change.

   In the Server Data And Log Files section, click the desired log file that you wish to change. Notice in the read-only text box, the current file location is shown.

7. Click Browse.

8. Select the desired new location.

9. Repeat for each desired location.

10. Click OK to save and close the dialog box.

Indexes

I discuss indexes in depth in Chapter 8. However, it is worth noting again in this chapter that one of the major ways to improve performance in SharePoint Portal Server is to dedicate one or more servers to allow users to search and one or more servers to crawl content and generate indexes. This way, the machines that provide searching capability to the users do not also waste valuable resources to crawl content. For more information about this, see Chapter 8 and the blueprint diagram in the center of this book.

Resource Usage

Two major bits of functionality that SharePoint Portal Server provides are very resource intensive. A *resource intensive* process consumes much processor time, memory, and/or disk activity (known as I/O). These bits of functionality are searching and indexing (also known as index creation). To instruct SharePoint Portal Server to use resources effectively, you can boost the priority of either or both of the searching and indexing processes.

SharePoint Portal Server allows you to configure either of these processes to work with dedicated resources (which boosts the priority), background resources (which lowers the priority), or somewhere in the middle. How you decide which setting to use depends on how your server is configured. By default, each process is configured exactly in the middle so that resources are neither dedicated nor background. To help you decide how you should configure these settings, see Table 11-3, which outlines different scenarios. Note that these are not a definitive solution, just a guideline.

TIP: You must be a domain or local administrator to adjust resource usage values for the server.

Altering resource usage is exceptionally easy once you decide what you want to do. Just follow these steps:

1.   Open the SharePoint Portal Server Administrator.

Scenario	Search Resource Usage Slidebar	Indexing Resource Usage Slidebar
Workspace performs both indexing and searching with nothing else running on the server	Dedicated or Near-Dedicated. Must be set to the same value as the indexing resource usage slidebar.	Dedicated or Near-Dedicated. Must be set to the same value as the search resource usage slidebar.
Workspace performs both indexing and searching with other applications running on the server	Middle setting. Must be set to the same value as the indexing resource usage slidebar.	Middle setting. Must be set to the same value as the search resource usage slidebar.
One workspace performs indexing and another performs searching with nothing else running on either server	Background on the index workspace. Dedicated or Near-Dedicated on the search workspace.	Background on the search workspace. Dedicated or Near-Dedicated on the index workspace.
One workspace performs indexing and another performs searching with other applications running on either server	Background on the index workspace. Middle setting on the search workspace.	Background on the search workspace. Middle setting on the index workspace.

Table 11-3.   Resource Usage Scenarios

On the SharePoint Portal Server computer, choose Start | Programs | Administrative Tools | SharePoint Portal Server Administrator.

2. Expand the tree until you see the name of your server.

3. Right-click the desired server.

4. Click Properties.

5. Click General (shown by default).

    Clicking this tab brings up the dialog box shown here:

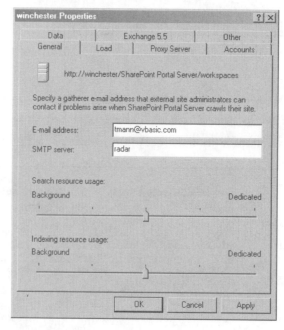

6. Move the resource bars to the desired position.

7. Click OK to save and close the dialog box.

Query Timeouts

When a user issues a query (also known as a search) to a SharePoint Portal Server, it must process the query. The processing consumes resources on the server. The more complex the query, the more time it can take to process, thereby consuming resources for a longer period of time. Just imagine lots of users doing the same thing. Resources can be tied up for quite a while. Therefore, you can adjust the query timeout value for each workspace.

NOTE: Timeouts don't apply to index workspaces because they are not used for searching. They're used for crawling content to create indexes, so searching is not performed against an index workspace.

Timeout values are expressed in milliseconds (or 1/1000 of a second). The default value for each workspace is 20,000, which is the same as 20 seconds. There are pros and cons for changing this value. The pros for lowering this value are that server resources are tied up for a shorter period of time. The cons for lowering this value are that complex queries might timeout before completing. Raising this value reverses the pros and cons. Microsoft has determined that 20 seconds is generally adequate, but if you wish to change this value, follow these steps:

TIP: You must be a workspace Coordinator to change the timeout value.

1. Open the SharePoint Portal Server Administrator.

    On the SharePoint Portal Server computer, choose Start | Programs | Administrative Tools | SharePoint Portal Server Administrator.

2. Expand the tree until you see the name of your server.

3. Expand the tree further until you see the name of the desired workspace.

4. Right-click the desired workspace name.

5. Click Properties.

6. Click Index.

    Clicking this tab brings up the dialog box shown here:

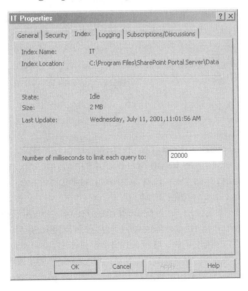

7. Change the timeout value.

The timeout value is represented by the text box labeled Number Of Milliseconds To Limit Each Query To. Enter the number of seconds you wish for the timeout value, multiplied by 1000 to convert to milliseconds.

8. Click the OK button to save and close the dialog box.

Scalability

Scalability refers to the ability to add on to a server when its resource capacity is reached (or at least leading in that direction). There are two types of scalability: scaling out and scaling up. Each of these is discussed in the next two sections.

Scaling Out

Scaling out refers to the ability to add more servers as the need arises. You can also think of scaling out as horizontal scaling. Scaling out in SharePoint Portal Server is somewhat limited. If you are familiar with scalability with other Microsoft products, like Internet Information Server (IIS), you can actually create a series of servers that distribute the load across those servers. This is known as a web farm. However, SharePoint Portal Server cannot take advantage of this.

The only way to scale out with SharePoint Portal Server is to place workspaces on separate servers. You can create an index workspace on a dedicated server to crawl content for searching. This is covered in Chapter 8. You can also create non-index workspaces (which I've referred to in this book as "regular workspaces or portal workspaces") on dedicated servers. This can help to reduce consumed server resources because each workspace is limited to a specific server. However, you should know that this is not necessarily required. Determining this need is based upon how many resources a workspace consumes. You might actually get a "better bang for the buck" by scaling up regular workspaces, rather than scaling out. Conversely, it's probably a better investment to scale out index workspaces, rather than scale up. Scaling up is discussed next.

Scaling Up

Scaling up can be considerably easier to achieve than scaling out. *Scaling up* refers to adding more hardware resources to one or more existing servers. You can also think of scaling up as vertical scaling. If you add additional hardware, SharePoint Portal Server will automatically take advantage of that.

The most common way to scale up is to add more memory. Memory is cheap! The reason why adding more memory can make a server faster is because the more memory you add the less virtual memory is used. Virtual memory is a dedicated area on the disk drive that Windows manages automatically and is used to swap data from physical memory. This is necessary because operations must take place in memory, not on disk. Therefore, if areas of memory aren't being used, they can be swapped to disk to free-up the memory.

If you add more memory, less disk swapping has to occur. That's why adding memory can speed performance.

In addition to adding more memory, scaling up can refer to:

▼ Adding hard disk space

■ Increasing processor speed

■ Adding processors

▲ Replacing motherboards with faster boards

CHAPTER SUMMARY

In this chapter, you learned how you can optimize your SharePoint Portal Server installation. There are some simple configuration changes that you can make to give a big impact on performance. There are also some less simple changes that you can make, like scaling out or scaling up your SharePoint Portal Servers.

Additionally, in this chapter, we touched the surface on how to monitor your server. This is quite an advanced topic, so it wasn't covered in too much depth in this book. If you want to learn more about using the Performance Monitor, I suggest that you buy a good book on Windows 2000 administration and troubleshooting.

CHAPTER 12

Backing Up, Restoring, and Deploying

In this short chapter, you'll learn how to back up and restore your SharePoint Portal Server computer(s). In addition, I'll discuss how to deploy a SharePoint Portal Server installation into production from your development or test environment. You'll be surprised how simple that is.

OVERVIEW

There is one thing in common with backing up and restoring your SharePoint Portal Server computers. That one thing is the program used to perform the backup or restore. There are no separate backup and restore programs. Throughout the rest of this chapter, I'll show you how these are used.

To back up or restore a SharePoint Portal Server installation, you must use a VBScript file called MSDMBack.vbs. This script file is installed automatically on the SharePoint Portal Server in the BIN folder wherever you installed SharePoint Portal Server. By default, this is in the directory:

```
C:\Program Files\SharePoint Portal Server\Bin
```

A VBScript file, such as MSDMBack.vbs, will be executed when you double-click the name of the file in Windows Explorer. However, if you simply double-click the file, the required parameters won't be specified. Therefore, you don't want to back up or restore by double-clicking the file. You need to assign it parameters, as noted later in this chapter under the heading, "MDSMBack Usage".

The MSDMBack.vbs file works by invoking, or instantiating, an object called MSDMBack.MSDMBackupWrap, which is located in the WSDMBack.dll file. The MSDMBack.dll file is also located in the directory with the MSDMBack.vbs file. This object is used to allow you programmatic access to the backup features of SharePoint Portal Server. Although this book is not about programming, it can be very useful to understand the mechanics of how the backup and restore utility works. Chances are that if you are reading this book, you have at least some understanding of Visual Basic or VBScript. The MSDMBack.vbs file contains hundreds of lines of code, so I'll show you only a few lines that really are the "meat" of the code.

The first significant thing that happens in the code is that an object of type MSDMBack.MSDMBackupWrap is invoked, (also known as being instantiated). This object is installed when you installed SharePoint Portal Server. This object is then used in both backup and restore operations. Here's the code that instantiates the object:

```
Dim objMSDMBackupWrap

Set objMSDMBackupWrap = CreateObject ("MSDMBack.MSDMBackupWrap")
```

Warning about the Windows Backup Utility

Do not use the Windows Backup utility to back up a SharePoint Portal Server computer. This utility does not back up all of the necessary information that you'll need to restore or deploy a SharePoint Portal Server. To accurately back up your SharePoint Portal Server, you must use the MSDMBack utility. Before you use any other backup utility, such as Veritas BackupExec Server, you want to check with the vendor as to the viability of backing up a SharePoint Portal Server.

Next, if you are performing a backup, the Backup method is called. If you are performing a restore, the Restore method is called. In either case, arguments relating to the operation are passed to the called method, like this:

```
If fBackupMode Then

    objMSDMBackupWrap.Backup strBackupPath, strPassword,
strMachineName, L_BackupCaption_Text, L_Abort_Text,
L_BytesTransferred_Text

Else

    objMSDMBackupWrap.Restore strBackupPath, strPassword,
fOriginalPaths, strMachineName, L_RestoreCaption_Text, L_Abort_Text,
L_BytesTransferred_Text

End If
```

Using the MSDMBack utility will take all of the security settings, SharePoint server settings, workspace settings, and web storage system content into a single nice and neat file. However, this file is actually quite large. To give you an idea, two small workspaces can easily be backed-up in a file that is greater than 100MB. Therefore, be prepared with a huge hard drive if you have to back up a large server.

MSDMBack Usage

To use the MSDMBack.vbs file, you must supply arguments so that SharePoint Portal Server knows how to back up your system. It can use one of two different syntaxes. Each is described in the next two sections. In either of the syntaxes shown in these sections, the following standard conventions are used:

▼   []   indicates an optional argument

- ■ | indicates that you specify an argument on the left side of the symbol *or* the right side of the symbol
- ■ / switch that acts as a flag to the program that a command will follow
- ▲ <> indicates that an argument or path needs to be substituted for the variable name

BACKING UP

If you don't back up your SharePoint Portal Server, you will eventually regret it. In fact, this is true of all of your computer systems that contain business critical or personal data. Also like your other computer systems, you should normally be concerned with only backing up your data and settings, not the programs themselves. In the case of SharePoint Portal Server, you would want to back up your security settings and data, not the SharePoint Portal Server program files themselves. Backing up the SharePoint Portal Server program files takes additional time and drive storage space. In addition, there may be COM objects (DLLs) that you forget to back up. If you ever need to, you can always reinstall the SharePoint Portal Server from the CD-ROM anyway.

The use of the MSDMBack.vbs script for backups requires that the path to the backup file must exist at the time of backup. In other words, the MSDMBack process will not create any directories or paths, but it will create the backup file that you specify.

Syntax 1

The first syntax is used to begin the backup of a SharePoint Portal Server installation. It is used like this:

```
MSDMBack </b> <Path> [Password] [/m MachineName]
```

The following arguments must be substituted in the syntax above:

- ▼ **/b** Specifies that you will back up your SharePoint Portal Server installation.
- ■ *Path* The path that will be used to back up your SharePoint Portal Server installation. The path should include the name of the file that will contain the backup, not just the path itself. Also, the file must not already exist.
- ■ *Password* Optional parameter used to encrypt the backed-up files with a password. This makes your backup more secure.
- ■ **/m** Optional parameter that indicates a remote machine will be backed up. You must specify this parameter if the script is being run from a server that is not the one you wish to back up.
- ▲ *MachineName* Optional parameter used in conjunction with the /m parameter. This is the name of the server you wish to back up if the script is not run on the machine you wish to back up.

To run the script file and arguments, you can type any of the following examples at the command prompt or the run line. Here are some examples of how you would use the first backup syntax:

This backs up your current SharePoint Portal Server (where the script is run) to a file called SPBack06012001 in the SPBackup folder on the C: drive of the server:

```
MSDMBack /b c:\SPBackup\SPBack06012001
```

This backs up the SharePoint Portal Server called winchester to a file called SPBack06012001 in the SPBackup folder on the C: drive of the winchester server:

```
MSDMBack /b c:\SPBackup\SPBack06012001 /m winchester
```

As a final example of backing up, this backs up the current SharePoint Portal Server to a file called SPBack in the Backup folder on the C: drive of the hawkeye computer:

```
MSDMBack /b \\hawkeye\c\Backup\SPBack
```

In case you need a refresher course, you get to the command prompt by choosing Start | Programs | Accessories | Command Prompt. To get to the run command line, choose Start | Run.

If you omit required arguments, you will receive error messages accordingly. These messages are quite descriptive and obvious which arguments are missing. For example, if you omit the path of the backup file, this error message appears:

As another example, this is the error message that appears when you provide a path to the backup file, but it is invalid:

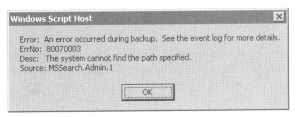

Furthermore, this is what you see if you provide a server name with the /m switch followed by a server name that is invalid or the server is offline:

On the other hand, some error messages are not so clear. For example, can you guess what would cause this error message?

Well, this error message is caused by running the MSDMBack utility on a computer other than a SharePoint Portal Server computer. For example, suppose you have a drive assigned to the letter S:, which maps to the C:\Program Files\SharePoint Portal Server\ Bin directory on the SharePoint Portal Server computer. Therefore, you would think that this would work just fine:

```
S:\MSDMBack /b c:\SPBackup\SPBack06012001
```

This sounds good, but in this case, the MSDMBack utility would be running on the computer where the S: drive is mapped, not the server. That's why you get the error message. It must be run on the server, which is where all appropriate COM objects are registered.

Syntax 2

The first syntax is used to save a user's backup account and password. This is helpful if you are running the MSDMBack.vbs script file from a web page or by other means where you don't want to store your user name and password in that web page. The second syntax is used like this:

```
MSDMBack </a> <Domain\User> <Password>
```

The following arguments must be substituted in the syntax above:

▼ **/a** Indicates that you will specify a user name and password. The VBScript will store that for future use.

- ■ **Domain\User**   The domain name and user name of the account that has security permission to back up the SharePoint Portal Server. If there is only one domain, you can omit the Domain\ in the syntax.
- ▲ **Password**   Password used in conjunction with the domain and user name.

You can run the script file in any of the means specified in the section, "Syntax 1" earlier. Here is an example of how you would use the second syntax:

```
MSDMBack /a sps\amann pword
```

The above syntax stores (in an undisclosed location and format) and validates the user name amann in the domain sps with a password of pword.

Likewise, if you only have one domain, you can omit that part of the syntax like this:

```
MSDMBack /a amann pword
```

RESTORING

Restoring is basically the opposite of backing up. For a restore to work, you must have used the MSDMBack.vbs to back up your SharePoint Portal Server installation. Likewise, you must restore by using the MSDMBack.vbs VBScript.

Restoring is useful in two different scenarios:

- ▼ Recovering from a damaged or corrupted SharePoint Portal Server installation
- ▲ Deploying from a development and/or testing environment to a production environment

It goes without saying, but the use of the MSDMBack.vbs script for restores requires that the backup path and file exist prior to attempting the restore.

To restore a SharePoint Portal Server, again, you can use one of two possible syntaxes. The first syntax is used like this:

```
MSDMBack </r> <Path> [Password] [/o] [/m MachineName]
```

The following arguments must be substituted in the syntax above:

- ▼ **/r**   Specifies that you will restore a SharePoint Portal Server installation.
- ■ **Path**   The path that contains the backup of your SharePoint Portal Server installation. The path must include the full path, including the file name.
- ■ **Password**   Optional parameter used when you backed-up a SharePoint Portal Server installation.
- ■ **/o**   Restores a SharePoint Portal Server using the original file locations.
- ■ **/m**   Optional parameter that indicates a remote will receive the restored SharePoint Portal Server installation.

▲ **MachineName**   Optional parameter used in conjunction with the /m parameter. This is the name of the server that will receive the restored SharePoint Portal Server installation.

Following are some examples of how to use the above syntax to restore a SharePoint Portal Server installation:

This restores a backup from a file called SPBack06012001 in the SPBackup folder on the C: drive of the server to the same server:

```
MSDMBack /r c:\SPBackup\SPBack06012001
```

This restores a file called SPBack06012001 in the SPBackup folder on the C: drive on the current server to a SharePoint Portal Server called winchester:

```
MSDMBack /r c:\SPBackup\SPBack06012001 /m winchester
```

This restores a file called SPBack06012001 in the SPBackup folder on the C: drive of the current server to a SharePoint Portal Server called winchester, but uses the original file paths, as specified with the /o parameter:

```
MSDMBack /r c:\SPBackup\SPBack06012001 /o /m winchester
```

As a final example of backing up, this restores a file called SPBack in the Backup folder on the C: drive of the hawkeye computer to a SharePoint Portal Server called winchester:

```
MSDMBack /r \\hawkeye\c\Backup\SPBack /m winchester
```

DEPLOYING

After you have read (and understood) the sections on backing up and restoring your SharePoint Portal Server installations, deploying your server becomes quite simple. Deployment generally begins from your development or testing environments. The deployment is generally a matter of copying data from the testing environment to the production environment by performing the following steps:

▼ Clean out bad data or test data from your testing environments

■ Remove unwanted or unnecessary security permissions from your testing environments

■ Back up your testing environment

▲ Restore to your production environment

Syntax 2

The second syntax for restoring a SharePoint Portal Server file is exactly the same as it is for backing up a server. This second syntax is used to set and store the security credentials for the restore command. If you need more information on how to use this command, see the earlier section, "Syntax 2."

If you don't remove unwanted data and permissions, you will have bogus data or permissions in your production environment. You definitely want to avoid this!

The backup and restore procedures are the same as those in the earlier sections in this chapter. Alternatively, you may opt to simply setup a server by installing the SharePoint Portal Server software and creating workspaces and security on that server without going from the testing environment. In this case, the deployment scenario described above does not apply.

CHAPTER SUMMARY

This chapter explains the nitty-gritty of backing up and restoring a SharePoint Portal Server installation. It showed you syntax and scenarios of when you would use this functionality. You also learned that it is very important not to use any other backup program, such as the Windows backup utility. This utility does not back up everything necessary to restore a SharePoint Portal Server installation.

CHAPTER 13

Troubleshooting

In a perfect world, you wouldn't need to read this chapter. However, as Murphy's Law states, whatever can go wrong...will. Therefore, this chapter is dedicated to helping you get around problems with your SharePoint Portal Server. There are many things that can go wrong during the course of using SharePoint Portal Server, but depending on your installation, you may not experience all of them. For example, if you are not using a proxy server, you may not experience problems with communication, but you might experience problems with using Netscape as a browser. Because of this, you may want to use this chapter as a reference when you need it, instead of reading it from start to finish.

GENERAL INFORMATION

For virtually all problems that you experience with SharePoint Portal Server, you should first check the following:

▼ **Prerequisites**   Refers to things like disk space, memory requirements, number of possible workspaces, software coexistence issues, etc. Prerequisites are covered in Chapter 3.

■ **Security**   Refers to Windows NT, Windows 2000, Windows XP, or Windows .NET Server domain accounts that have access to specific resources. Also, security refers to the ability of specific users or groups to perform certain actions. Security is discussed in detail in Chapter 10.

■ **Event Viewer**   Allows you to view specific details about errors that occur on the SharePoint Portal Server computer. The event viewer is discussed later in this chapter, under the heading, "Event Viewer." This is a good place to go to determine if any required services failed to start.

▲ **Error Messages**   Many times error messages in the form of dialog boxes are presented on the screen and we simply click Enter to dismiss the dialog without actually reading it. This is true of most people. I'm guilty of it also. If one appears while using SharePoint Portal Server, make sure to read it. It is possible that the message appears on the screen, but is not written to the Event Viewer.

For specific tips and tricks, refer to the appropriate section throughout the rest of this chapter. As the types of errors that can occur that need troubleshooting are infinite, this chapter focuses more on the tools that can help you rather than specific errors that you could possibly encounter.

SERVER PROBLEMS

There are two types of logs that are kept on a SharePoint Portal Server computer. They are the Windows Event Viewer logs and SharePoint Portal Server logs. If you experience any problems with SharePoint Portal Server at all, refer to these logs. You may receive very detailed information to point you in the right direction.

Event Viewer

The Windows Event Viewer is a standard tool that comes with all versions of Windows servers that reads three categories of logs:

▼ **Application**   Contains events logged by applications that have registered themselves as event providers.

■ **Security**   When auditing has been enabled it contains events relating to security, such as failed attempts to log into the server.

▲ **System**   Contains events logged by the operating system and it components, as well as third-party software that has been registered as a system event provider.

In addition, certain programs may install other categories in addition to these three. Within each of these three categories of logs, there are five types of events that can be logged:

▼ **Information**   Provides data about a process, application, or service, but does not indicate that a problem exists. Figure 13-1 shows a sample of an information event message.

■ **Warning**   Indicates that a process, application, or service caused an error (or a potential error), but not one that is so severe that the operation halts. Figure 13-2 shows a sample warning event message.

■ **Error**   Indicates that a process, application, or service cannot continue because a severe or critical error occurred. Figure 13-3 shows what a sample error event message looks like.

■ **Success Audit**   If auditing has been enabled, indicates that an individual has successfully logged into a computer or domain. Figure 13-4 shows a sample of a success audit event message.

▲ **Failure Audit**   If auditing has been enabled, indicates that an individual has failed to log into a computer or domain. Figure 13-5 shows a sample of a failure audit event message.

NOTE: Depending on the software that you have installed on your server, you might see additional logs, such as DNS, File Replication Service and Directory Services.

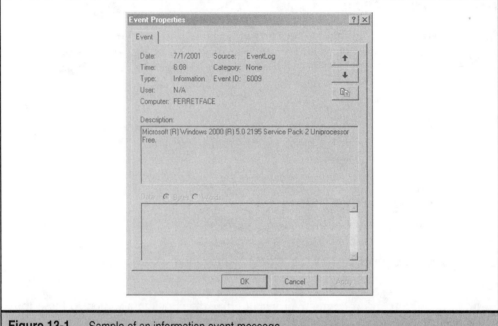

Figure 13-1. Sample of an information event message

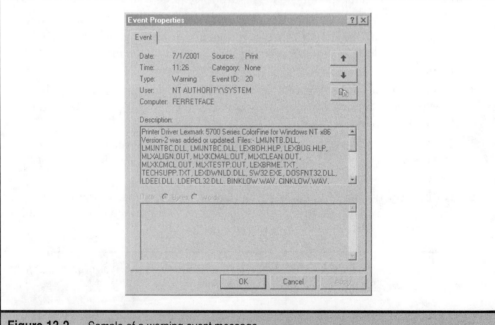

Figure 13-2. Sample of a warning event message

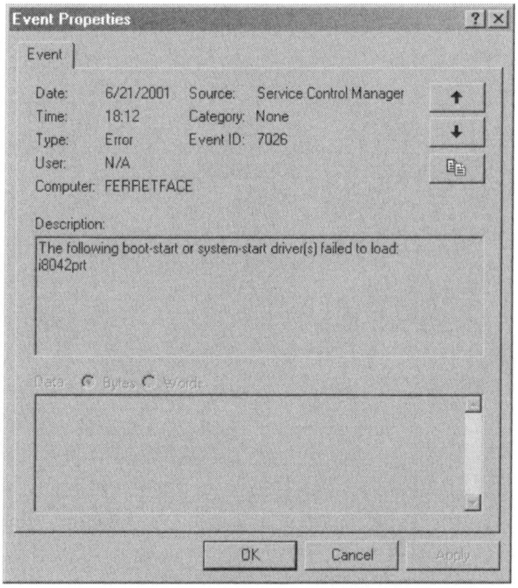

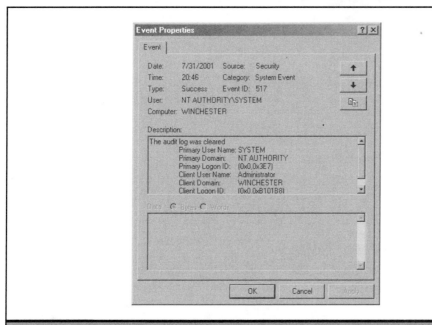

Figure 13-3. Sample of an error event message

Figure 13-4. Sample of a success audit event message

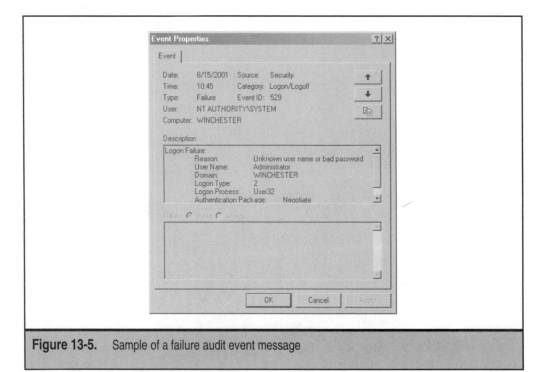

Figure 13-5.   Sample of a failure audit event message

To use the Windows Event Viewer, follow these steps:

1. Open the Event Viewer.

   On the SharePoint Portal Server computer, choose Start | Programs | Administrative Tools | Event Viewer. This brings up the Event Viewer, as shown in Figure 13-6.

2. Click the desired log.

3. View all error events for the selected log.

   Double-click the desired error event to receive further information about the message. You should view all error messages and perhaps all warning messages to help you troubleshoot server issues.

SharePoint Portal Server Logs

SharePoint Portal Server generates its own logs outside of the event viewer. These logs are located, in the \Program Files\Microsoft Integration\SharePoint Portal Server\Logs

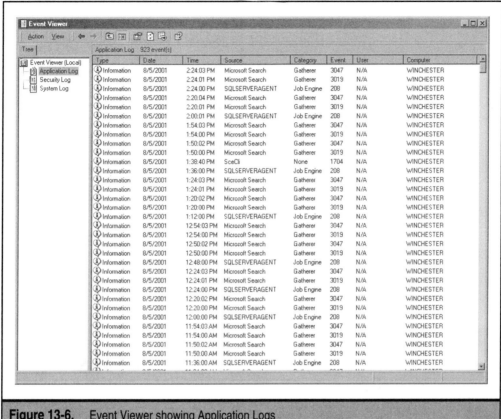

Figure 13-6. Event Viewer showing Application Logs

folder on whatever drive you installed SharePoint Portal Server. The following logs will be contained within that directory:

▼ **errorlog.txt** Logs all error events that happen in SharePoint Portal Server.

■ **eventlog.txt** Logs all informational events that happen in SharePoint Portal Server.

■ **setup.log** Logs the status of installation. If the installation failed prior to creating the \Program Files\Microsoft Integration\SharePoint Portal Server\ Logs folder, this file will exist in the TEMP folder, whose location is specified in the operating system.

▲ **spsclient.log** Logs the status of client extension installations.

The above logs can be viewed with a simple text editor, such as Notepad. Typically, if you simply double-click the name of the log file, it will automatically be opened with Notepad.

Client Problems

You may remember from Chapter 3 that there is no actual program that is installed on a client computer. However, Microsoft Office 2000, Microsoft Office XP, and Windows Explorer extensions do get installed for communication with SharePoint Portal Server. Therefore, there can be issues that arise when attempting to install these extensions.

If you have problems with the client computer, it is a good idea to resolve the problems by troubleshooting in this order:

1. Ensure that you have met the minimum requirements.

2. Ensure that you have administrative privileges on the client computer. It is a good idea to log in as the local administrator of the computer if you are not sure. This ensures that you have the appropriate privileges to install software on the client machine.

3. Check the spsclient.log file in the \Program Files\Microsoft Integration\ SharePoint Portal Server\Logs folder on the server. It may contain additional information.

4. Create a detailed client log file.

A detailed client log file can be created by following these steps:

1. Open Windows Explorer.

    Select Start | Programs | Accessories | Windows Explorer to bring up the Windows Explorer program.

2. Map a drive to the SharePoint client extensions.

    Click Tools | Map Network Drive. Browse for the location of the client extension installation program. For English, this program is located in the Program Files\SharePoint Portal Server\ClientDrop\Languages\enu folder on the drive where you installed SharePoint Portal Server. Don't forget to assign a drive letter to this network drive. For this example, we'll call it F:. Click Finish to map the drive. Note that if you don't already have a public share to the drive that contains the enu folder, you'll have to do that before you can map drive F:.

3. Open the command prompt.

    The command prompt can be opened by clicking Start | Programs | Accessories | Command Prompt.

4. Start the setup program in logging mode.

    To start the setup program (which is now located in the F: drive), use this syntax (followed by ENTER):

    ```
    drive:\setup /L* path\filename
    ```

You can substitute the following for the parameters above:

- *drive* The drive letter that you have used to map your network drive. Following the above example, you would substitute F:.

- *path* The path of the log file that you wish to create. For example, if you wanted to place the newly created log file in the Logs folder on the C: drive, you would substitute c:\logs.

CAUTION: The path must exist or an error will occur. The setup program will not create it for you. Also, in case you were wondering, the /L* parameter is used to specify that the setup program should use logging mode and log all possible events.

- *filename* The name of the log file you wish to create. For example, you may want to create a log file named SPSClient.log.

Putting this all together, you would execute this statement at the command prompt:

```
F:\setup /L c:\logs\SPSClient.log
```

You can view this log file by using a text editor, such as Notepad. Typically, if you simply double-click the name of the log file, it will automatically be opened with Notepad.

NETSCAPE NAVIGATOR

By default, when you install SharePoint Portal Server, the virtual directories that are installed (which represent workspaces) within Internet Information Services (IIS) authenticate access by using Integrated Windows Authentication, formerly known as NTLM. Integrated Windows Authentication uses an encryption algorithm when it verifies login information from a Windows NT domain or Windows 2000 Active Directory. Netscape Navigator does not work with Integrated Windows Authentication, so your only other

Netscape Discussions

If you want to use discussions with Netscape Navigator, the same problem exists where Integrated Windows Authentication, or NTLM, is not supported. You must follow the same procedure noted in this section, "Netscape Navigator," with only one exception. In step 4, you click the MSOffice virtual directory instead of the desired workspace. Every other step stays the same.

option is to use Basic Authentication. This is a less secure way of authentication, as passwords are sent in clear text across the network, unless you use a Secure Sockets Layer (or SSL) Certificate. If you don't, anybody with a network "sniffer" can see passwords transmitted in clear text.

To enable Basic Authentication, follow these steps:

1. Open the Internet Services Manager on the SharePoint Portal Server computer.

   Select Start | Programs | Administrative Tools | Internet Services Manager to bring up the program. This is shown in Figure 13-7.

2. Expand the name of your server.

3. Expand the Default Web Site folder.

4. Right-click the desired workspace.

5. Select Properties.

6. Click Directory Security.

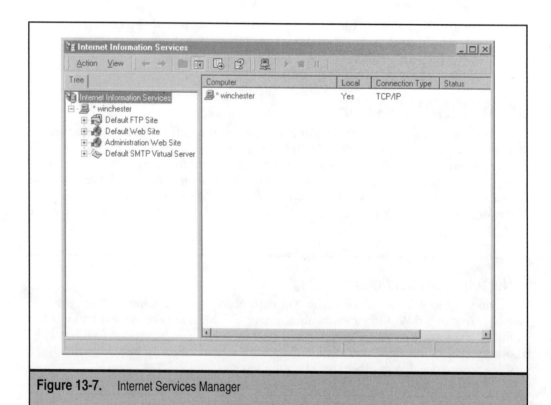

Figure 13-7. Internet Services Manager

7. Click Edit under Anonymous Access And Authentication Control.

    Clicking Edit brings up the dialog box shown in Figure 13-8.

8. Click Basic Authentication (Password Is Sent In Clear Text).

    You will receive a warning message stating the security issue that I mentioned with Basic Authentication. Click Yes to continue.

9. Click OK to close the Authentication Methods dialog box.

10. Click OK to close the Properties screen.

Another issue with Netscape Navigator has to do with advanced searches. For more information on this, see section "Q274711" later in this chapter.

INDEX CREATION

There are a few things that can go wrong when dealing with indexes. The problems mainly focus on crawling content to create indexes and propagating indexes. It is a good idea to solve problems with indexes by checking:

▼   Event Viewer for detailed information.

■   Security accounts for crawling content sources or propagating indexes. For example if you are using the Default Access Account (discussed in Chapter 10),

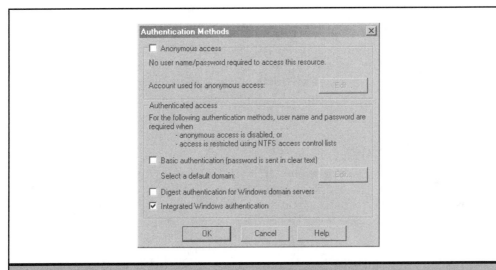

Figure 13-8.   Assigning authentication methods in Internet Information Services (IIS)

what if that account does not have administrative privileges and cannot actually access the content source for crawling?

■ File paths.

▲ Disk space on either the SharePoint Portal Server that contains the index workspace or the workspace that receives propagated indexes.

SUBSCRIPTIONS, NOTIFICATIONS, AND DISCUSSIONS

Notifications are alerts to subscriptions that a user has requested. For example, if a user requests to be notified every time computer.xls changes, when that file actually does change, SharePoint Portal Server sends out a notification to the user. However, there are a few reasons why this notification doesn't get to the user. These reasons include:

▼ The document, such as computer.xls was renamed. The notification does not get renamed also. The user must resubscribe to the notification.

■ The authentication method was set to allow anonymous users. Earlier, under the heading, "Netscape Navigator," you learned how to set authentication methods. Because a notification goes to a specific user or set of users, SharePoint Portal Server must know which user is logged in. If IIS allows anonymous access, it doesn't know who is logged in. Therefore, the subscription will not work.

▲ The subscription must be set to notify a user by using a specific domain user account and not a group account.

One additional problem with discussions in Internet Explorer is when a double-byte character set is used on the SharePoint Portal Server. A *double-byte character set* is typically used for East Asian languages that require more than 256 characters. Such languages include Chinese, Japanese, and Korean. Double-byte character sets are incompatible with Internet Explorer.

PROXY SERVERS

If you are using a proxy server to connect to the Internet, you must configure your SharePoint Portal Servers to use those proxy servers. Chapter 10 discusses this in detail, as well as showing you error messages and resolutions for those errors. Refer to this chapter for more information.

PERFORMANCE ISSUES

Troubleshooting performance-related issues can be the most challenging type of troubleshooting. If your system is slow, you might ask yourself these questions?

▼   Does my server have enough power?

■   Are there too many transactions going on at the same time?

■   Is(are) my server(s) set up correctly?

▲   Can SharePoint Portal Server handle my needs?

Well, some of these questions can be answered by using System Monitor (such as the first two listed above). You learned how to use System Monitor in Chapter 11. Some other questions, however, are harder to answer (such as the last two listed above).

Is(are) your server(s) set up correctly? There are many ways to setup a SharePoint Portal Server installation. You can have a single server or multiple servers. If you have multiple servers, what will they do? Will each have its own workspace? Will one server be used for index workspaces only? Perhaps System Monitor will help answer this, but it is likely that common sense and available budget will dictate which is the right answer for you. Chapter 11 includes information on optimization which might help point you in the right direction for this question.

Can SharePoint Portal Server handle my needs? Of course, the answer to this question depends on what your needs are. Microsoft does not appear to be marketing SharePoint Portal Server to be the "be-all, end-all" to portal or document management solutions. They seem to be targeting it towards small and mid-sized enterprises or departments within large enterprises. Part of this question can be answered for you if you determine how to configure your workspaces by reading Chapter 11. The other part of this question, perhaps, can be answered by going to Microsoft's web site **http://www.microsoft.com/ sharepoint** and reading about their latest recommendation and to see if they have any benchmarks available.

"Q" ARTICLES

Microsoft posts Knowledge Base articles to its web site and assigns them all unique numbers. Each article begins with the letter "Q," hence the title of this section. Under this heading, I want to point out a few specific known issues with SharePoint Portal Server. I don't want to duplicate the information presented in the Microsoft Knowledge Base, so all of the details are not listed here. Instead, a basic synopsis of the problem is presented, along with a URL of where to go for more detailed information.

Q291835

This "Q" article describes an issue that can present itself when filtering TIF or TIFF files. If you use these files with Windows Components Wizard on your SharePoint Portal Server computer and your server uses the Windows 2000 Indexing Service, TIF and TIFF image file filtering breaks. TIF and TIFF file filtering allows you to crawl Tagged Image File Format file properties. In addition, if Optical Character Recognition (OCR) is installed on the server, SharePoint Portal Server will attempt to index the actual content of a TIF or TIFF file. However, this "Q" article describes the conditions which will render the filter inoperable. To fix the problem, you must edit the registry as described in the article. The knowledge base article can be found at **http://support.microsoft.com/support/kb/articles/ Q291/8/35.ASP**.

Q275274

This "Q" article describes a security-related problem in SharePoint Portal Server. You may recall that only a coordinator can change a user's permissions on a folder within SharePoint Portal Server. The article states that because a coordinator can remove permissions on a folder, a coordinator can actually remove himself/herself from having permissions on the folder. Once this is done, only a different coordinator can reassign the permissions. This shouldn't happen too often, but you can obtain more information on the knowledge base article at **http://support.microsoft.com/support/kb/articles/Q275/2/ 74.ASP**.

Q275188

The Web Storage System has a problem where properties stored with documents cannot have a space in the property name. There is no actual fix for the problem at this time. You simply must not use spaces in the name, although there will be no errors that prevent you from doing it. For more information about document properties, see Chapter 9. For more information on this "Q" article, see the knowledge base article at **http:// support.microsoft.com/support/kb/articles/Q275/1/88.ASP**.

Q274711

This "Q" article describes a problem with using Netscape Navigator. More specifically, you cannot perform advanced searches when using this browser. Netscape allows you to perform basic searches, as shown in Figure 13-9, but not using advanced search features, as shown in Figure 13-10.

    You can find more information on the knowledge base article at **http:// support.microsoft.com/support/kb/articles/Q274/7/11.ASP**.

Q295721

As mentioned in Chapter 3, SharePoint Portal Server cannot be installed with Exchange 2000 Server. However, you might think that if you have installed the administration tools and removed them again, everything would work fine. This is great in theory, but when you uninstall software, it does not always revert the system to the way it was before the installation. This Microsoft "Q" article describes in detail how you fix this exact situation. You have installed, then uninstalled the Microsoft Exchange 2000 Server administration tools, but you receive errors when installing SharePoint Portal Server.

    To fix the problem, you must edit the registry as described in the article. The knowledge base article can be found at **http://support.microsoft.com/support/kb/articles/ Q295/7/21.ASP**.

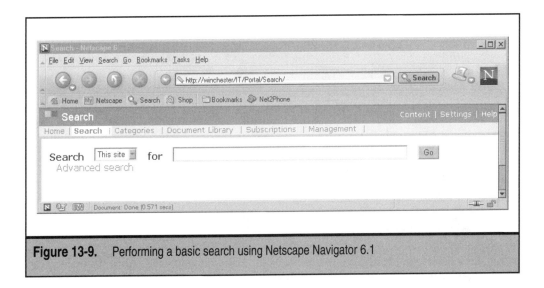

Figure 13-9.   Performing a basic search using Netscape Navigator 6.1

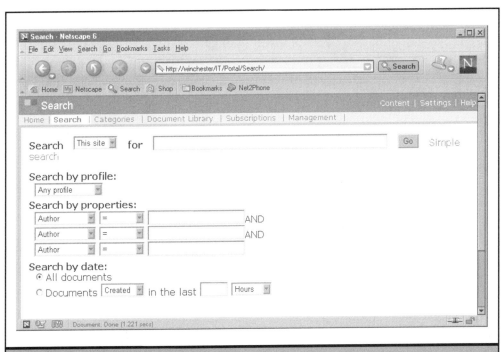

Figure 13-10.   Performing an advanced search using Netscape Navigator 6.1

ADDITIONAL RESOURCES

Since it is impossible for this chapter to answer all possible questions that can arise during the course of administering SharePoint Portal Server, at least you can be pointed in the right direction for solutions.

One of the most useful resources is the Microsoft Knowledge Base. Microsoft's Product Support team carefully scrutinizes and verifies the technical accuracy of the knowledge base. The knowledge base can be searched by pointing your web browser to **http://search.microsoft.com**.

Another useful resource is Microsoft TechNet. TechNet is a subscription-based resource whereby Microsoft sends CDs or DVDs to you in the mail, as well as provides a web site for up-to-date technical information. TechNet is not free, however. To find out what your price would be (based on subscription level, region, etc), visit the Microsoft TechNet web site at **http://www.microsoft.com/technet**.

Additionally, you can ask questions about SharePoint Portal Server to your peers by using Microsoft newsgroups. To use the Microsoft newsgroups, you can either use a web browser or a news reader. To use a web browser, point your browser to the URL, **http://communities.microsoft.com/newsgroups**. To use a news reader, the newsgroups can be located at msnews.microsoft.com.

CHAPTER SUMMARY

As you have seen from this chapter, there are many things that can cause problems with SharePoint Portal Server. The intent of this chapter was to get you to think about issues relating to these problems and the tools that are available to help diagnose and troubleshoot those problems.

INDEX

D

J

K

L

M

N

Q

R

▼ W

INTERNATIONAL CONTACT INFORMATION

AUSTRALIA
McGraw-Hill Book Company Australia Pty. Ltd.
TEL +61-2-9417-9899
FAX +61-2-9417-5687
http://www.mcgraw-hill.com.au
books-it_sydney@mcgraw-hill.com

CANADA
McGraw-Hill Ryerson Ltd.
TEL +905-430-5000
FAX +905-430-5020
http://www.mcgrawhill.ca

GREECE, MIDDLE EAST,
NORTHERN AFRICA
McGraw-Hill Hellas
TEL +30-1-656-0990-3-4
FAX +30-1-654-5525

MEXICO (Also serving Latin America)
McGraw-Hill Interamericana Editores S.A. de C.V.
TEL +525-117-1583
FAX +525-117-1589
http://www.mcgraw-hill.com.mx
fernando_castellanos@mcgraw-hill.com

SINGAPORE (Serving Asia)
McGraw-Hill Book Company
TEL +65-863-1580
FAX +65-862-3354
http://www.mcgraw-hill.com.sg
mghasia@mcgraw-hill.com

SOUTH AFRICA
McGraw-Hill South Africa
TEL +27-11-622-7512
FAX +27-11-622-9045
robyn_swanepoel@mcgraw-hill.com

UNITED KINGDOM & EUROPE
(Excluding Southern Europe)
McGraw-Hill Education Europe
TEL +44-1-628-502500
FAX +44-1-628-770224
http://www.mcgraw-hill.co.uk
computing_neurope@mcgraw-hill.com

ALL OTHER INQUIRIES Contact:
Osborne/McGraw-Hill
TEL +1-510-549-6600
FAX +1-510-883-7600
http://www.osborne.com
omg_international@mcgraw-hill.com

ABOUT THE CD-ROM

The CD-ROM contains a 120 day trial version of Microsoft SharePoint Portal Server 2001.

This program was reproduced by Osborne/**McGraw-Hill** under a special arrangement with Microsoft Corporation. For this reason, Osborne/**McGraw-Hill** is responsible for the product warranty and for support. If your diskette is defective, please return it to Osborne/**McGraw-Hill** which will arrange for its replacement. PLEASE DO NOT RETURN IT TO MICROSOFT CORPORATION. Any product support will be provided, if at all, by Osborne/**McGraw-Hill**. PLEASE DO NOT CONTACT MICROSOFT CORPORATION FOR PRODUCT SUPPORT. End users of this Microsoft program shall not be considered "registered owners" of a Microsoft product and therefore shall not be eligible for upgrades, promotions or other benefits available to "registered owners" of Microsoft products.